quietly **hostile**

samantha irby

quietly **hostile**

Samantha Irby is a humorist and essayist and
the author of three previous essay collections.

quietly **hostile**

quietly **hostile**

essays

samantha irby

VINTAGE BOOKS
A Division of Penguin Random House LLC
New York

A VINTAGE BOOKS ORIGINAL 2023

Library of Congress Cataloging-in-Publication Data
Name: Irby, Samantha, author.
Title: Quietly hostile : essays / Samantha Irby.
Description: First edition. | New York : Vintage Books,
a division of Penguin Random House LLC, 2023.
Identifiers: LCCN 2022042843
Subjects: LCSH: Irby, Samantha. | Bloggers—United States—Biography. |
Authors, American—21st century—Biography. | African American women
authors—21st century—Biography. | African American comedians—
21st century—Biography. | Comedians—United States—Biography. |
American wit and humor. | GSAFD: Essays. | Autobiographies.
Classification: LCC PN4587.2.I73 A3 2023 (print) | DDC 814/.6—dc23
LC record available at https://lccn.loc.gov/2022042843

Vintage Books Trade Paperback ISBN: 978-0-593-31569-9
eBook ISBN: 978-0-593-31570-5

Book design by Anna B. Knighton

vintagebooks.com

Printed in the United States of America
10 9 8 7 6 5 4 3 2 1

This book is dedicated to Zoloft.

CONTENTS

i like it!

This is not an advice book. And I don't know anything.

I don't make a lot of goals because it's hard to do things that are different from what you are currently doing. It's also embarrassing when you fall short, especially when that shit is easy.

Drink more water? Can't do it.

Go to bed earlier? But what about my shows?

Give up sugar? Not possible.

Save more money? But what about buying stuff?

Learn a new skill? Where and also how and also with what brain?

Get organized? But I love mess.

Lose weight? Is there a pill for that, and if so can I take it in cheese like a dog?

Eliminate bad habits? Who would I be without them?

Have compassion for myself? But I'm a dumbass who sucks at everything and is unworthy of love.

I don't have a lot of coping mechanisms that aren't wholly self-destructive, but here is one good one that I will recommend: saying I like things that I like. At first blush, this doesn't sound revolutionary, I know, but let's get into it.

One of the tools that people who are shitheads use to make people who are not feel like shit is the casual dismissal of things those people like. We all know some total fucking asshole who's like:

"Ew, *that's* your coffee order?"

"You stayed at *that* hotel?"

"You're going to *that* party?"

"Why do you use *Vaseline*?"

They say things in a way that makes you feel like you have to apologize for liking them, that puts you on the defensive, that sends you down an internal spiral thinking, *Why do I like the dumb shit I like?* and questioning your entire life's history of tastes and choices, all because you had the nerve to . . . express enjoyment of something mundane.

Or the interaction can go something like this:

ME: I thought [*name of innocuous movie that is perfectly fine*] was good!

THEM (*feigning shock*): You did? Well *I* thought it was sophomoric garbage with no character development and an implausible ending. [*Seriously, we're talking about a thoroughly enjoyable popcorn movie here.*] I can't believe you're into it!

This is where they stop—a satisfied smugness spreading across their slimy face—and wait expectantly for you to conjure a defense for a movie (or a book or a television show or the store where you buy shirts or the place where you get your cat groomed or . . .) you didn't make and have no emotional attachment to. Whenever this happens to me, my automatic reaction is to feel stupid and ashamed, like I should apologize for not understanding that a thing I enjoyed was poorly made or offensive to people who actually know what quality is.

I get embarrassed for being a person with basic tastes who does not interrogate things very deeply, a person who needs to be smacked in the face with the subliminal message because I absolutely will not suss it out for myself. Can someone explain *Parasite* to me, please?

The embarrassment usually leads to my second-guessing both myself and my interpretation of whatever it is we're talking about: "Oh so what you're trying to say is that I'm *not* supposed to think *Mission: Impossible—Fallout* is intellectually stimulating and the greatest film of all time?" This then devolves into an even more embarrassing apology: "I'm so sorry for not understanding what 'good acting' is!" And that continues until I shrivel into a husk and die, vowing with my dying breaths to never again publicly express joy or excitement.

Some friend of my wife's said to me—who am I, a balding stand-up comic in 1987??—after using the dry cleaner recommendation she'd asked me for a week earlier, "That strip mall where you told me to get my pants hemmed is so depressing. I can't believe you go there."

I leaned against my open front door, in a fraying hoodie and soiled pajama bottoms, blinking at her over my first Diet Coke of the day. What did she want from me? What was I supposed to say?

"I can't believe you go there!" she repeated, and it became clear to me that she wanted . . . an explanation. An apology.

Unfortunately, I was in no mood to be forced to atone for a place I:

- did not conceptualize.
- did not build.
- do not own.
- do not live in.
- do not profit from.
- frequently use with satisfaction.
- told her about as a courtesy because she asked me!

Wanting to keep this early-morning interaction as brief as possible, my brain cycled through the possibilities of how to respond. I could:

- apologize for, uhh, helping her and solving her problem?
- apologize for having poor taste in local shopping plazas?
- apologize for being alive?
- apologize, then snarkily ask how her dry cleaning turned out, and then immediately and reflexively apologize for being snarky?

Imagine me saying, "I'm sorry that the home of Bill's Greeting Card Hut and Lucy's Luxury Lashes wasn't up to your exacting standards, and I apologize for making you look at dull brown bricks." I would rather live inside the Value City that's next door to Glamour Nails! But I didn't say anything, and she chuckled again, saying, "It's so ugly!" followed by an anticipative pause.

And I dunno, man, the smoothie spot is pretty good and the out-of-business DVD store is oddly comforting to me, so I arranged my face into something resembling cheerfulness and said, in my highest octave, "I like it!"

Gotcha, bitch.

I watched as she searched for something to say next since I'd dodged the trap she'd set and whatever further insults she had prepared to hit me with. "I like it!" I chirped again.

"I like it! I like it a lot!"

I don't remember if I slammed the door in her face or kicked her backward down my concrete steps, but what I do know is, that day a new person was born, an upgraded version of myself that no longer felt shamed by some smarty-pants making fun of the John Grisham novel poking out of my backpack.

I'd need a sociology degree to write about this in a real way, but we live in such a hilariously stupid time, where everyone is just hurling expectations of justification at each other constantly, and I'm sorry, lads, but I don't like it. I have no idea what news is real or which celebrity is an actual good person or what zeitgeisty show most deserves my attention or which cause is the correct one for me to text my $10 monetary support to, but I do know that if I pick the wrong one, someone I don't know very well, or maybe don't even know at all, is going to demand to know "WHY?"

I can't live in hell *and* make excuses for ravenously consuming a shitty reality show produced by a person I don't know personally on a network I am unaffiliated with. You can use "I like it!" (the exclamation point is necessary) any time some freak questions a regular-ass thing you enjoy, and it'll swipe their legs out from under them every single time, and you can stand over their quivering body with your subpar tastes and laugh your face off. Deploy it whenever you want, then sit back and watch your judgmental friend splutter and try to choke out a response, because what people like that really want is to show off how much more cultured and evolved they are than you, and saying "I like it!" (include the exclamation point, I mean it!) robs them of that opportunity. They want to fight and pick apart the shaky defense you had to come up with on the fly for, I don't know, the place you get coffee from just because it's close to your house? Let's practice:

"Why are you listening to Justin Bieber?" I like it!
"I can't believe you still drink milk." I like it!
"Why haven't you replaced your shitty car?" I like it!
"Gross, you still use Instagram?" I like it!
"That shirt is so ugly!" I like it!
"You're watching that dumb show again?" I like it!
"Your dog is so naughty." I like it!
"I can't believe you go to Trader Joe's." I like it!
"Ugh, another Samantha Irby book?" I like it!!!!!!!!!!!!!!!!!!!!

the last normal day

The day before the last normal day, I was sitting in a bland, sparsely furnished corporate apartment in Chicago, strategizing the fastest and least physically taxing way to pack up all the unnecessary purchases I'd made in the six weeks I'd lived here and drive them to Michigan while somehow managing to avoid the many deadly germs threatening to implode my lungs between there and here.

I was in Chicago to work on the recently canceled (sigh!), brilliantly funny, and heartfelt television show *Work in Progress*, which I thought meant that I was going to spend six weeks luxuriating in nice restaurants and getting wasted with all my friends from high school every night, but the job actually required my full un-hungover attention and, oh yeah, it was also WINTER IN CHICAGO and no one wanted to even leave their houses, let alone put on lipstick and pants with a zipper to meet me near where I was staying all the way in freaking River North for an overpriced drink in a pitch-black room in which we'd have to scream ourselves hoarse over thumping beats to catch each other up on our lives.

Oh, the halcyon days of February 2020, when we had no idea just how much our future selves would regret not hauling our asses out in the snow to expectorate in each other's faces while pressed uncomfortably close together in some dark and overly sexy bar.

I like to have the news on in the background when I'm puttering around at home because I find the tone-modulated droning of newscasters oddly soothing, and my preferred way of learning what's happening in the world is to absorb it via osmosis, never directly because that feels too stressful. So in the weeks prior to mandatory lockdown (Is that even what it was called?), I hadn't panicked because, like, when everything is breaking news absolutely nothing is breaking news? How do you know if it's nuclear war or if it's just a celebrity getting divorced when all you hear echoing from an adjacent room every single time anyone does anything is *dun DUN dun!* [*the serious news intro theme*] "Breaking news at the top of this hour [*in an animated yet sober newscaster voice*]. Good evening, America, I'm Brick Shetland, reporting live from the newsroom . . ."

By March, cable news was breathlessly reporting that people in Europe and Asia were coughing to death from some new easily transmissible virus unlike any the world had ever seen and that airports were shutting down, but then with the exact same urgency an anchor would be reading a rundown of the then president's angry tweets, and no one I knew *really* understood the magnitude of the crisis that was about to be upon us because none of my friends are epidemiologists and we all have access to the same CNN. In Chicago, I would go to work at a studio in Edgewater in the morning then return to my temporary home overlooking the screeching L and cheerfully lit Merchandise Mart at night, and I did all that again and again and again and again, and then suddenly the headlines screamed.

WASH YOUR HANDS

ORDER DELIVERY FOR EVERY MEAL BUT OPEN THE DOOR FOR THE DELIVERY PERSON AT YOUR OWN PERIL

SPRAY YOUR MAIL WITH LYSOL, BLEACH YOUR GROCERIES

CANCEL ALL YOUR RESTAURANT RESERVA-TIONS

IF YOU SO MUCH AS LOOK AT AN UBER YOU WILL DIE

WASH YOUR HANDS

ORDER EVERYTHING YOU POSSIBLY CAN ON-LINE AND BURN YOUR PARCELS UNDER THE SUN BEFORE THEY CROSS YOUR THRESHOLD

IF YOU ARE NOT AT HOME, GO TO YOUR HOME AND DON'T LEAVE, UNLESS YOU NEED TO GO TO WORK AND—FINE, OKAY, SWING BY THAT BIRTHDAY PARTY IF IT LOOKS FUN

GOOD LUCK FINDING SANITIZER!

GLARE AT ANYONE WHO SO MUCH AS CLEARS THEIR THROAT IN YOUR GENERAL VICINITY

STOCKPILE TOILET PAPER FOR NO DISCERNIBLE REASON

PEOPLE ARE DYING AND WE'RE GONNA LET THEM

SHOULD YOU BE WORRIED THAT YOUR CAT HAS COVID????????

PURCHASE THE DIGITAL VERSION OF *CONTAGION* ON AN IMPULSE AND TRY NOT TO SCREAM TO DEATH IMAGINING THAT AS OUR COLLECTIVE FUTURE

MAYBE IT'S FINE FOR YOU TO GO TO THAT OUT-OF-TOWN WEDDING?

WASH YOUR HANDS

But no one really *knew* anything. At least not definitively, from what I could tell through my passive consumption of broadcast news. Everyone in the writers' room kept going to work because our employer, Showtime, was expecting a season of television from us in exchange for all the Thai food and LaCroix they'd paid for, and also because the papers were casually like "Maybe Steam Clean the Shit You Bought at Walgreens When You Get It Home, If You Feel Like It" and not "WARNING WARNING DO NOT BREATHE COMMUNAL AIR."

Remember how reporters-cum–preschool teachers taught us to sing the words to "Happy Birthday" while washing our hands as we coughed into our friends' mouths??? Nobody knew shit! When we switched to working remotely (OH GOD, the early days of Zoom!!!!!!), I figured it was pretty serious, this Corona-whateveryoucallit. At the same time, we were led to believe it would blow through like a foul wind if we just hunkered down and laid low for a few weeks. Then things would go back to normal. But also, what the fuck is "normal" anyway, and is it actually a thing we wanted to get back to?

A few days after we'd gotten used to where to focus our dumb eyes on a multi-person video call (I participated then as I continue to do now: stare intently at my own visage, horrified by its many flaws and hoping no one has the kind of crystal clear resolution that amplifies my upper lip hairs), our boss emailed us something to the effect of "Fuck this job, pack up your tiny dorm rooms and flee the city before it's too late!" Sure, I'd been trying to open doors with my elbow for a week at that point, but *that's* when it really hit me that it wasn't just a bad flu other reckless people who just couldn't resist a St. Patrick's Day bar crawl were catching; Covid was in this country and rapidly spreading across the city I was in, and I needed to hurry up and get back to my hermetically sealed bunker in Michigan before I caught it from a grocery cart or a high five.

I read the email from the building manager telling us

where to leave our keys and reminding us that we would be heftily fined if we had done visible damage to any of the three forks we'd each been allotted (one day I would like a job as the person who decides what amenities should come standard in short-term corporate housing; imagine being the dude who's like, "Nine hand towels, no corkscrews." What power!!!!!!!!!!!!!!!!), and I had less than a day to pack my shit and hit the road so I could ride out the lockdown with all of my books and shirts and cats—and my wife, I guess. AND YET: rather than immediately throw everything in a suitcase and haul ass home as fast as I could, I instead sat on the side of the bed and googled "coronavirus symptoms" while hoping the tickle in my throat was just allergies (IT WAS) and wondering how in the world I was gonna get all the stuff I'd bought out of my temporary home and into the car without a single box to carry it all in.

The thought of multiple trips up and down in a highrise elevator crawling with other people's potentially deadly spores filled me with doom while also forcing me to examine how one person could contain so many different types of emotional wreckage. My contract said I was supposed to work for six or *maybe seven* (unlikely, though!) weeks. A month and a half, at most. Why on earth had I purchased:

- an Anthropologie fruit bowl made from surprisingly heavy wood that I got off the sale rack during a late-night spiral at Nordstrom, which was beautiful but honestly the six pears I let rot inside it could have turned to mold just as easily on the fucking counter;
- several different varieties of scented luxury candle,

for an apartment with only two distinct rooms and a bathroom;

- the biggest pack of paper towels they sell at the store;
- a bunch of Trader Joe's snack foods that always sound good theoretically but once I get them home it's always like: "But who actually *wants* these brussels sprout–flavored tortilla chips, and who was I buying this *for*?";
- a modest stack, but a stack nonetheless, of books that I bought at the Women & Children First bookstore because books are my friends, but also because I thought they could warm up the soullessness of a place I mostly used for sleeping;
- a tub of collagen powder????? (My knees hurt.);
- a set of washcloths and towels because the apartment came equipped with an all-white set, and I didn't want anyone to get mad at me when I inevitably ruined them;
- some sweaters I panic-ordered in the middle of the night after opening my suitcase to discover that everything I own is gross and ugly, but joke's on me because if you get a package delivered to one of these high-tech buildings that offer things I don't care about like communal work spaces and indoor dog parks, you have to ask the twenty-four-hour doorman to interrupt whatever he's looking at on his phone to go collect your package while you stand there awkwardly, dying of shame . . . and those sweaters were ugly!!!!!!!!; and
- a ninety-six-count container of Tide PODS, literally the kind you buy for your large family of offensive linemen?

Nothing feels more ridiculous than needing to pack in a hurry and confirming that you are a frivolous person who makes terrible decisions yet doesn't have time to, ummm, *unpack* all that because a deadly virus is barreling directly toward your sensitive lung tissue. Every time I walked past the hall closet containing the mop bucket (???) and an extra coat (?????) I thought I'd need, carrying armloads of shit I was hoping not to contaminate between my apartment and the parking garage, they silently mocked me. Someone reading this who understands how broken brains work is probably formulating a theory about the connection between my impoverished, unstable childhood and my burning need to create a cozy home in a space I was going to be in for the time it takes a fractured toe to heal, but I only have a high school diploma so it's not gonna be me.

During my Chicago stay I was driving this rental car that was nicer than anything I'd ever seen in real life: a silver Cadillac SUV so fancy it didn't even have a name, just a combination of letters and numbers that probably translated to "this bitch is too broke to be driving me" in Morse code. I hadn't even picked it out; when I reserved a car online I chose the very sensible and economical "midsize SUV" option, only to arrive at Enterprise and be presented with this brand-new, super glossy carjack-bait by a cheerful salesman. He tried to make me feel lucky when he told me that he was giving me a car that would make everyone stare at me in curious disgust and was gonna cost twice as much to fill up for the same price as the "Ford Escape or similar" I'd signed up for. Cut to me smiling apologetically at the building manager like, "Yes, sorry, these are my real clothes, I'm not actually rich" when I showed up on move-in day.

I was trying to Jenga all the unnecessary garbage I'd surrounded myself with into the back of that fancy car whose automatic seat positioning I had yet to figure out (a feature the Enterprise salesman had enthusiastically sold me on without ever teaching me how to use) at midnight in the parking garage of my fancy dorm that I shared with one of those acoustic-guitar, young-people churches (you know the kind I'm talking about) while hoping no one came out and either (1) caught me looking like I was stealing my own stuff in the middle of the night or (2) infected me with a deadly virus they had recently caught on an airplane.

What is it about me that feels compelled to make a concrete box filled with generic furniture somebody else already slept on feel "cozy" when I'm just going to sleep and eat microwaved gluten-free frozen dinners in it? What mental illness is it that makes you buy multiple bottles of wine and a case of mineral water for a place furnished with only two drinking glasses, especially when you don't even drink wine? *What is my fucking damage, Heather???* I thought as I wedged the Pendleton throw blanket I had purchased to make a living room I literally never sat in look like the inside of a special-edition *Kinfolk* magazine into the back seat next to the angled broom whose cellophane wrapper I hadn't even had a chance to remove. I tucked paper bags filled with shelf-stable pantry foods (How much chickpea pasta does a person actually need?) into the passenger seat footwell and crossed my fingers that no one would find smashing a car window to steal a discount vase I got from the Crate and Barrel clearance section worth the considerable effort.

On that last normal day, Illinois had pretty much shut down as I tentatively piloted my whisper-quiet rental SUV down the winding maze of the deserted parking garage out onto Franklin (empty) and left onto Grand (also startlingly empty) then right on Orleans (okay, scary empty???), past all the barren sidewalks and storefronts. The highway was postapocalyptic horror movie desolate too, which, if we're keeping it all the way real, was kind of a relief. Pandemic cons? Death, uncertainty, economic collapse, the fall of society. Pandemic pro? Absolutely zero traffic on eastbound I-94 at rush hour on a Wednesday. I'm sorry! I hate merging!

But it was also bone-chillingly creepy, speeding down the expressway with seven other cars at 9:00 a.m. on a weekday. I kept waiting for the sky to turn black or zombies to surround the car and drag me out from behind the wheel so they could peel all the flesh off my bones. Does the add-on insurance the salesman talked me into cover destruction by the undead? But none of that happened, just me and a podcast about how social media destroys your brain barreled toward Michigan going ninety miles per hour and hoping not to get pulled over by an infected state trooper.

I didn't want to stop to pee (or poop, can you fucking imagine?) because in those early days, before we knew officially that people couldn't cough near you or breathe in the same room you were in, avoiding touching your face and singing "Happy Birthday" while you washed your hands was the thing, and no place on this planet is worse for trying to keep bacteria off your goddamn hands than a gas station bathroom some stranger barfed in and pissed all over. I had wanted to get a coffee as big as my head on my way out of town, but I resisted, resigning myself to the two swallows of water it took to get a couple of Advil and an allergy pill down my throat so I could make the two-plus-hours drive back to Michigan without stopping. An hour into the trip my sluggish bladder and nonexistent pelvic floor were like, "Hey, babe, isn't your favorite truck stop near here?" and I sighed, but not too hard because I didn't want to mess around and piss my pants in that nice-ass car.

I took the exit. My reward for working and packing and driving and making it halfway to my house was going to be a delicious gas station corn dog before I inevitably ended up in an ICU. I'd earned it.

The Flying J Travel Center in Lake Station, Indiana, is basically an all-purpose gas station where you can take a shower and wash your clothes and get fountain drinks, but it's also a restaurant and an electronics store and most definitely a hub for trafficking of some variety. I didn't even know a magical wonderland like it even *existed* until a few years ago, when I was regularly driving back and forth between Kalamazoo and Chicago (before I finally left the big city for good, only to sporadically go back because I never have enough time to see everyone who gets mad when I don't). I stumbled upon it while looking for someplace clean to go to the bathroom that (of course) offered both a fully stocked assortment of canned Arizona beverages and also live ammunition.

The Flying J is always teeming with grimy, unwashed truckers grunting racism at you as you squeeze past the freestanding Cinnabon kiosk to get a look at the chafing dishes of congealed barbecued-rib goo rapidly decomposing under the heat lamps at the hot bar next to the cigarettes and porn. If you are lucky, there will be one (but hopefully two!) glistening, grease-soaked, golden-brown batter-dipped carcinogen logs rotating on a crisping spit, or whatever they call those rolling curling irons they steam sausages on, manned by delightful women named Brenda or Donna who say things like "Looking good today, sweetie" even when you are not, in fact, looking good.

The corn dogs are two for two dollars because it's Indiana for God's sake, and if they have two available you fucking! buy! two! They are meant to be consumed alone, without condiments, while you softly weep behind the wheel of the regular-person car that you were forced to park next to a BIGFOOT 4×4 affixed with both Confederate vanity plates and a "Baby on Board" sticker, as the hot juice from ground chicken lips and cat meat scorches your chin on its path to your shirt.

I had a mild panic attack while filling up the car: touching a gas pump feels like a dare even under normal circumstances, but having to wrap my moist, sticky hand around the visible dirt and invisible disease at the onset of a mysterious, rapidly spreading global pandemic?! I was so nervous I could hardly fucking breathe. I could *feel* the germs slithering onto my skin, oozing into my open pores. I watched the numbers on the pump tick upward and did the deep-breathing routine my nurse practitioner had taught me and imagined someone at my funeral rolling their eyes like "Of course that dumb bitch stopped to get a fucking hot dog." But listen, I was down to a quarter of a tank and I'm a forty-three-year-old woman who has never done a single Kegel exercise, I didn't want to wet myself, okay?????

I walked into the station with my hands up like I was

under arrest, trying not to accidentally touch anything or let anything accidentally touch me, and I scrubbed my hands and went to the bathroom and scrubbed them again afterward while casually breathing in a billion droplets hanging in the damp, potpourri'd public bathroom air. I bought a tallboy of Diet Coke and two corn dogs and one pocket-sized Purell for every pocket of every single item of clothing I own, and I took all this to my car full of shit I didn't need, slid behind the steering wheel, and cried from the stress and confusion of it all.

Then I got worried that the virus had somehow attached itself to my corn dogs between the station and the car I had to return to Enterprise with a minimum half a tank, so I tossed them in a nearby trash can just in case those rumors about stomach acid killing Coronavirus weren't true (they weren't, imagine that, and even if stomach acid were the cure, how would you bypass all your infectable organs to submerge the Covid in its frothy death bath?), and I drove the rest of the way home without stopping, thinking about the bleach bath I would need to take once I got there.

david matthews's greatest romantic hits

People always pretend to be shocked when I say I unabashedly love Dave Matthews, but . . . why? Sure, I don't play hacky sack or whatever (Is that how you do it, do you "play" hacky sack?) so maybe I don't look like I fit his target demographic, but I've played bags before. That's gotta count for something!!

I love Dave Matthews for real, passionately and without shame. Every time I make that declaration in public someone says, "You're doing a bit, right." I see why you might think so, but I promise you I am not. Here's a thing people who are not me don't talk about enough: Dave Matthews can write the shit out of a love song. I know everyone thinks his albums are made up of twelve-minute-long jam-band odes to tie-dye and weed. But he has so many gut-wrenching songs about love and heartache and regret and desire, and I know it's hilarious to make fun of the bus poop and clown a dude who has flutes in his music. BUT: my man has an undeniably gorgeous voice (His falsetto!!!!!!!!! Sorry, but it rules!) and makes music that is extremely listenable.

Stop fronting like he's not great! Why am I forced to petition on this man's behalf like he's my son filming himself playing the recorder and I need him to get some likes, and not a person who has been (mostly unsuccessfully) nominated for fourteen Grammys?! Here is my list of the greatest Dave Matthews songs to swoon over:

1. "If Only"

most romantic lyric, to me: "So help me get my way back to you"

I do not believe in helping a man, AND YET . . . When Dave asks this woman I'm sure he dumped with neither cause nor due process to take him back, please—it breaks my cold, dead heart. I cry to this song a distressing amount, as I am interested in sex-weeping, especially because he does this plaintive keening near the end that sounds like he's crying for his woman to take him back, a position I have never been in but feel like I would deeply enjoy. Regret is such a powerful emotion!!!!! Did he do something fucked-up to this lady? Probably! But that doesn't matter now because he's distressed about it and he wants back into her life, which is probably a very bad idea! But the thing about romance is that in general it's a bad idea, so this is actually fine.

2. "That Girl Is You"

most romantic lyric, to me: "Oh, hallelujah"

How can you not like a song that uses shakers or maracas or whatever the beginning noise is? This song is about how Dave saw some hot girl on the dance floor and enjoyed the way she moved so fucking much that he went over and introduced himself to her and then wrote a song about how sexy she looks on the dance floor. But because it's Dave you know this broad is not, like, JLo slithering across a strobe-lit disco, this girl is in a dirty gravel parking lot with her shoes off doing that hands-above-her-head, eyes-closed, "ladies who wear scarves" dance, and Dave is sweating through a multicolored Baja hoodie (a drug rug, come on now) while mirroring her moves, hoping she notices him and comes over to ask if he will share his joint with her. Hallelujah, indeed.

3. "Little Thing" (*Live at Luther College* two-disc set)

most romantic lyric, to me: "Weighted by the memory of /
The memory of a love that never got born" </3

Okay, so this is my favorite record, a live recording that's just Tim Reynolds and Dave and a couple of acoustic guitars playing a bunch of hits in front of a friendly college audience that doesn't scream out any rude stuff. Dave starts by telling this story about how he saw a hot, very small—but *not a child*—adult human woman on the street and he asked her for directions, and she gave them to him and left. After she'd gone he was like "DAMN, THAT GIRL WAS FINE," but it was too late. He couldn't ask her name or suggest they get a cup of coffee, his chance for romance with this woman he met on some grimy New York City street was dead, and now her voice was going to echo in his ear, tormenting him until he dies or until he sees another hot young elf on a different street. I love this song because Dave spends a lot of it singing in his gorgeous falsetto, and also because I, too, like to project a complicated fantasy onto a person I saw on the street for approximately nineteen seconds.

I once had to wrestle my original 1994 CD of *Under the Table and Dreaming* from the greedy clutches of a dude who had broken into my room to try to steal my shit at the boarding-house where we both lived. The only other thing of value I had at that time was a used, scorched-up Rowenta iron. The album meant that much to me, and also my car had broken down. And I didn't want to take the bus all the way to Best Buy to replace it, and if we're being honest—I would absolutely fistfight him again today. My love for "Typical Situation" knows no bounds.

So here's the thing, women of a certain age (forty-three years old, to be precise), who no longer get their period and can't eat dairy anymore, need romantic music to vibe to. Of course, when I was a wee lass of twenty-two freezing my face off waiting for the L at Granville at seven thirty in the morning, I did so while listening to Trina rapping about grinding on a dick. But listen, I use a retinoid before bed every night now. I am officially in my smooth-jazz adult contemporary years! And yeah, I listen to a lot of metal or whatever in the daytime. But I like to sit in my chair with my eyes closed, swaying to gentle songs and imagining Dave is singing to me when it's the middle of the night and I'm spiraling.

4. "Here On Out"

most romantic lyric, to me:
"When you laugh, it's like a light / That fills me up"

This song has a lot of guitar plucking but also a whole orchestra playing on it, which is how you know it's a "Very Serious Love Song." Anytime you hear a French fucking horn?????? Babe, you are being wooed. I heard myself laughing on a podcast once and damn near projectile vomited. Having a nice-sounding laugh is nearly impossible, even beautiful famous people mostly have gross discomfiting laughs that make your skeleton want to jump out of your body, so the thought of someone saying "your laugh fills me with light" is astonishing. Oh yeah? Your heart beats for the seal barks that escape my throat every time I hear a good joke? I'm yours forever.

5. "Stay or Leave" (the live Vegas version)

most romantic lyric, to me: "Remember we used to dance /
And everyone wanted to be you and me?"

Okay, this is not an example of my best self, BUT: Wouldn't it be cool to be a couple that everyone else wants to be? Not to rub it in anybody's face, of course, I just mean it would feel good to know you're admired by other people who aren't as happy as you. They're not doing choreo; they're at home, glaring at each other over plates of roast chicken! Obviously their jealousy would be built on whatever lies and artifice you presented to the outside world, but still. I feel like when people see me and my old lady, they're like, "Sheesh, Kirsten is probably tired as hell of dealing with that," and YES SHE IS. No one is watching us dance and thinking anything other than *Is Sam using her wife as a human walker?* And the answer is DUH, OF COURSE. No one wants to be their partner's sexy cane!

6. "You & Me" (Planet Hollywood acoustic version)

most romantic lyric, to me:
"We're gonna take a boat to the end of the world"

I'm not one of these freaks who thinks you can survive off the love of one regular person for the rest of your life. No friends? No bitchy coworkers? What if my sister has some juicy gossip about one of our other sisters?! But I do like the overall sentiment of the song, which is basically: "Let's move far away from everyone we know so they'll stop bothering us." Or at least that's how *I* interpret it.

I got to see Dave live for the first time in my life in 2021, at a ripe old forty-one years of age, and, yes, it was an excruciatingly long time for me to wait to go see this absolute legend. But in my defense, I wasn't trying to stand in the middle of a field in the western Illinois suburbs watching people on shrooms grind on each other in the grass, and also I didn't reliably have a car until a few years ago, and I do not have the kinds of ride-offering friends who are also willing to suffer an interminably long evening of listening to me sing "Ants Marching" at the top of my lungs while shouting "ISN'T THIS SO FUN?" directly into their faces between each song. The show was at Van Andel Arena in Grand Rapids, which is a big enough place that we could see Janet Jackson there (which we did) but small enough that we could make out her facial features without having to squint at them on the jumbotron. It was my first-ever everyone-in-attendance-is-at-least-thirty-nine-years-old concert, and can I say I never want to see a young-people show again? Dude started right on time at 7:00 p.m. and played for two and a half solid hours and then everyone quietly filed out to their minivans in an orderly fashion. I mean, it might've still been light out. That is the ideal concertgoing experience!

I wore soft pants with an elastic waistband and an official DMB sweatshirt I ordered from the merch website, and I didn't feel underdressed or out of place for even a minute. Your dad drank three twenty-seven-dollar lite beers and danced to "What Would You Say" with every ounce of energy in his body, his L.L.Bean fleece jumping and gyrating as if it had a life of its own, and I sat behind him with tears in my eyes, overwhelmed to be at a show with hundreds of people who were likely on the same arthritis medication I am.

7. "I'll Back You Up"

most romantic lyric, to me: "Do as you please, I'll back you up"

This is all I want. Someone to tell me to do whatever I want no matter what and even if it's reckless or horrible they'll still be there to have my back. No one will ever tell me this because I am not to be trusted. I would try to commit some kind of low-stakes crime and immediately turn to Dave, like: "Did you really mean what you said in that song on 1993's certified-platinum album *Remember Two Things*, or were you lying?" Me, brandishing the keys to the getaway car: "I dissected every single song on that mixtape you made me, get your ass up and help me rob this goddamn bank."

8. "Say Goodbye"
(might be too depressing to bone to, not for me though)

most romantic lyric, to me: "Lovers for a night, lovers for tonight"

THIS SONG IS SO HORNY, and that's hilarious because dude is literally saying, over and over and over again, "Hey, friend, I would love to bone you, I'm feeling wild, sexy sex sex, but just for tonight because tomorrow we're saying goodbye." Tonight? Lovers. :) Tomorrow? FRIENDS. :(

It's so funny and honest and literally the way dirtbag men are in real life, which is as rare a thing to find in a pop song as it is when some dude is unbuckling his belt on your couch. He will have his tongue buried in your asshole up to your fucking pancreas saying, "We're just friends, right?" He'll be flipping you on the mattress like a pancake and pause with you in midair like, "I don't want to be tied down in a relationship, this is just for fun, okay?" It's infuriating in practice but hilarious in song form, a man crooning about smoking you down and loving you up in his sweetest coo and then at the end being like . . . tonight only, though.

. . .

If I made music this is the kind of music I would make. I don't mean jam-band-y saxophone solo music, I mean sensitive songs full of howling and begging. In my singer-songwriter phase in my teens (I'm still in that phase, quit playing), I daydreamed I was gonna get a guitar, somehow develop the patience to learn how to play it, then travel around singing my little plaintive songs in smoky coffeehouses as people sitting cross-legged on dusty fake Persian rugs wept into their cappuccinos, even though I had no idea what a cappuccino even was. I thought that I, a person who requires three different soaps in the shower and very specific bedsheets, was gonna stuff a backpack full of drugstore underwear and Salvation Army jeans into whatever kind of terrible used car I could afford and drive around the country playing open mics and sleeping, where, in a hostel? Little Miss Allergies and Bowel Disease is gonna survive on a road diet of gas station snacks and no prescriptions?! In what world?!

9. "The Space Between"

most romantic lyric, to me: "Love is all we need, dear"

Now, I do not believe in this; I believe we need shelter and clothing and shoes and a strong Wi-Fi hookup and an income stream and cell phones and a linen duvet cover and air-conditioning and a coffee machine we both know how to use and separate dressers and similar furniture preferences and a car with all-wheel drive and some cats and designated

sides of the bed and a shared belief on how many refriger-
ated condiments is too many and good dish soap and decent
towels and a gas grill and a tall sturdy couch and lamps and
throw blankets for every season and books and subscriptions
to smart magazines nobody ever reads and a snack cabinet
and gel pillows and cookbooks and a drink fridge and green
plants that require no care and never die and rakes and vac-
uum cleaners and hangers and noise-canceling headphones
and a medicine cabinet and storage bins and dryer sheets and
the occasional night out and charger cords and frying pans
and flower vases and shoe racks and Clorox and a good mop
and postage stamps and chairs and vibrators and a TV in the
bedroom and kitchen utensils and a Bluetooth speaker and a
lawn mower and an ugly dog and a wine cabinet and a computer and Saturday matinees and, and, and . . .

10. "Steady As We Go"

most romantic lyric, to me:
"When I don't say a word / And you know exactly what I mean"

This, to me, is the summit of the mountain that is a relationship.
I've been married for seven years and I'm not itchy but I *am*
out of things to say. And that's okay! Preferable, even! We gotta
normalize the idea that people who live together and work
near each other and know all the same people are eventually
gonna run out of shit to say to each other and acknowledge
that that's natural and healthy. I don't have any new ideas, it's
not like I'm actively learning things all the time; why would a
person who saw me get up in the morning, watched me Han-

sel and Gretel my little bits of life garbage around the house all day every day for nearly a decade want to, I don't know, need to have regular philosophical conversations with me?

"Hmm, while I was at work, Sam had an oat milk latte from Dunkin' at 9:47 a.m. according to this sticker on the side of the cup she left in the sink, forgot her AirPods in the downstairs bathroom, left some wet Crocs in the mudroom, tried and failed to hide a Sephora box in the outside trash, let the dog mess up the bed and tried to cover it up, wrote a grocery list but didn't go to the store, and watched three episodes of *Brooklyn Nine-Nine* without me, even though I told her not to skip ahead" is a sentence I'm sure my wife utters, or at least some variation of it, at least twice a week. Why would she need to talk to me after seeing all that? What else could she possibly need to know?

I want to push back against this idea that it's not real love if you're not passionately chattering at each other all the time, that it's just as valid (and romantic!) to know instinctively when to shut the fuck up.

11. "If I Had It All"

most romantic lyric, to me: "If I had it all, you know I'd fuck it up"

I love that he can admit this! Isn't it fucking refreshing? Every song is like, "I need you so bad / Blah blah blah / Please get with me and cure my depression / I swear I'll always let you use the bathroom first in the morning / I will do the dishes until the end of time / Please fuck me, I promise I won't do anything bad." But here's Dave admitting right out the gate that if he gets you, because you are "it all," he will destroy you. And if you're into that . . . by all means.

I was listening to the Smashing Pumpkins' *Siamese Dream* in the car the other day, a record I have a visceral response to and one that transports me right back to my locker in the freshman wing of Evanston Township High School, jamming my dirty gym clothes on top of the algebra book I never opened. I hear "Soma" and immediately panic that I haven't done my Spanish homework, but here's another weird thing: it doesn't sound old or outdated to me. Despite my having a crystal clear memory of listening to this on cassette while riding the bus, it didn't sound like an antiquated relic; it just sounded cool. Then the Cranberries came on the terrestrial radio classic rock station a couple of days later, and I almost drove my car off the fucking road. Excuse me? "Linger" is fucking classic rock??? I'm sick. This must be how our parents felt. Am I my own mom?!

Every time my dad was putting a Betty Wright LP on and cranking it up so loud it drowned out the Smurfs on TV, I'd be feeling sorry for him. "Ugh, this old brontosaurus thinks this music is still good." But I get it now, your jam is always gonna sound like your jam, timeless and relevant even if the youths fail to appreciate it.

12. "Let You Down"

most romantic lyric, to me: "I'm a puppy for your love"

Here I am, wagging my lil fluffy tail, thumping it against the hardwood floor, covered in microscopic bugs, eating my own poop, just desperately trying to get you to kiss me!

13. "Crush" (Radio City version)

most romantic lyric, to me: "Lovely lady / Let me drink you, please"

This is about eating pussy, right? There's an earlier lyric in which he says "I am at your feet," and listen, there are not enough songs about a man getting on the floor and worshipping at his woman's feet, then working his way up to suck her vaginal fluids dry. That's so hot. Plus, I love a song about having a crush. I love thinking about crushes. I love the idea that he has a crush on someone but maybe he doesn't, because there's a later lyric where he sings, "Crush me, come on, oh yeah," and he's definitely talking about her squeezing his head like a juicy plum between her thighs, right? Either way, don't ever let anyone tell you this dude is not an absolute freak who loves *S-E-X*.

14. "Belly Belly Nice"

most romantic lyric, to me: "You can't get too much love"

I mean, CAN YOU???

My friend Wil Blades, whom I have known forever—literally from back in the days when white kids like him had ill-advised dreadlocks and smoked weed before class and taped Bob Marley posters over their beds—lives in Oakland

and plays the Hammond B3 organ, and he's always touring with cool groups. Dude texts me and is like "GIRL
WE'RE OPENING FOR DAVE MATTHEWS BAND
AT ALPINE VALLEY THIS SUMMER YOU GOTTA
COME." He told me that if I did, he could get me backstage
to meet Dave. Do I want to? No, because I don't want to
humiliate myself. But do I have to? I think I do. Can't wait
to cry on my king while blubbering, "I love you, you're so
romantic!"

chub street diet

Samantha Irby had the most boring week of all time because she doesn't live in a culinarily adventurous town, and we told her we wouldn't publish this if it was just detailed descriptions of every menu item at Olive Garden. Honestly, we aren't sure why we even asked her to participate in this in the first place, other than that we thought she might have something funny to say about Midwestern casseroles. We reached out to several other writers (you know the ones), but she's the only one who replied to our email. Damn, she uses a lot of exclamation points. The eagerness to please was palpable. What a huge mistake.

[grotesque illustration of Samantha Irby looking pained]

Wednesday, February 9

I wake up in a panic at eight thirty because it scares me when I've slept straight through my wife getting up, dealing with the cats' breakfast and litter boxes, taking the dog out in the blizzarding snow, feeding the dog, taking a shower during which the dog squeezes out the poop he refused to do in the cold on the bathroom floor before tunneling his way back under the covers next to my sleeping carcass, turning every light on in the house to get dressed, loudly grinding coffee beans, clanging around making a lunch to eat cold at her desk, and noisily gathering all the important papers and files she needs for her real job before leaving the house. Whenever I wake up in a completely silent house after all that, it makes me wonder if maybe I died for a couple of hours, because what kind of creature that isn't a hibernating bear can sleep like that?

Every other Wednesday we pay a service to come and do a surface clean of our shitty house. The dog is a maniac who goes berserk when anyone walks in because we got him during quarantine and couldn't train him not to aggressively protect his Lamb Chop stuffy or whatever it is he gets so bonkers about, so I like to get him out of the house before they arrive so they don't call animal control on me. The problem with this is that I never know when they're going to arrive; sometimes they come at nine, other times they've rolled in at eleven thirty, and one anxiety-inducing time they didn't come until four in the afternoon. I am deeply uncomfortable with the idea of picking up a telephone to ask a person, "Hey, did you forget to clean my house today?" and will never do that ever, so I just try to get out early and not return home until after dark.

Before I do that, I bolt out of bed and drink a bottle of water in the shower after I pour these <u>cucumber-flavored probiotic crystals</u> down my throat. I don't know what they do or if they even work, but my friend who might actually be in an MLM scheme sells them, and they come in these convenient little stick packs. The box has a lot of scientific mumbo jumbo on it about balancing microflora and gut colonization, and that kind of phrasing is catnip to me, a gullible idiot. After throwing on the same clothes I wore yesterday and digging the dog out from under the duvet on my bed, I pause in the kitchen and consider not spending $84 on coffee for once, but rather than google "how to use an AeroPress" for the hundredth time, I instead do some light precleaning so the company that charges me $75 will have less to do.

After dropping the dog off at school I drive to a different part of the strip mall parking lot where no one who works at the dog school can see me having a panic attack, then I park the car near the karate dojo that isn't open yet to watch men go in and out of BJ Benjim's Big and Tall—"Big Buys for Big Guys"—for an hour until I feel less nuts. I drive past the fancy coffee place where last week the dude at the window said, "A cranberry orange scone again?! You must really like those!" and drive five miles out of the way to go to Dunkin', where the rotating cast of disaffected teens who man the intercom could not give a *shit* what the fuck I order there. I leave the drive-thru with my iced oat milk latte feeling like Ben Affleck. I think about how to waste some time before I go back home to waste some *more* time, and I decide to drive out to Ric & Stan's, my favorite car wash because they have a hippie dog wearing cool shades in their logo, and also they use pink soap during breast-cancer-awareness month. They do not serve food there.

Thursday, February 10

First thing in the morning (ten o'clock, come on now), I'm supposed to have a work meeting with a person I've never met before, and I decide to go to my temporary office so this lady won't have to see all my cats swarming in the background while she talks to me about Very Important Television Show Business. Just kidding, nothing I do is important, but you can't tell that to Hollywood people or it literally short-circuits their brains. Every meeting I've ever had involves my agent's assistant emailing me something to the effect of:

Hi Sam, available times for Dirk Dirkwood at [*a network I've never heard of*] or [*a production company that sounds fake*] who would *love* a meeting:

Monday June 37th from 6:00–6:07 p.m. PST
[*9:00 p.m. my time*]

Wednesday March 116th 11:37–11:52 p.m. PST
[*2:37 a.m. my time*]

Thursday September –41st 7:02–7:07 a.m. PST and that's a hard out for him he will literally die if he has to talk to you for more than five minutes

Let me know your avails and I will set it up. Thanks!

I usually read these emails three or four times, racking my brain to remember if I've met Dirk Dirkwood before or if I'd previously agreed to meet with him and am therefore contractually obligated to follow through, trying to read between the words to figure out what this proposed meeting could possibly be about. When nothing turns up in my brain I write back:

hey what is this for

The response is instantaneous:

Hi Sam, it's just a general! They're huge fans over at [*imaginary network full of people who are absolutely not "fans"*]! So can I schedule this for Tuesday July 93rd at 13:54? (please learn military time, lol) Does that work for you?

Then I say:

am i selling them something are they giving me a job

i don't have any ideas please don't make me do this

And finally, I receive:

Relax! No need to prepare anything! They just want an introduction! You're all set for Novembruary 92nd at 2100 GMT, here are six identical-looking Zoom links! Good luck figuring out which one to click before your meeting that absolutely must begin on time!

I don't like to eat or drink during Zoom meetings because I can't stop staring at myself and scrutinizing every little thing my face does. Plus if you eat on camera that invites the person you're talking to to inquire about what was so goddamn irresistible that you had to be shoveling it into your mouth right in their fucking face. Because whatever I'm eating is never, say, "a crispy dukkah-spiced chickpea salad with frizzled shallots and turmeric tahini dressing." It's always something like "a chunk of cold meat I pried off the leftover rotisserie chicken in the fridge smeared with dill mustard and a brown banana I mashed into a cup of blue yogurt marketed to children." I don't want to admit that to someone who lives in Los Angeles!

To keep my stomach from roaring like a tiger and embarrassing me on a hot mic, I decide to make one of my favorite signature meals: <u>hot bread</u>. I'm not talking about toast, which is its own delicious invention, I mean a little stack of raisin bread microwaved for twenty seconds, then spread with a thin layer of fake butter to be quickly inhaled off a single-ply paper towel while standing next to the sink. To wash it down, I drink a bottle of <u>BIOLYTE</u>, which bills itself as "the IV in a bottle." Man, I love intravenous fluids. If I could be hooked up to a bag of saline every morning when I wake up and every night before I fall asleep, I would be thrilled. It's the best part of going to the hospital! I know little kids are like, "When I grow up I wanna be rich so I can buy a hundred cars," but my lifelong dream is to get rich so I can afford top-notch in-home health care. It's wild to me that the Amazon dude is out here building spaceships when he could be hiring doctors and nurses to move in down the hall and attend to his every physical need. This might be a sick-person-specific desire, but I'm telling you, it's real. Let me trip over a million-dollar bill one day. I'd have a port in my arm before I even got to the bank to deposit it.

After my morning meeting, I'm mentally exhausted from coming up with a decent-sounding answer to the question "So [*dramatic pause*], any potential projects or ideas you want to throw at us?" that I was promised I wouldn't be asked, and my face is sore from smiling so hard in an effort to appear friendly and nonthreatening. I take a couple <u>extra-strength eight-hour Tylenol</u> washed down with some steaming <u>Throat Coat tea</u> I lace with spicy honey to soothe my aching vocal cords from their hourlong "high-octave excitement voice" performance.

It's my night to cook dinner, which I prefer to do in the morning, but since I had to panic about the meeting while staring into space for an hour beforehand and then waste time doing an extended improv bit through the meeting itself, I'm off my schedule, which zaps my ambition to prepare anything complex. I have dozens of fancy cookbooks and will attempt to make almost anything, but only if I start working on it before 10:00 a.m. Since it's already after noon, I only have the energy to make one of my regulars. I crack open a <u>Diet Coke</u> and shuffle-play this banging yacht rock Spotify playlist I made from my phone. It's the best music to cook to, because it's upbeat without demanding choreographed dancing, and the nostalgia is comforting. I like a song I can sing along to while pretending it's 1987, just crooning in harmony with Bread while trimming my little beans and shucking my little corns. I hit shuffle-play and "Dance with Me" by Orleans comes on, and I sway in front of the pantry, figuring out what I can make with ingredients we already have so I don't have to deal with the store.

By the time George Benson's "Turn Your Love Around"

starts blasting out of the Bluetooth speaker we keep in the dining room, I've gathered all the ingredients I need to make this kale and white bean soup that everyone knows means: "Sam had a stressful day today." First, I cut up a kielbasa into skinny coins, then toss it into a heavy soup pot with a couple of glugs of the <u>cheapest olive oil they had at the store</u>. I add a tablespoon or three of minced garlic from the jar, because I am never mincing my own garlic.

"'You're puttin' a rush on me / But I'd like to know you better,'" I sing with Stephanie Mills as I turn the heat on medium high. While that's cooking, I dump two cans of cannellini beans in a colander and rinse them with cool water, then I stir the sausages so they don't stick to the bottom of the pot. "Biggest Part of Me" by Ambrosia starts playing, and I let out an auntie scream and drop everything I'm doing to step across the kitchen, but the garlic is crackling, so I come to my senses and stir the pot, then I dump in a large can of diced tomatoes and fill the can with water and add that, too. I crank in some salt and pepper, and ten-plus dashes of <u>Cholula</u> while playing air saxophone. I played the saxophone in marching band in middle and high school, so my fake saxophoning is extremely realistic.

I add the beans to the pot and turn up the heat, stirring again for good measure. I take a break to close my eyes and let Bette Midler serenade me with "Do You Want to Dance?" Damn, this bitch can sing. I get the bag of <u>kale</u> that seems to be ever present in the refrigerator and wash the whole bunch, because have you ever tried separating kale?! It's a nightmare, and this music has me feeling too good to wreck my Tylenol buzz, so the whole thing is going in. Who cares. I take a big, sharp knife and chop off the rough stems to the beat of "Laughter in the Rain" by Neil Sedaka, and then I cut the rest into ragged chunks.

I like to make soup because nothing has to be precise. You can literally just put cut-up pieces of whatever into some spicy water and add some oil and alliums to it and cook it for a while and then you have a filling meal whose warmth you can hug to your chest as you eat it—if you have the right kind of bowls. "Your Sweet Love," a monster of a jam by Al Jarreau, comes on, and I add the kale to the pot, let it simmer for the duration of the song plus the five minutes Paul McCartney's "No More Lonely Nights" takes, and then I turn off the heat and cover the pot until dinnertime, when I decide I want <u>a fish dinner from Culver's</u> instead.

Friday, February 11

I agreed to do a podcast today even though I always regret agreeing to do podcasts, because I always sound like an idiot and I have no control over how I am edited, which is fine but also reckless as hell. Lucky for me the podcast people cancel, so all that's on the agenda is taking the dog to his little school and then sitting in front of the computer pretending to be doing some meaningful work. After I drop the dog off, I decide to go to this office I rent across town to feel like I have a reason to occasionally leave the house, although it often comes in handy when I have to talk to people who might be disgusted by our circus of pets yowling and barking as they somersault off the furniture behind me in my living room corner "office."

There's nothing but a Family Dollar and some <u>abandoned</u> <u>train tracks</u> near the building where my office is, and I hate leaving in the middle of a productive workday. When I get a good early-morning spot in the parking lot, I can't stand the thought of losing it if I were to go out to get rations. So, like a squirrel, I try to gather all my nuts before I get there so I don't have to fight any of the hipster bros I'm too afraid to introduce myself to when I buy lunch. I go to Panera because it's the only place that's open in the morning where you can get a breakfast sandwich and a lunch sandwich at the same time, and it looks like I'm not the only genius with that great idea. The man ahead of me is ordering a Greek salad with extra onions (hold the olives) at 9:00 a.m., and I like his style.

Bored in the wraparound Starbucks drive-thru line with my Panera sandwiches warming on the heated passenger seat beside me, I take some more of those probiotic crystals because Past Me was looking out for Future Me and threw a few packets in my bag. Then when I get to the speaker, they're out of oat milk (WHAT?!), and I can't get that shaken espresso drink or whatever it's called, so I scramble and end up ordering a . . . . venti iced green tea "with a little mango in it?" The silence on the other end of the intercom lasts long enough to make my cheeks hot, roasting me from the inside with the embarrassment that I've said some wrong thing. Thirty agonizing seconds later, the disembodied voice tells me my total—$200.14—and I scooch closer to the minivan full of toddlers in front of me.

After staring at the computer in my dim basement office for eight hours, I decide to pack my stuff and go stare at the computer in my home. It's a Friday night and my wife's kids aren't home, which means we can get wild and treat ourselves to dinner prepared by someone other than either of us. I love ordering takeout. I will pick up food from a dark and foreboding alley if it means I don't have to cook for children whose constant disapproval causes me physical pain. I'd rather listen to you calling me the c-word than hear one of them say "Can I be excused?" in an annoyed tone while pushing away from the elaborate meal I slaved over to go eat stale Fritos and drink room-temperature Arizonas in front of the Nintendo in their bedroom.

We don't have a single Thai restaurant in this town but there *are* seventeen different styles of pizza, so I make my lady choose between thin-crust Chicago pub cut or a slightly thicker thin-crust Detroit style. She chooses the latter, so I pull up the <u>Buddy's</u> menu online and order us two separate personals because I don't like beets and kumquats and shit all on my pizza.

Saturday, February 12

Tomorrow is my birthday, so to celebrate I spend the entire morning in bed with a blanket over my face and a fan blowing directly on me, then I get up and decide that to celebrate for real, I would like to spend forty-five-ish minutes driving to Grand Rapids to get a gyro from this good-ass Bosnian restaurant there called <u>Bosna Express</u>. I don't know what the hell they do to make the food so good but GODDAMN. I like to order an O.G., which is gyro meat and tomatoes and onions stuffed into lepinja bread and a side of special fries, which are seasoned and served with tons of chopped herbs and fresh garlic on top. I'm never trying to eat forty-five-minute-old fries, so my lady and I split the order in the car in the parking lot, wolfing them down like animals as people walk by watching us in horror, then kill the sandwiches while they're still hot. I also get a salad for dinner later because, surprisingly, lettuce with a bunch of shit on it is the only thing that will still be good after touring southwest Michigan in the back seat of my car.

I wake up screaming at 3:00 a.m. with a charley horse from hell in my left calf, and I roll out of bed and hobble gingerly to the kitchen to get a glass of water. A long time ago my friend Melissa told me about this stuff called <u>DripDrop</u> that you can get at Walgreens that turns a regular glass of water into nutrient-rich, less-gross Gatorade. You just pour this little flavored powder (I'm partial to mango) into your water, stir it up, then drink it without gagging because it doesn't taste like salted asshole like every other sports drink. I had to fly to New York a few months ago, and since I only feel comfortable traveling when I am dehydrated and starving, I brought a bunch of DripDrops in my carry-on to make my mini plane waters more hydrating. The box says it has three times the electrolytes and half the sugar of regular drinks, which legally makes it health food. I perform some chemistry—stir the powder in cold water until it mostly dissolves—and drink the whole thing, including the unincorporated silt at the bottom of the glass, while checking my text messages to see if anyone texted me at midnight since it's officially my birthday. No one has.

Sunday, February 13

Today is the Super Bowl. I'm too old to need a whole lot of birthday fuss, so this year I took it easy and demanded that Kirsten make an array of dips and assorted dip vessels, oh, and also a cheesecake to celebrate my many years cheating death on this rotten planet. I start the day doing a yoga sun salute, then drink a liter of warm lemon water, thanking God for allowing me to see another sunrise. I follow that by feeding myself some avocado on sprouted grain bread with fermented sprouts; which is to say that I drink a <u>Fresca</u> in one long swallow and take a shower just so I might feel like I put some effort into being alive before settling into the couch for thirteen straight hours of pregame coverage.

I love dip dinner. It's my favorite of all the novelty meals, mostly because I don't know anyone who isn't downright delighted when presented with a steaming bowl of cheese-mixed-with-other-shit-but-pretty-much-just-cheese to dunk a <u>sturdy chip</u> in. There's a Southwest-style, vaguely Mexican spicy corn dip; an inscrutable tomato-based concoction that is very scrumptious; and the <u>Alison Roman labneh with fried scallions dip</u> that tastes like fancy ranch dressing. Don't let this menu fool you. I would have been just as happy with a tub of store-brand French onion with a bag of Ruffles. I'm glad we had bougie dips, though. It made me feel like a slobbery-fingered princess.

Monday, February 14

Valentine's Day dinner is always an enormous letdown, because it usually falls on a day when Kirsten has to go to work, which is also a day she's gonna come home mad and tired, so my doing anything "special" without it involving pajama bottoms and a sweatshirt that doesn't require a bra is gonna get side-eyed. So I ordered some flowers from the internet (I cannot walk into a florist, I do not know what to say, I have no idea what to do with my hands) and they arrive intact, and our marriage will live to see another day, which is wild because I immediately offer to make her a peanut butter sandwich for dinner, basically undoing all my hard romantic work in a split second. She refuses, and I find an expensive sushi spot on DoorDash that will deliver thawed-out frozen sushi rolls because we don't live anywhere near the damn ocean and save the day. I fetch her loosest pajama bottoms and a hoodie I bought from the Erykah Badu merch store because I am too agoraphobic to go to shows anymore and we sit on the couch and watch the little digital car pinwheel around the app's digital map in search of our house. Love wins!

my firstborn dog

I was talking to a man (first mistake), reminiscing about old shit (that's a trap, never do it), and he said to me, with the kind of brazenness only handsome people can get away with: "Level with me, baby: Don't you wish we'd gotten serious back in the day and had a kid?" I damn near choked on my own tongue.

Excuse me, sir? What are you asking me? Do I wish that instead of talking about weed strains you and I were instead arguing about summer camp fees and community college applications?

What is it about being comfortably ensconced in middle age, deep in the cozy confines of his sweatpants-in-the-middle-of-a-Tuesday years, that makes a man who should be on an aspirin regimen say something like that to a woman who is no longer shedding eggs and endometrial lining? Is it boredom? Regret?? Dementia??? I stared slack-jawed at my phone, wishing it was 1998 and I had a receiver I could slam into its cradle.

"Don't you wish you'd had a kid?" Do I wish I could stand

idly by and witness all the things I hate about myself mani-
fested in, and mirrored back to me by, a person it's against
the law for me to kill? I absolutely do not!

Imagine, if you will, my child:

FAT, which is great, who cares, it's in his DNA and can't
be helped, but also I would serve themed dinners like
"bread night" or "every pizza from the store," and that's
fine by me, but you know some fucking hater who hates
fun would hear about it and report me to child services.

SICK. I mean, I'm sick, so I probably could only produce a sickly child? I'm not an epidemiologist, but that
just feels true. I don't think any of my various conditions
is even hereditary, but I know in my weakened bones that
any offspring I produce would be riddled with maladies. I
don't mind, but I am two-plus years overdue for a mam-
mogram and a full checkup right now, and if you are
that lax with a child, I'm pretty sure, once again, you go
to jail.

CAN'T READ. We'd be a TV house because I love TV
and also—have you ever tried to talk to a child? I've never
met a little kid with good jokes or opinions! And reading
to them is like "cat rat bat shat," and that's a big snooze.
So we would just watch shows all day, and the kid would
grow up with no clue what the alphabet even *is*. So yeah,
like I said: jail!

UNDISCIPLINED. Though I am an ardent rule fol-
lower, I possess zero personal discipline and have no idea

how to instill that virtuous quality into another human being. Cut to Future Me and Future Baby eating chips and not doing laundry. Every day.

BAD TEETH. I got my shitty teeth from my mother, and my kid would get them from me, and I wouldn't have enough money for proper orthodontia because there's *never* enough money for all the shit a kid needs, and then there'd be *two* of us sitting around with buck teeth and discount crowns and every time that little yuckmouth wailed in my face about a toy, the sight of his rotting gums would make me sad.

QUIETLY HOSTILE is how I would describe my public personality; I am mild-mannered and super polite, but just beneath the surface of my skin, my blood is electrified and I am one inconsiderate driver away from a full *Falling Down*–style emotional collapse. I don't know how to teach a child not to seethe and instead to develop a healthy coping and communication style, because I do not know how to do that for myself.

Are these all just words that describe . . . me? One hundred percent yes, and they describe my illiterate, toothless mother as well, which is how I know with absolute certainty that this is what any one of the millions of unfertilized eggs I've reabsorbed into my body would have evolved into had ol' enlarged prostate and I ever foolishly attempted to procreate "back in the day."

When I was an actual kid growing up on welfare with a sick mom and expired Tuna Helper from the dollar store, the future and its infinite possibilities stretched before me like a sumptuous buffet I couldn't afford to go to, one I'd be forced to watch other people enjoy from where I stood: outside, pressing my sebum into the glass and drooling. Even at nine years old I knew there was no way I was gonna ruin my chance to fill my adult life with overpriced candles and designer lip balms by giving birth to a baby with a bad personality whose needs I'd be legally required to place above my own for eighteen-plus interminable years.

I have never been pregnant. I'm not saying to brag but to let you know I would wrap a dick in plutonium if I could, just to make sure there's no earthly way a human child could wriggle its way through any protective barrier and swim past all my sluggish organs to implant its rapidly multiplying cells in my inhospitable uterine lining.

I had an ablation five years ago and thank God it worked, so even if I accidentally slipped and fell on an ejaculating penis, all those spermies are gonna find at the end of their .18-meter relay is an empty haunted house overtaken by gooey floating cobwebs. Honestly, *you* should thank God too that you don't have to watch Me and Me Junior trying to put each other in a headlock in the middle of Saks to determine which one of us was gonna get the one small bottle of Jo Malone Me could afford! Or hearing about Me seething watching Me Junior get the one good entrée at the steak place while I make do with the sides! Me Junior wearing shoes with holes in the soles because Me couldn't resist the siren song of a perfect deep coral blush from Pat McGrath!

We got a pandemic dog because our local SPCA really turned up the advertising juice with everybody stuck at home looking for a reason to get even three lousy minutes of fresh (masked) air. One morning my lady logged onto Facebook for her daily dose of Russian disinformation and saw a post about a mangy little gremlin dog named Granny who was in need of a loving home. *Our* loving home, where I would be happy to shift my endless search-scroll for "good Zoom lipsticks" to "cute chew toys" and "little dog shirts."

Granny was the perfect theoretical dog. According to our local SPCA's GeoCities looking-ass website, Granny was a teeny tiny gooey-eyed seven-year-old chihuahua whose likes included sitting, sleeping, lying down, relaxing, cuddling, being comfortable, warm blankets, snuggling, and resting, and her dislikes consisted of one thing: walking outside. Kirsten called me into the uninsulated sunroom, a corner of which she'd converted to an "office" that didn't have a door or any privacy. I stood over her shoulder, squinting at the grimy little dog on her laptop as our cloudy breath hung in the frigid air between us, and said, "She's perfect. Let's get her."

Did I want a dog? Not really! But neither of us was particularly enjoying this preview of our retirement years, bumping into each other while shuffling our feet from room to room after having run out of interesting things to talk about months earlier, and at least if we got a dog we could talk to each other about every little thing the dog did?

"Look, she blinked!"

"Hey, did you see that big yawn?"

"How many kibbles did she eat this afternoon?"

"Wow! What a big poop!"

All this would take the pressure off of us having to be interesting or finding something new to say, and thus it would save our relationship. Not that our relationship needed a rescue, but come on, what if we used up all possible conversational topics in year four because we were trapped together without a tiny chihuahua to otherwise keep us distracted from our shortcomings and entertained?

It was a Saturday when we saw the listing for Granny online, so I spent the rest of the weekend fantasizing about all the places I would sneak a tiny dog into: picture me rolling up to your birthday party at the club and whipping eenie weenie Granny out of the kangaroo pocket of my hoodie like "SURPRISE!!! You're forty-seven! Look at my little-ass dog!" That would rule. Also, these cats are emotionally withholding, and I'm sick of humiliating myself for a crumb of their affection. Granny was going to ride in the cupholder of my car, smooching my palm every time I reached for my Starbucks cup, nodding along to whatever musical selection was bumping from the speaker. Yes, she would be a gross and obnoxious dog, *but* she'd be the cat version: small, snuggly, and doing her business in a box in a corner of the bathroom!

We called the SPCA Monday and were told that, unfortunately for us, Granny had already been scooped up. I mean, of course. I can't be the only bored piece of shit in southwest Michigan who is allergic to being outdoors and looking for the company of a tiny immobile dog. The cats all screamed, "THANK GOD!!!!" in unison and were sure they'd won this round, but I remained undeterred.

A couple of weeks later another chihuahua was featured on the SPCA personal ads, this time an eight-year-old named Felicity. "Damn, I loved that show," I said, looking at her crooked little smile. We called to inquire about her and were told that she, too, had been adopted immediately. They just hadn't had a chance to take down her picture. I'm never gonna buy a dog, and two strikes is plenty for me, especially when it comes to something I don't care about. I mean, dogs are gross and bad, I'm not gonna break my neck trying to get one? The cats, satisfied that whatever spell they'd placed on our adoption chances had worked, retreated back into the shadows where they plot their mischief.

I'm not even sure how Bubbles ended up on Kirsten's radar—she's doing something in the other room right now, and I don't feel like asking—but one day, she texted me a screenshot of this pale, sad-looking dog and: "This guy is available??!!?!" Apparently she'd found his listing while digging through the bowels of the website. He wasn't featured prominently like Granny and Felicity had been. He was tucked away a handful of slow-loading pages deep, after all the animals who need surgery and special care. "Ew he's ugly," I texted back, "but let's get him anyway."

At the end of that school day, we piled into the car and I drove like a madwoman, determined to not have another rickety dog snatched from my grasp at the last second. We burst into the door, looking wildly around for a volunteer to help us. When one appeared, Kirsten and I both shouted "IS BUBBLES STILL HERE?" at the harried woman, who looked us over pitifully before guiding us toward the visitation room. She told us she'd get him, and the feeling I'd been hoping for, victory over imaginary adoptive parental competitors, washed over me. We waited in silence until the door opened and Bubbles, a scrawny guy wearing a too-small camo fleece cape, came trotting in, glaring at us.

"Here he is!" the volunteer exclaimed, bubbling over with fake enthusiasm.

She closed the door, and Bubbles stood there, looking bored. He didn't really engage with us, just stood there looking uninterested in both the treats and the love we offered him. Two minutes after she'd gone, the volunteer tapped the door and let herself in.

"Here's the paperwork!" she said cheerfully. "Just fill all this information out and he's yours! Is there a credit card you'd like me to run for the adoption fee?"

Hold up, what happened to all that time we were supposed to have to get acquainted and decide whether he seemed like he'd be a good (i.e., stinky and nonpaying) roommate? I looked down at him skeptically.

"Something's not right with this dude," I said to Kirsten, but she waved me off, picking him up and trying to snuggle him even though he'd gone stiff as a board. She told me to shut up and fill out my information, so I picked up the clipboard from the table and started writing, watching Bubbles out of the corner of one eye. I paid his ransom and glanced tearfully in the direction of the cat room. We left with our new dog, whom I thought we should call Abraham because it sounds regal and distinguished. I drove while the dog stood rigid on Kirsten's lap, surfing the potholes and uneven roads, clearly freak behavior.

"Why do you think she was so quick to push him out the door?" I asked as I slid into a parking spot in front of Chow Hound. "We didn't even get a good look at him before she was busting in with the papers." I looked over at where he was standing cemented to her thigh. "He's weird. I don't like him."

"He's just nervous!" she said. "Now go get some dog stuff."

I gave him one last look before putting on my mask and

going into a store where a bunch of teenagers were gonna lecture me on stuff I already knew about dogs and their care. I got a cart and walked up and down every aisle, throwing in a bed and leashes and toys and a crate, and no one talked to me until I got to the food section, where a person I could've given birth to said, "Are you sure about that Royal Canin? Let me talk to you about Purina One!"

Listen, I don't know anything about history or geography, I don't know who invented lightning or what plants are poisonous, I can't tell you anything about any movie that does not feature Tommy Lee Jones prominently in it, but the one thing I *do* know? Shit about dog food. I answered the phone at an animal hospital for fourteen years, which is why I knew enough to get out of that conversational death trap by telling my daughter that I wanted "a breed-specific kibble for its palatability and chewing ease." Maybe I should have gone to vet school.

In any case, here's an abbreviated list of why, I assume, this dog was left in a bassinet outside the SPCA doors like Baby Moses by that biblical river:

- He barks at everything.
- He's very dumb.
- He's very dumb and very naughty.
- If you put him in a crate he screams.
- He's a picky eater.
- He barks at everything.
- His eyes leak constantly.
- He stinks.
- If you take him out of a crate he screams.
- He's too loud.

- He fights the cats.
- If he sees a squirrel during a walk, he will spin in a circle ninety-two times before you can move.
- He jumps on the dining room table and buries his face in your dinner.
- He barks at everything.
- If the doorbell rings, he goes apoplectic.
- He stands on the corner of his indoor pee grass and pisses off the side and onto the floor.
- He steals cat food.
- If you leave for longer than he likes, he scratches paint off the door.
- He will not walk if it's raining.
- He commandeers every blanket in the house for himself.
- He refuses to sleep in any of his many beds at night, preferring the human bed.
- He barks at everything.
- His one trick is "shake," and he's bad at it.
- He screams at the vet.
- He tries to get tough with dangerous wildlife.
- He only likes Kirsten.
- He insists on being in your lap in the car.
- He's always trembling, even when it's hot.
- He's so fucking bossy!
- If you're chopping vegetables on a cutting board, he thinks someone is knocking on the door and loses his mind.
- He'll bark his head off at a precious blade of spring grass if it is ruffled by a gentle breeze.
- He is not cuddly.

- He's always aggressively cutting his eyes at me.
- He is rude to guests.
- He won't take his various medicines without making it into a whole production.
- He is impervious to calming measures.
- If he slips out the door, he will run so far and fast that you have to get in the car to hunt him down and bring him back.
- HE BARKS AT EVERYTHING, CONSTANTLY.

Our vet told us that it would take a year to potty train Abe because his smooth walnut brain is too small to learn things fast, and I am proud to say that it's been almost three years, and I just found a lake of urine with two turds bobbing on its surface in the basement this morning, literal minutes after he'd enjoyed a luxurious twenty-minute walk through the nearby forest preserve. We took him to a puppy-training class at PetSmart, where a young, half-asleep stoner kid taught us how to teach him his name and to come to us from the other side of a training pen in exchange for a delicious Rachael Ray treat, which we could conveniently locate in aisle seven for purchase. Unfortunately we got kicked out of class before we could make much progress because Abe could hear other dogs as they calmly shopped alongside their owners and devolved to the point where he stood there yapping at the ceiling, hoping all the dogs he couldn't see over the side of the barrier would quake at his high-pitched shrieking.

The first daycare I called had a waitlist several months long, and the second one didn't even answer the phone, which is a business model I honestly respect. The third one said they'd be happy to have him, on a trial basis, which they could revoke at any time. The morning of his first day I woke up filled with dread, worried that this creature whom I was responsible for and was also a reflection of me was going to show his fool ass and humiliate me in front of a bunch of strangers who would be right to judge me. I loaded him into the car and drove to daycare, scolding him the entire way: "Don't bark too much. Don't play too rough. Don't eat anyone else's lunch. Don't pee where you're not supposed to. Don't talk back. Don't bite anyone. Don't get up during naptime." This is exactly like parenting a child, right? Threatening a small creature with limited cognition into doing what you want, ostensibly for their own good?

I deposited him into the arms of a very nice and unsuspecting stranger, and then I peeled out of the parking lot before she could change her mind. Of course, I treated myself to a $6 coffee for being such a good mom. I turned my ringer all the way up and waited all morning for a call telling me to come get my bad-ass son, but none came, so I relaxed a little and put my phone on vibrate and kept an eye on it throughout the afternoon. They never called. Somehow, we'd made it through an entire day of school without my having to deliver the apology I'd rehearsed in the drive-thru while waiting for my oat milk latte. I was proud of that little rascal!

I waited in line at school pickup with the other moms, who chatted about, I don't know, the best brand of harness, excited to hear about Abe's first day of kindergarten. His little classmates paraded past me, beautiful, well-trained springer spaniels and golden retrievers with luscious blond coats. They sat patiently waiting to be leashed and led to gleaming Volvos and Mercedes-Benzes into which they jumped without struggle or complaint. One graceful papillon even leapt into the *crate* in the trunk of his dad's car! I shook my head and glanced back at my crusty, dirty Honda, whose seats were caked with Abe's sharp, spiky hairs from when I'd tried, and failed, to wrestle him off my clean lap at a red light earlier that morning. Abe was vigorously tongue-bathing his empty nuts as the teacher carried him out to me, and I tried to cringe not too loudly.

"So, he had a great day?" I asked, leading the witness.

"Well . . ." She hesitated, and I glared at the dog in her arms, still consumed with his penis. "He's a very spirited guy! [*That meant he was bad.*] And wow, so vocal! [*He was loud and bad.*] And he loves to be a leader! [*He was bossy and loud and bad.*]"

I waited for her to tell me to try that place that wouldn't answer when I called the first time because he was no longer welcome, and when she didn't, I asked, "Um, is he allowed to come back?" I braced myself for a rebuke.

"Oh, of course! We love him!"

In the car he looked at me like "Bitch, you doubted me?" and whipped around to bark at some other, better-behaved dogs as they subserviently trotted in lockstep with their owners.

Daycare emails me a report card at the end of every session, and every day I recoil from the pictures of placid, happy dogs terrorized by my scrawny, watery-eyed offspring. I swipe through photo after photo of good-boy-sitting dogs being choked, manhandled, swatted, barked at, chewed on, and mounted by my wild-ass son who has zero discipline and also? THE BOY CAN'T READ!!!!!!!!!!!!!!!!!!!

"Level with me, baby: Don't you wish we'd gotten serious back in the day and had a kid?"

"No way, man! I have a fucking dog!"

body horror!

In my mid-to-late twenties, I had one of those mid-to-late-twenties epiphanies you have when you get your first twinge of sciatica or when some other age-related corporeal break-down makes itself known to you. It triggered the crushing realization that I was not going to be young and lubricated for much longer and caused my brain to fry like a Partnership for a Drug-Free America egg: "Wait a minute, my lower back aches? I should probably start paying my bills on time."

When I was a teenager, I thought twenty-seven was the definitive, full-stop age I needed to have my shit together by based, I'm pretty sure, solely on this article I'd read in a magazine that said you have until age twenty-seven to shrink the fat cells in your body or be stuck with them forever. Imagine this world, where it seemed plausible that I could be fat for the first twenty-six years of my life then go on, I don't know, the Atkins diet, eat hot dogs for a year, and then magically become skinny for the rest of my life. Think of how hopeful you gotta be to believe some shit like that. I wish I still had that optimism.

I made a list of things I should do that real grown-ups do, like "make preventative dental appointments" and "learn to enjoy unsalted squash." But, look, I don't remember that I even *have* teeth until the holes in them start radiating shock-waves of incandescent pain through my skull, and I cannot imagine being put together enough to do things like take care of the jagged mouth bones I use every single day *in advance*. I think it's hardwired in you from childhood that you are either a person who painstakingly maintains things from the moment you remove them from the package, ensuring they remain nice and reliable for their intended life span, or, otherwise, you are like me, already damaging your bright new shiny thing as you take it out of the fucking box. I was born strangling myself with the cord; I continue passively trying to kill myself to this day.

At that time, one of the resolutions I'd made in my attempt to conduct myself more like a grown-up person was to stop hooking up with people who didn't value my jokes or the wide range of varying interests I'd adopted to look cool and interesting in front of them. This, of course, was a total flop because no one had ever been interested prior to then. Plus I felt desperate in my need to catch up. Catch up to what, or to whom, I can't be sure. I needed to make all my romantic mistakes in one day—okay, one weekend—so I could get them out of the way and get to the good stuff that was sexy and fun. Except I didn't realize they were mistakes until after they'd already given me chlamydia, not to mention I would've kept dating that particular mistake if he hadn't acted like such a freak about it.

One night four or five weeks into my sneaking downstairs to have emotionally unfulfilling intercourse in a sparsely furnished apartment below mine (its contents: a soup pot, a card table, one chair, assorted milk crates, a television, a bed in the living room, a bed in the bedroom) with a different mistake—a niceish man who was fanatical about soccer but not about the idea of a girlfriend—I left said mistake passed out across his bed and got up to pee and squeegee his semen out of me before quietly masturbating into the toilet and seeing myself out like I always did. But this time, dude jumped out of bed to follow me.

Was he worried I was going to drink his last Muscle Milk? Steal the plastic crate he used as an end table? I grabbed a blanket to hide the myriad embarrassments of my body in the light of the television, whose eerie blue glow he insisted on keeping on while "making love" (sir, if you refer to it as "lovemaking," then it's against the rules to have the TV on), and stammered, "Oh, okay, this is what we're doing?" while we both groped for the bathroom light switch. I tried to pee as he babbled about something dumb while standing sentinel outside the door, then I thought to myself, "This is kind of nice, does this mean he's my boyfriend now?" as I tried to hot-water-rinse whatever UTI-causing bacteria he'd deposited inside me down his sink.

It only took another two weeks of late-night creeping for him to regularly start asking if he could come into the bathroom and watch me as I went. I am not one to make a value judgment on anyone's fetish, but he couldn't really *see* anything through the opacity of the toilet and the density of my human hips and thighs, so what was even the point? Was he soothed by the sounds of trickling water? Aroused by the sight of a woman struggling to make conversation while trying to will her bladder empty?

It was awkward, especially when coupled with the hurdle of my newfound performance anxiety. It's one thing to psych yourself up enough to put on a dog collar (did that once) or take a bite from a doughnut with a penis through its center (did that more than once???), but peeing on command is difficult! I was nervous! Like what if I tried forcefully pushing out my pee and a huge squelching turd slipped out at the same time, you know how that sometimes happens? What if my butthole ruined someone's fantasy?! My dude would perch on the edge of the bathtub expectantly, drooling lustily in anticipation, night after night after night as I failed to produce much more than a handful of droplets or a tepid stream.

He was so eager to get me to piss for him—truly the most enthusiastic he'd been about having anything to do with me since we'd met in the laundry room months earlier, when I caught him using my Tide powder—that I really wanted to make it happen for him. Picture me, a human puppy, staring blankly at the wee-wee pad my owner is crouching near, encouraging me to "go on, be a good girl." I was like an ailing quarterback who desperately wants to get the win for his long-suffering coach.

We moved our meetings to the daytime. I would down a bottle of water as soon as he called to tell me he was leaving his office. Then, when he'd text me from the parking garage, I would hustle down three flights of stairs, waves of urea crashing against the walls of my bladder. I'd run into his apartment and get out of my pants and onto the can as fast as I could, desperate to relieve the pressure in my lower abdomen, only to find that the pressure of his eyeballs searing into me (not to mention the distraction of his hand moving around inside his pants) completely shut off the spigot. Not even a drop. I had no idea where the urine went, it just disappeared, reabsorbed into my body, where I was sure it would eventually poison me. I was absolutely going to go into renal failure.

We went together to the Glenwood Avenue Arts Fest, this outdoor hippie street fair around the corner from our apartment building, one afternoon in a desperate attempt on my part to move our relationship beyond the forty square feet of his bathroom. I drank approximately nineteen pints of Old Style while burning to a crisp under the summer sun, walking and walking and walking around booths packed with tie-dye dresses and woven hemp bags I was never gonna buy, and the second we walked back to the building I had to pee. I had to piss so bad my vision got wavy. I could barely get my ass on his toilet seat before the floodgates opened, and it was one of those orgasmic pees, the rapturous kind where you've held so much for so long that you almost weep when it comes torrential downpouring out of you. Little did I know, that orgasm was reciprocal; I'd looked up to find dude jerking off into the sink as I reached for his one-ply toilet paper.

From that day forward, he always just happened to have a six-pack around whenever I came over, and drunk jerking off to the sound of me pissing became a regular sexual event. If I were smarter, I would have known that eventually he was gonna ask me to urinate on him. That hadn't even occurred to me? Because even though I'd had sex, I wasn't exactly having, like, *adventurous* sex. The dog collar/doughnut thing was an anomaly, suggested by the same person who I thought had just watched too many dirty movies and had a vivid imagination. I didn't know people outside of porn apartments in the San Fernando Valley were pissing on each other and doing other freaky stuff.

When he finally made the casual suggestion—"What would you think about making *me* your toilet?" in the same exact tone he might've said, "What would you think about getting nachos *and* burritos?"—it took a minute for me to conceptualize how this might physically happen. It wasn't even that I thought it was gross, I've just taken enough unnecessary pregnancy tests to know what messy business targeted urination is when you don't have the luxury of a penis. I've pissed all over my hand and down the back of my pants and on the floor of every hospital bathroom I've ever fumbled that disposable sippy cup in. I couldn't even begin to imagine how I was going to get urine anywhere near this dude.

Well. Things sort of crystallized for me as I stood over his naked body stretched the length of his crumbling, lead-painted Rogers Park bathtub, Lamaze breathing while relaxing my pelvic floor in an attempt to produce a strong, steady flow instead of weak spluttering droplets. It's kind of impossible to contort a human body without some sort of funnel attached to it into whatever position is optimal for spraying urine into a dude's face within the confines of a coffin-sized apartment bathtub. I almost broke my fucking teeth on the edge of the sink falling out of the tub trying to make sure the piss ended up somewhere in the vicinity of where he wanted it rather than running down the insides of my legs before pooling along the sides of his torso. Over the course of many unsuccessful attempts, I mangled three shower curtains, destroyed a bottle of dandruff shampoo, and gouged my cheek on the faucet, skating and slipping and sliding around in my own liquid waste.

I'm not sure that I mastered a technique, but I did figure out how to sort of get some pee near his body once out of every third try? That's a decent success rate! Early one pitch-black winter morning I pissed on him before I went to work (undiluted morning pee was his favorite), and he jumped up to turn the shower on and grabbed my hand like he wanted us to take a shower together, which is an activity I do not believe in. I really had to get to work, i.e., go upstairs to my own apartment where all my bath products lived in close proximity to my many forks and cups. As I started to step out of the shower, he pulled me back in to kiss me good-bye. That's romantic, isn't it? From a man who told me that kissing on the lips "wasn't really his thing." Super nice, huh? That is, until he proceeded to discharge a mouthful of urine down my unsuspecting throat.

I should've known, man. I should've heard it collecting in his mouth! Aren't your other senses supposed to be heightened in the dark? Only a chaotic evil person would hold someone else's piss in his mouth for like two real minutes before expectorating it down that someone's throat. And I know you're thinking you would've beat that dude's ass, and that's easy to say because no one is piss-snowballing you right now. But at the time, I just stood there, in bewildered surprise, thinking about how I'd just swallowed three table-spoons of my own salted uric acid. I tried to spit some out, but he'd vomited it into me with such force. Needless to say, our relationship sort of dried up after that. And I made myself a new golden rule. (Piss onto others as you would have them piss onto you.)

. . .

Now, I am forty-three years old, and I no longer have control of my bladder. Twenty years ago, I was at this club called Slicks in Chicago on two-dollar-Corona night, and even back then in my "youth," my party strategy was to get there by nine so no one takes the good chairs. This is what I liked to tell my friends when they scoffed at the idea of arriving at a nightclub while it was still light out, but the truth is that if I sit too still between the hours of 7:00 and 8:30 p.m., I will clinically die until noon the next day, so if I'm gonna go out, I need to have a bra and shoes on by 6:55 at the very latest or that shit's not fucking happening. Okay, anyway, it was deep house night, and I had been guzzling lukewarm water-beers for four hours straight in a pair of unforgiving jeggings when my kidneys started pulsing in time to the beat. It was already too late. I looked in the general direction of the single-stall bathroom, its line snaking halfway around the back of the club, and breathed a sigh of relief that I was wearing urine-absorbing socks and sensible, closed-toed shoes.

Yes, I pissed my pants at the club, but that was VERY COOL back then because it made me seem fun and spontaneous—like it was my choice, and not an involuntary consequence of my managing to avoid death these many years. I thought the spoils of reaching middle age relatively unscathed would be better than unrelenting anxiety and loss of control over my various nerves, joints, limbs, and bodily fluids. I wouldn't have taken so many antibiotics if I'd known I was just gonna grow up to fall the fuck apart the same year I finally nursed my credit score over the seven hundred line.

What is the point of taking handfuls of unsexy vitamins and paying my secured card on time if I'm extending a life spent examining stains on the clothes I wore all day while wondering aloud, "What hole did that come out of?"

What I wouldn't give to have that old urethral elasticity back. What misery it is, being a person and existing in a human body over whose chemicals and hormones and cells you have very little control. With all the evidence you've gathered for this experiment otherwise known as life on this dying ball of garbage, level with me: Would you choose this again? You spend your whole youth eating french fries and fucking up and crying, praying for stability and confidence, and then, as soon as you get close to something resembling self-sufficiency, your nerves get bad and you spend the better part of most days covered in at least a microscopic bit of your own waste. While you contemplate your mortality and endless human suffering, weighing it against [*name me one good thing*], I present to you an exhaustive list of things I've peed on over the past few years:

Seat 3B on Delta flight 2734 to LAX

I used to never have to pee on flights, due to a carefully calibrated combination of claustrophobic terror and forced dehydration, but now, every time an airplane touches down with me on it, a little pee squirts out to christen my arrival in a new location.

The recumbent elliptical machine at the YMCA

I had to buy special "moisture-wicking" compression leggings because it's nearly impossible for me to engage my core (My WHAT?!) while also pushing pedals at a super-high resistance for forty-five minutes *and* trying to read the closed captioning on whatever episode of *NCIS* is playing on all the wall-mounted TVs *and* securing the contents of my bladder safely inside my body. Honestly, I would just quit going, but it helps my shitty knees, and you gotta see fourteen specialists to get so much as a Tylenol these days, and fuck that. So sometimes I leave the gym with a very "sweaty butt." Anyway, it could be worse, I could be emptying my entire bladder onto a squeaky wood floor to a Pitbull song during Zumba Gold. Although I bet they'd probably relate.

My pants as I approach literally any bathroom ever

I understand the Pavlovian response to seeing an outline of a toilet on a little plastic sign, but even if I could shield my eyes from it, it's like the minute my tiny brain hears "Bathroom . . . ," my sphincter muscles relax whatever grip they have on my urethra and it's all downhill (downleg) from there.

The gravel driveway outside the house we rented once in LA

I briefly lived in this house at the very top of an inconvenient mountain in the Hollywood Hills, and one night I drove my rented Toyota Camry up the steep and winding too-narrow path with a bunch of kombucha and alkaline water pooling in my bladder (FUCKING LOS ANGELES), and by the time I finally reached the garage, I was just about to burst. I slammed my hand in the car door because a dog I couldn't see in the dark barked at me, and my response to the screaming pain was to cry, from my pee hole.

My office chair

I share a big, airy space that gets tons of natural light and is very peaceful with two people who can absolutely hear every echoed noise coming from inside the adjacent bathroom, so sometimes I try to hold it until they have a phone call or go to lunch, and, listen, holding it is no longer a real thing.

The floor right in front of my very own home toilet, while trying to extricate myself from a complicated jumpsuit

I'm not even sure why I own a single article of clothing with buttons, let alone something you gotta hike up to your cervix just to get it over your goddamned shoulders, but listen: I am not immune to trends. I, too, am vulnerable to the algorithm. And that's how I wound up shuffling from foot to foot, as urine coursed discreetly down my pants that are also a shirt, while unsuccessfully trying to dislocate my left arm to hasten the process of sitting down fully naked to try to squeeze everything out of my suffering bladder.

I cough, I pee.

I sneeze, I pee.

I laugh, I pee.

I fart, I pee.

I sit down, I pee.

I stand up, I pee.

I cry at a dog food commercial, I pee.

I walk five steps, I pee.

I step out of the shower too hard, I pee.

I bend over to pick up the newspaper, I pee.

I reach for a bottle on a high shelf, I pee.

I have too good of an orgasm, I pee (and then it's a bad orgasm).

I frown at a news story on my timeline, I pee.

I chuckle at a cute news story on my timeline, I pee.

I pull up to the pharmacy drive-thru window, I pee.

I take a bite of something crunchy, I pee.

I have to call customer service, I pee.

I drop the remote and bend over to retrieve it, I pee.

I google a meme I'm too out of touch to understand, I pee.

Remember when you only pissed yourself for sexy reasons, like drinking too many bottomless mimosas at brunch or during literally any kind of penetrative sex? These days, I can't look at a picture of a lake without leaking a little at that mere suggestion of a body of water, even if it's one filled with E. coli and horrible bugs! I woke up at four in the morning yesterday, wide awake and drenched in sweat with a dry vagina, moody as fuck, burning up as if I had just dragged myself from the mouth of an active volcano, smelly, anxious, depressed, allergic to everything, on the verge of pissing myself: What should I have done before twenty-seven to get out of all this?!

I watched that "Naomi Campbell cleans an entire airplane with a Clorox wipe" video in its entirety at least twice when it first made rounds on the internet, thinking, "Is this before or after she dribbled a little bit in her travel pajamas after too many unlimited Diet Cokes?" Because I've had to fashion a makeshift diaper out of the complimentary blanket they hand out on planes since I turned thirty-fucking-five. That's even if I've managed to drink nothing but the swallow of water it takes to get an Ativan down my throat during takeoff!

How do the properly hydrated among you get through the goddamned day? Are you just pissing in those Thinx panties all the time? I've been following this hipster nutritionist on Instagram (fuck you, an actual one is incredibly expensive and will actually hold me accountable, which is a little too panic-inducing for my current frame of mind), and she was like YOU SHOULD DRINK THREE LITERS OF WATER EVERY DAY BEFORE NOON, and, first of all: Who is out of bed before noon, let alone chugging water? But also, just listening to her even say those words, my bladder muscles reflexed so forcefully that you could hear the waves in the next goddamn room.

How do you stay hydrated without (1) urine just slowly leaking out of you all the time with no warning or (2) alienating everyone who loves you because you have to pull the car over every three miles to squat over the Super Big Gulp you've designated as the urine catcher? Does it really help your skin look better, or is that just some bullshit the suits over at BIG WATER are trying to sell us? What was

I so busy doing when I was a kid instead of training my Kegels for my progressive-lensed years, in a mirror somewhere practicing the *Real World* audition submission I would never make? Committing petty larceny in the home of a child I was babysitting? Where is the young woman who could hold her pee for hours even when sitting atop a toilet that, frankly, could've used a thorough bleaching?!

It's too late, that ship has sailed on a pungent ocean of excreta, and now I spend my whole day tinkling on trees in broad daylight while whoever I'm with hovers nearby with an inside-out plastic bag stretched over their hand in case it turns into a poo. I'm gonna keep being hydrated, and being damp 75 percent of the time, if for no other reason than the other nightmare thing that comes with the collapse of your decaying meat suit: all the fucking pills you gotta choke down to keep the fucking thing working. See you in the pharmacy aisle with the Poise pads.

two old nuns having amzing [sic] lesbian sex

I'm a masturbator. Some people are sex people and other people are masturbation people, and I am a masturbation person. Which is not to say that I don't know how to have a good time fucking another person, but my absolute favorite person to have sex with is me.

I'm not even that good at it, there's just no performance pressure, and if I fall asleep in the middle it's not like I'm gonna spend the next morning passive-aggressively pouting at myself while I put the coffeepot on. I just got this ad in my email for Valentine's Day–themed underpants: "Sometimes flowers and candy aren't enough. Say 'I love you' with ravishing red lace." I would prefer to show my love by putting the cell phone bill on autopay, but even if that wasn't enough, I can't think of anything that feels less special and romantic than having my right underbutt shredded by tiny lacy razor blades all day in a feeble attempt to be "sexy."

Consider, if you will, this copy describing an article of clothing advertised to me as a reward for my longtime (read: sick and tired of years of my bullshit) lover on Valentine's night:

Celebrate every inch of your gorgeous skin in this ultra-strappy and revealing teddy! This Juicy-Hot Teddy is made from super stretchy nylon and spandex, so it stretches comfortably and clings to your sexy curves in all the right ways. Watch your lover's jaw drop as you work your mojo and reveal naughty amounts of skin through all those sexy cutouts. Make sure to flash your rear view, too! The Juicy-Hot Teddy's thong back knows just how to tease with great views of your sexy booty. After a steamy night, wash by hand in cold water.

Is this what you have to do to have sex when you're a boring married person? Is this what daytime talk shows mean when they say you have to keep things spicy in the bedroom? Is "spicy" code for "elaborate and embarrassing"? If I put a thong on, I would get diarrhea on it, then throw a tantrum when I couldn't fish it out of my butt at the end of the evening. Also, what do you do once it's on? Twirl around the bedroom? Put music on and do a humiliating striptease? And when do you do the cold-water-washing part? Is that something I can double task while digging through the expired medicines under the sink looking for some Uristat?!

This is why I like to have sex with myself, because here are a bunch of sentences describing an actual article of clothing marketed to a "naughty temptress" who is trying to fuck someone else. *AM I THAT????* Your lover won't be able to keep their hands off you in this versatile lingerie set! The flexible fishnet top is designed so that you can wear it with your breasts showing or with them covered up. Underwire helps separate your breasts, making the twins stand out more and giving your cleavage a helpful boost at the same time.

The twins!!!!!!!!!! Distant relatives, more like, at best. You're the star of your own sensual adventures. Experience natural stimulation with every thrust as the panty's delicate stretch black lace encircles your waist and holds a loop of ten smooth beads against your nether lips. *I'M SWEATING.* When he slips inside, the beads roll and massage you both for intense orgasmic sensations that make sex even more amazing. Wash the thong panty by hand in cold water, do not iron. *Who is out here ironing their crotchless beaded thong?!* The paddle, pasties, and stockings are not included but the leather-look stretch-mesh fabric stretches four ways, for your comfort! *OH OKAY, THEN, AS LONG AS IT'S FOR MY COMFORT.*

A verified purchaser with the username BusyOnTheBeaver gave it five out of five stars and added, and I quote, "very complimentary to the female form, i love my wife." Good for Mr. Busy!

I'm so embarrassed by everything all the time, humiliated even by the need to breathe air where other people can see me. There is just no universe in which I could stand at the foot of a hastily unmade bed, laced up tight like a kindergartner's gym shoe, and not sweat through my "crotchless beaded lovers thong" while fully melting down about hyperpigmented butt folds and coarse, unruly pubic hair. I am on so many pills, so many dusty-pink and white tablets crowding my end table, the foot soldiers in my losing war against premature death that grind my libido to a spluttering dribble, it feels like a tall ask to expect another person to remain patient through twenty minutes of dry chafing to see if something happens. Much easier to instead wait to feel something down there ("Is this overactive bladder or sexual arousal?") then slink off, pretending I have to take a shit, so I can deal with it on my own.

There are a few (extremely specific) genres of porn I prefer to masturbate to, chief among them:

- "middle-aged man jerking off while being gently pegged"
- lovemaking with kissing
- public (Hear me out: Have you ever seen people fucking on a bus?)
- big ass
- compilation
- "fat lady being worshipped"
- videos where you just watch a dude's boner grow
- cuckold
- massage (maybe what I actually need is a nap)
- "dudes who fuck like Xavier Thicc"
- BBW
- hand job
- mature lady riding to orgasm
- KISSING

But "Two Old Nuns Having Amzing [*sic*] Lesbian Sex" is my favorite pornographic piece of cinema. I don't even remember how I found it years ago now. I'm sure I searched "senior citizen real orgasm" or something like that, because I like to see an orgasm, but also I can't watch a person engaged in any sort of sexual activity unless I am absolutely certain, beyond a shadow of a doubt, that person is of legal car-renting age. Imagine me going to jail because I clicked on a video called "Hot Teen Squirts on a Banana" or some shit, and said hot teen turns out to be an actual child, *and* it just so happens to be the day the FBI agent assigned to monitoring my phone activity is awake and paying attention.

That shit is terrifying to me. I won't even watch an obvious thirty-seven-year-old with crow's-feet and low bone density if she's in pigtails and fucking braces! Maybe that lady in a plaid school uniform with her pussy waxed down to the bone is old enough to have weird hip pain, or maybe she has an actual backpack full of tenth-grade chemistry homework just out of the camera's view. Won't be me finding out!

Let's break down the tags.

HD Porn

The video quality is exceptional here, it's true. I can't decide whether it makes me feel creepier to rub one out to a high-definition piece of ~cinema~ or a grainy POV shot in the dark on an Android phone, but high-definition television in general is kinda gross to me. I don't need to see every hairy mole in crystal clarity, I'd actually prefer not to be able to zoom in on a crumb of feces stuck to someone's anus.

Lesbian

You already know what this means, but I'll tell you what it doesn't: two butch dykes with leg hair fisting each other while talking about what's on sale at Menards, which is honestly the lesbian sex scene I would most like to watch.

Mature

This is a nice way of saying fifty-plus, and is easily my most used search term. This isn't a scientific observation, but I do think the older the participants, the more authentic the sex is . . . ? I hate all that hysterical shrieking and grunting that young people do, that high-pitched unrealistic yowling that is supposed to sound orgasmic but honestly just sounds like I want to watch people who are having sex to distract them from the reverse mortgage commercial playing during a *Mork & Mindy* rerun at 7:30 p.m.

Porn Star

Is every person who stars in a porn a "porn star"?

Pussy Licking

Okay, sure, but why the distinction from "pussy eating"? Are these two different things??? Wild question for me to be asking as an active pussy licker, but do men know that one doesn't actually "eat" pussy? That, within this context and probably when men do it too, pussy eating = pussy licking? Or are there men who are out here literally using their teeth to bite the labia minora of the women they are having sex with?

Nun

Self-explanatory!

Romantic

I love romance, I do, but I wonder in this context how that word applies. When I think of ~romance~ the things that come to mind are: elaborate floral arrangements that make your allergies flare up, high-quality fancy chocolates in gilded heart-shaped boxes that the UPS man drop-kicks to your doorstep, a humiliating meet-cute, overpriced dinners by candlelight that you can't even really eat because your shapewear is too tight and cinchy, bubble baths during which you almost drown, desserts crammed into your private parts, tacky jewelry that doesn't fit right, a lacy, strappy piece of lingerie that chokes you to death, a bottle of wine you try not to vomit all over his erection. This movie doesn't have any of that, just discomfiting religious imagery and a soundtrack better served in an "oh no, she's dying" montage in a movie of the week, which maybe qualifies as "romance" to a different kind of person than I am.

Story Line

This does not matter to me. At all.

Scissoring in Lesbian

Judging by a quick poll of most of the lesbians in my phone, no human lesbians without a director and camera crew are doing what people who make porn call "scissoring." Scissoring is a position requiring you and your partner to lie on your sides and intertwine your legs like two pairs of opened scissors and awkwardly grind your genitals together until either you have an orgasm or you ignite a flame. Grinding atop a thigh like it's a fleshy pommel horse is a thing I'd maybe be into, but there aren't enough, umm, firm parts around the vulva to provide the level of friction I require. What, am I supposed to get some kind of traction from a urethra hole? Quit playing! Not to yuck anyone's yum if you can derive sexual pleasure from grazing your uncomfortably tilted labia majora against someone else's while trying not to fall off the bed, but all I can think while watching it is: "This screeching is fake, there's no way she's gonna come from that." Theoretically I understand why watching people ram two aux cords with the same import port (hire me, RadioShack) together can be fun, but in practice I have found it to be very weird!

British

No one in this film (LMAO) speaks with a discernible British accent.

Mom

Hmm, I don't love this. Or maybe I *would* love it if the "mom" tag guaranteed a stream of videos featuring very nice ladies bringing hot soup to other ladies in bed or giving them an allowance or something. This is probably the orphan in me talking, but I would happily watch any number of short clips of short-tempered, tired moms cutting sandwiches into triangles and impatiently tapping their feet at the open passenger door of a minivan while shouting, "Hurry up! I'm late for my ballroom dancing class!" I would watch your mom arguing over the price of mortadella at her local discount-meat counter, putting on her reading glasses to scrutinize the fine print on the side of a bottle of supplements, calling the cable company to ask why she's being billed for Showtime when she never signed up for it in the first place, grilling the librarian about why her hold on the new Glennon Doyle is taking so damn long: GIMME IT ALL.

Old

Maybe this doesn't seem nice on its face, but I appreciate the distinction since it appears that people who make porn have multiple definitions of what the word "mature" means. When I search "mature" on xxxxxvideos dot com, I'm looking for wobbly-assed seventy-three-year-olds on an aspirin regimen, but sometimes smooth, taut, poreless young people will pop up, and I'm like "Wait, do they mean emotionally mature?!" And, like I said, if I can't tell you're old, then that leaves the door open for you to be criminally young, and I can't do that. So "old" is a welcome relief.

Big Tits

I have these, so I get it. It's fun to watch them bounce and get smooshed.

Mother

Ew, I don't know, man, "MILF" doesn't bother me at all, but there is something about "MOTHER" that makes me want to jump off a fucking building. Who is logging on to jerkmydick dot com and typing "mother" into the fucking search bar? "Mom" is one thing, but "mother" is another, worse thing, and I hate it. Also who's in charge of the internet? When are we gonna get dot cum?

Nun Lesbian

I suppose this is necessary to distinguish it from other varieties of available nun porn? I am scared to search, but I'm sure there are probably, you know, hard-core priest-nun skin flicks out there.

Fake Tits

Rude!

Granny

Okay, I'm gonna sound like a hypocrite, but this I understand, because sometimes "mature" doesn't quite get you what you need when it comes to wanting to watch a hot bitch get her nut in the retirement home, so sometimes you really have to be specific.

Passionate

I would give all (most) of the money currently in my bank account for a porn site that consists 100 percent of people doing passionate lovemaking during which you don't have to see any gross stuff like spitting or dislocated shoulders. The worst thing is when you're watching some straightforward, nice sex and then all of a sudden the dude slaps the woman he's fucking in the face, and then you dry right up because that's not what you were expecting. If I made a porn, it would be virtually indistinguishable from a steamy Lifetime movie, except there would be cursing and testicles. I'd leave in all the other shit, the longing and the pining and the suffering, the deep staring into each other's eyes, the non-sensical underdeveloped subplot. And then when it came back from the fourth commercial break, there would be hot, sweaty, grabby sex that looks like it feels good. That's maybe my biggest gripe when it comes to dirty movies, that so much of it looks painful or uncomfortable. Sometimes these hits and slaps look like the start of a fucking fight, and that makes me nervous!!!! If you like getting your ass slapped hard as hell, I love that for you, but I gotta be treated like a two-hundred-year-old haunted doll in bed.

Movie Scene

Well, this is definitely that, but I'm not sure why this is a category people are interested in, *unless* it's the kind of thing where people post extended clips from actual sexy movies? Like if you didn't want to waste time scrubbing through your DVD of *Blue Is the Warmest Color* to get to the hard-core parts, it might come in handy (PUN INTENDED) for some knowledgeable internet person to have uploaded them to this sketchy website.

MILF

I know a lot of both my friends' moms and my mom friends are reading this, and I'm sorry, but those big milkies and that wrinkly I-had-a-child-nineteen-years-ago lower belly is extremely sexy to me, and don't tell me, for real, but this is because my mom died when I was a kid, right?

Reality

It's hilarious that *this* is a tag on a video that is both longer than an episode of prestige television and opens with a sweeping Spielbergian wide shot of the Italian countryside. I like a lot of "real" or "amateur" stuff, mostly because I don't like thinking about a guy in the corner whose job it is to squirt baby oil on a dry torso between takes. I also don't like the idea of takes, because it's sexier and less creepy to feel like it's just me and my pals in a rented room down at the hourly motel having a little innocent fun on a Saturday night. Just me (fully clothed, saying nothing, feeling no hands on my body except for my own) and my pals (Bob, the manager at a furniture store in the one strip mall you avoid going to, and Harriet, who works at the neck-pillow store at the airport) getting our blood pressures up for seven minutes and not a second longer at the end of a grueling week.

Scissoring

So nice they had to list it twice.

If I was into role-play I'd literally be like, "Let's do the one where we play hot dog vendors at the Tigers' stadium who get home late and are too tired to touch each other's genitals so they just fall asleep in matching recliners, fully clothed," but I do understand the transgressive appeal of fucking in a nun's costume, even though I have had just enough African Methodist Episcopal indoctrination that even the idea of initiating ass eating while wearing God's uniform makes me feel phantom flames from hell lapping at the back of my neck.

My ultimate sex fantasy would be something like: I want to rig the sky so it rains and thunders for three days (but not scary thunder) and the rain magically doesn't flood anything or make the roads too treacherous to get a pesto-based pizza delivered in a reasonable amount of time, also the power doesn't ever go out and the Wi-Fi stays strong, plus I get to wear the same threadbare sweatshirt I always wear, without a pinching-ass digging-ass bra, and we watch thirteen straight hours of television and then make out in the dark and go to sleep in separate rooms and maybe I'll use my high-tech vibrator that simulates sucking human lips alone (you need one of those!), if I'm not too exhausted. You're lying if you say that doesn't sound like the best night of your life. No one is actually fantasizing about figuring out which leg hole is which in the Sexy-Illusion Bodystocking!

I can't find this on Pornhub anymore, so I've got "Two Old Nuns Having Amzing [*sic*] Lesbian Sex" queued up on a site purporting to have "the best in lesbian erotica." And I want to talk about how this porn movie you are supposed to furtively jerk off to in your linen closet, or wherever you hide from your family, is thirty-nine minutes and eleven seconds long. I am genuinely curious: Does anyone need this much time to bring themselves to orgasm, as they risk second-degree-burning the tops of their thighs from a blisteringly hot laptop? Also, are there people who watch porn like a show and, I don't know, take note of the cinematography and shit while they eat chips? Thirty-nine minutes is such a long time to keep one hand hovering over the pause button in case someone wakes up or comes home! I would like to be finished in a maximum of three minutes and nineteen seconds!!!!!!

Okay so, we open with a sweeping overhead shot of the Italian (?) countryside (??), and then we follow the camera inside the convent to find a very stern "nun" in a bright white habit, draped in large wooden beads and pretending to read a thick, old Bible. I typically fast-forward through this part because I can feel God watching me and shaking his head with disapproval. There's a knock at the door and another nun enters the room, eyes cast downward as she says, "I found the other book you wanted, in the archives." You know what just occurred to me? I could probably write something like this. I have no idea what it would pay or how permanent the (cum) stain on my career might be, but I certainly could come up with something more titillating than "I found this old book in the archives"???

The archival nun (work with me here, okay) is younger than the stern nun, who snatches the book away meanly from her hands while saying, "Let me see!" The room they're in looks vaguely churchy, with stark white walls, filled with old books and flickering votives in red glass holders. The stern nun sits to flip through the book as her nun apprentice leans curiously (and sexily!) over her shoulder, trying to get a peek. It's very Meryl Streep and Amy Adams in *Doubt*, if it was about hot sex instead of, ugh, well, not hot sex? The young nun is reading over the stern nun's shoulder about "modesty in the fifteenth century for cloistered sisters," and you just have to trust me that there is something worth grinding your pussy into the edge of the couch cushion coming up. The stern nun says, "Thank you, Sister Mona, you can leave," and I have literally never listened to that part before, and I am crying. SISTER MOAN-A, GIVE ME A BREAK OVER HERE.

Sister Mona turns around to face Mean Nun as she reaches for the door and holds out a white envelope. "This came for you," she says coyly, and because I'm disgusting, I thought, "And I'm gonna come for *you*."

There's a long, lingering shot of Mean Nun as some inscrutable emotions play across her face (Fear? Anxiety?? Heartburn from Taco Tuesday at the nunnery???) and then, it's the next day (I guess?) and Sister Mona and another young nun are outside collecting the wash from the line, and I need you to know that in this case "the wash" appears to be stiff white napkins that still have the crease marks from the package they were purchased in. There's water noise in the background, from either a babbling brook or because someone left the sink running or because these ladies are squirting so forcefully it's audible through ten pounds of black cloth.

The other nun stops doing her chores and says, "Sister Mona? I have a confession."

Oh shit! Are we about to find out God isn't real and there is literally no point to our stupid and painful lives atop this spinning rock as it hurtles through outer space?! Haha, no, she just wants to tell Sister Mona that she still "thinks of [their] night together." Sister Mona rolls her eyes like "Here we go with this shit again," and continues unclipping her cheap-ass napkins. Ugh, maybe whoever wrote this actually knew what they were doing because nothing is sexier than intense, unrequited longing. My heart is pounding in my chest!

Hang on, the camera pulls out (don't make me make the joke), and it's actually sheets they're pretending to fold? I imagine the morning after your first night in this sexy lesbo convent you wake up covered in a thousand papercuts because these sheets look like the definition of hell. Sister Mona coldly apologizes to Sister Mary, apparently, for "awakening temptation" in her, and Sister Mary is crestfallen, holding her basket of sandpaper with tears streaming down her face as Sister Mona walks around her to go back inside. Is this what Jesus would do?!

We're back inside and Mean Nun from earlier is in a confessional booth. I think. I don't know because I was raised in black-people church where we did not have to do this. God, I can't even imagine. How do you decide which sins to tell? According to my behavior in therapy, my answer would be the most entertaining ones that make me sound the least unhinged, but there is no universe in which I could divulge my grimiest secrets and then, just, let myself out of the booth and walk around normally in the world? The priest knows my voice! I would melt into the church floor if he even made accidental eye contact with me during the sermon. Back to our film, though, where Mean Nun says it's been a month since her last confession and she's been "having doubts." I don't know how often you are supposed to confess, but surely if you're a nun the answer has to be "more than once a month"?! What's she so busy doing, lighting candles and making weird faces while thumbing through dusty old books?

Mean Nun says that her doubts are about decisions she's made in the past, how she runs her convent, and her relationship with God. Let me tell you, I would *not* be masturbating to this if I had ever, even once, let this part play rather than fast-forwarding through it to the naked shit. The last thing I want to think about while cycling through vibrator settings is whether God is mad at me. She says that she's having trouble with the new addition to her convent, Sister Mona, who engaged in all sorts of perversions at her old convent. Mean Nun says that she tried to fix Sister Mona, that she took pleasure in brutalizing her, to no avail. Then, as she roughly fondles the wooden beads around her neck like she's trying to extract milk from them, she says that she just received "a letter from a very old friend" telling her that she's dying and wants to see her before she passes away. Oh no, this is a tearjerker! The priest starts reciting an actual Bible verse, and my skin just crawled off my body. Then Mean

Nun crosses herself, and holy shit, we are seven minutes in, and I haven't seen a single titty.

Beautiful cinematography in this next aerial shot of a large beautiful church that I hope they didn't actually film in because that feels a little blasphemous. A seventyish woman is sitting up in a plain wooden bed in a Vermont Country Store–ass nightgown, eyes closed, making little "I'm dying" coughs as she rubs a rosary. She calls out, "Charlotte? Is that you?" and then Mean Nun steps forward and bellows, "IT'S ME."

Sick Nun's eyes pop open in surprise (or maybe it's her thyroid), and she says, "Joan! Let me see you!"

Mean Nun comes over to the side of the bed and doesn't know what to say, then Sick Nun says, "I was so hurt when you left," as somber piano music twinkles in the background. They're really trying to make me cry, huh. Is that a kink?

Sick Nun says that Mean Nun opened her heart to a love she never knew existed, and the two of them get into a little forgiveness dialogue straight out of a Hallmark movie, but the most important thing to note is that Sick Nun's hospital-style blanket has been pushed down a little to reveal an enormous pair of Sick Boobs. They're still in her nightgown and this is what is sexy to me: the outline of a septuagenarian breast through a sensible cotton pintuck pinafore nightgown. Mean Nun is like, "My feelings for you are wrong, even if they still burn bright." And Sick Nun looks genuinely pained before extending her hand and inviting Mean Nun to sit next to her on what is absolutely a twin bed stolen from the set of *Little House on the Prairie*.

Sick Nun says, "I wasn't meant to be a nun, but I wasn't

meant for the outside world, either. So, I tried to make this the most pleasant prison I could." Are there . . . best original screenplay awards for pornography?

There are more *literal minutes* of talking, about choosing love and bravery and regret, and I wonder if this is what women want to watch, or if this is what whoever made this short film *thinks* women want to watch. I am trying to imagine even the most sensitive, kind, and thoughtful heterosexual men I know sitting through all this gentle-feelings talk, patiently waiting for the appropriate moment to pull his dick out. Frankly, I can't think of any women who would, either? Especially because we're busy. Who has time for all this boring chuffa when there are pizzas to order and slasher movies to watch? Finally, Sick Nun and Mean Nun rest their foreheads gently together and perform that hair-wiping thing across each other's faces while gazing into each other's eyes in a way that would immediately humiliate me if I tried it.

I would've guessed that Mean Nun was in a Party City sexy-nun outfit but as Sick Nun starts to remove each piece for her, I have to say the habit looks pretty real. First, she lifts off the veil and then there's a Velcro *rrrrrrip* as she unfastens the cap underneath, then there's more forehead touching and hair smoothing coupled with meaningful eye contact, and if this was me I would be asleep. The minute homegirl tried anything other than "vigorous digital stimulation," I'd be tapping the watch I refuse to wear like, "Come on, babe. I took an edible and a Benadryl an hour ago; we got fifteen minutes MAX."

There is some gentle kissing of foreheads and hands, and

I'm gonna contradict myself and say that this stuff is sexy to me, but only if I don't have to do the other stuff later. I'm bad in bed, man. I don't know if it's my depression or the meds I take to counteract my depression, but if I'm near a bed I want to lie very still on it for nine hours, not kiss a lady's hands for ten minutes and still have to do other stuff later. I mean, sure, let's make out, but also I got today's episode of *NFL Live* waiting for me on the DVR, and I can only remain conscious for forty more minutes, so pick a thing and let's do that and then stop!

Mean Nun is doing a hell of a job acting. She looks so pained by either her sex guilt or the fact that Sick Nun isn't doing well, and Sick Nun takes her face in her hands and kisses her in a way that would be hot if I wasn't wondering what disease Sick Nun supposedly has. Is "deathbed porn" a genre? These two do a solid minute of kissing, and I love that. Ten out of ten. A+. No notes. I will watch any video of people kissing, it doesn't matter who. I love being kissed. Kissing is the best. Wait, this is actually three minutes of fully clothed kissing only, and somehow this movie is better than I originally gave it credit for? Yes, we are 12:39 into it, but also why was I skipping past this loving, sensual part?

At 12:49 we get our first boob after a shockingly realistic struggle for Mean Nun to wrestle her way out of a top with absolutely zero stretch and a cheap quarter zip at the back of her neck. There's no easy way out of a top like that! Especially when you have a huge rack and aren't wearing a bra!! Okay, now they're doing some topless kissing—although Sick Nun still has her flimsy nightgown on—and hugging, which is funny to me because if I hug you with my shirt off that means I'm about to go to *sleep*. If the momentum slows for even a second, I will fall off a cliff into the deepest slumber possible because I am a cat. They're clutching each other, now they're rocking back and forth, and maybe this is why the video was tagged "mommy." It's giving very much "I skinned my knee, please make it better," and also like . . . . is Sick Nun okay? She really is leaning on Mean Nun like she's about to die of consumption. Have I accidentally stumbled across a movie from 1883?

Finally Mean Nun's scowl cracks, and she starts smiling! Then laughing! Sick Nun kissed her meanness away, and now she's happy enough to have sex!!!!!!! Sick Nun pulls her nightgown over her head and goes in for another gentle embrace, and now I'm wondering how wet her fitted sheet is because this is an awful lot of foreplay with very little digital insertion. Sick Nun commands Mean Nun to stand, and she yanks her black nun dress down and: OH SHIT, this is the first time I have ever seen my preferred style of underpants in a porn??? Mean Nun is wearing high-waisted white full briefs, and I have never felt more recognized by a piece of cinema.

Well, okay, now the video is kind of glitching. I've had to reload the browser a couple of times when the video refused to play and the sidebar ads keep popping up all over the screen. I tried to skip ahead to see if that would fix it, to the part at 17:10 when it starts to get good, when Sick Nun finally slips her moisturized hand into Mean Nun's Hanes Cool Comfort breathable cotton briefs and starts fiddling around, but all I'm getting is the spinning wheel of death that means I either gotta log off before my laptop explodes or someone in the matrix has zeroed in on my location and

Agent Smith is about to kick down one of these windows. Anyway, it takes these ladies approximately 22:01 to realistically orgasm together while moaning to their husband, God, about how good their sinning feels, and I guess now I'm a convert.

qvc, ilysm

**Isaac Mizrahi Live! Essentials Pima
Cotton Mock Neck Top #A462479**

*EXTREMELY PERSUASIVE AND IRRESISTIBLE
PRODUCT COPY:* It's the kind of top you need in every
color. You'll love the fit and feel of this mock neck done in
Isaac's signature (so soft!) pima cotton.

WHAT DID THE LADY IN THE VIDEO SAY?
Jayne is in studio standing next to a rack of colorful mock-
neck tops wearing the red version. Even though red is my
favorite color to look at, I don't wear red very often. When
I was a teenager, I worked with this dude who called me
"Benny the Bull" every time I showed up at the bakery in a
red shirt, which is a hilarious roast but has obviously caused
me permanent brain damage.

Jayne looks stunning, though. She says this is a good shirt
if you're looking for something in cotton (I mean, how
could you not be?) and want a top that will shine on its own

but would also be great to layer under a jacket or sweater that you can pair with a dressy scarf for the office or a casual lunch! I'm not trying to be an asshole, but that's the shit that sucks me in. I will buy practically anything if you can paint me a story about it. Do I eat casual lunch? Absolutely not, I eat my undercooked Lean Cuisines while wearing a fucking tuxedo. But the thing is, now I want to? Now I am dying to call someone at random and ask them to meet me at a Panera for a turkey sandwich so I can wear this shirt!

Jackie, who is wearing a sparkly bejeweled cardigan I would wear if I could burn this life to the ground and start fresh somewhere in the middle of Kansas, is tapping in over Zoom from what looks like her home studio. She is aggressively stretching and yanking at a shirt (color: evergreen) to prove to us that the shirt has the 4 percent spandex it claims to on the label. She explains the difference between pima cotton and the garbage regular cotton you're used to with the help of a high-tech CGI graphic presentation in which an empty white T-shirt (with boobs) morphs into two disparate piles of cotton that then morph into two different types of woven fibers. Jackie says, in her very compelling British accent, that the way this cotton is knit makes it "extra durable and buttery, luxuriously soft." Hmm, I'm sorry, but if I heard her describe a literal piece of human stool in this way, in this accent, I would buy it.

Glamorous Jackie goes on to call this top "an essential piece that forms the basis of your wardrobe. . . . These easy pieces that you throw on when you're running out the door automatically look pulled together and polished and are the answer to everything you need." And you know what? I believe her! My life simply does not require ever "running out the door" or "looking pulled together"—AND YET. I want a shirt that makes me feel like that. I want to make a plan, lie down in the dark with the sound machine blasting until one minute before I need to leave, then run around in a panic looking for my wallet and keys before snatching one of these shirts out of the dryer, where it's been sitting for three days, and tossing it on so I can look GREAT. Imagine my stupid-ass friends when I walk into a restaurant that doesn't seat incomplete parties late after fucking up the reservation, and instead of scorn and revulsion they embrace me like, "Wow! That semifitted, not-too-clingy top with a gorgeous side vent that follows the lines of your body with so much added wearing ease looks amazing on you! Not to mention, it gives you so much aging-neck coverage!!!" *Adds to cart*

WHAT IT COST ME: *Five Easy Payments of $7.64*

The pandemic hit and the first thing to collapse—before our collective sanity and physical virility came tumbling down in rapid succession shortly afterward—was my shitty internet. We had whatever country-ass internet you get when you choose to put an enormous satellite dish in the middle of your overgrown backyard, and that shit was not going to support three people trying to conduct very important jobs and online classes and one loser who has a blog.

One day a cable salesman knocked on the door, and we were still in the beginning *Contagion*-style stages of quarantine, when you'd threaten to kill anyone who stood at your door for longer than ten seconds. I stood behind the closed door and shouted, "WHAT DO YOU WANT, SIR?" while looking for something to hit this salesman on the head with if it came to that. The only items we kept next to our front door were mittens and hats, so what was I gonna do, snuggle him to death? He said he was selling "lightning-fast internet," which is so funny because the mental picture that creates is one in which my house burns down, but I'd risk it to make sure I don't miss even a millisecond of *Yellowstone*. Even if I didn't need my downloads to happen at the speed of sound, I would've signed up anyway because we live at the top of a steep and treacherous hill that the salesman had clearly parked at the bottom of, as evidenced by his sweat-sheer shirt and the way he leaned against the railing like his life depended on it. I couldn't invite him in because, you know, "spores" or whatever, so I passed him a bottle of water and told him he could walk around to the back deck and we'd figure it out from a distance of six feet or greater.

I know it's not cool, but I love having regular TV. I never cut the cord, and I never will. Everyone else who doesn't give a shit about sports or the soothing drone of CNN can enjoy squinting at the laptop balanced on their scorched knees. I am always gonna want an actual television set and a guaranteed way to watch the Super Bowl, okay?

One of the perks of reacquainting myself with the joys of basic cable, once we had succumbed and bought whatever internet our visitor was peddling, was finding QVC. On the first night after installation, I watched hours and hours and hours, Dyson and Sport Savvy Fashion and Gourmet Holiday washing over me like warm soapy water, lulling me into a deep, peaceful sleep in which visions of marked-down home essentials danced through my head.

You know what rules about QVC? In addition to the luggage sets and lawn tools, where else can a fat bitch see clothes on an actual fat body as it moves and turns and poses inside a fake living room with bright lights and no ceiling? I want to see a size 2 host skimming her shiny gel manicure over the sumptuous fabric of the button-front cardigan with floral embroidery she's modeling ("Just gorgeous!!" she coos, doing a little twirl) and then I want Suburban Mom straight out of central casting to stroll onto the set wearing the same cardigan in a damn size 22, and when she does, I gasp in surprise because it looks just as good on her as it does on the host. Then I want Isaac Mizrahi himself to come on and tell me all the fabulous places where I can wear that sweater fabulously. And he will! Do you know I purchased something called a "chore coat" because he made it sound so appealing? You know who needs a coat for chores? A hard-working lady who lives on a farm! And by that I absolutely do *not* mean me! But I wanted (and deserved, frankly) that coat, so I could live out my fantasy as a person who needs to throw a little something on to "dash to the market for fresh cream." I've never dashed anywhere a day in my life. But with this luxurious Deals on the Daily chore coat on my back? MAYBE I WOULD.

Peter Thomas Roth Anti-Aging Cleansing Gel Duo #A331311

EXTREMELY PERSUASIVE AND IRRESISTIBLE PRODUCT COPY: Two full-sized bottles of Peter Thomas Roth's luxurious facial cleansing gel produces a beautifully fresh, youthful-looking complexion with advanced pore-resurfacing action. These two cleansers contain 1 percent glycolic acid and other ingredients that help diminish the appearance of fine lines and wrinkles. Lemon, lime, and grapefruit extracts help to leave the skin ultraclean, revitalized, and invigorated.

WHAT DID THE LADY IN THE VIDEO SAY?

Lately my skin has been sensitive to the point of deep, sub-dermal pain, but I am watching this anyway because I am a sucker for the idea that a tiny dab of liquid that you mix with water and rub on your skin for approximately ten seconds before the shower rinses it all down the drain can somehow change the composition of my face. On screen, Julia starts this one off in a way that caught me so off guard I had to double-check that I wasn't watching a diet ad: "Over the summer you got lazy, you were *Real Housewives*–ing it, reading magazines on the front porch? Well, don't worry, everything you're gonna see tonight is a quick turnaround that's gonna get you back to where you should've been." I'm sorry but is this . . . . still a commercial for face wash??? I love it. Shame me, Mommy! Make me feel like absolute dogshit for spending the entire summer frying bacon on my forehead at high noon!

Julia has an aesthetician in studio with her today, and she is thrilled to be with us and can't wait to answer our stream of burning questions in the chat. Okay, I love QVC and watch it like I'm chilling with my pals, but even I am not cool or confident enough to kick it with the heavy hitters in the chat. That's for the real QCard insiders. The as-yet-unnamed aesthetician enthusiastically details a full antiaging skincare routine, but Julia interrupts her to tell us that this best beauty product–nominated cleanser typically retails for $75, but they are cutting me, their best friend, a deal by offering two bottles for less than $50! I don't care so much about that, as chances are I'm gonna be back to using Ceta-phil from the bottom shelf of Walgreens within a matter of days anyway, but I love that she's doing math.

The aesthetician says you can keep one for yourself and give the other to your significant other, and I broke out in a full-body sweat like "HOLD UP, THEY GOT LES-BIANS ON HERE????" But, no. She is just talking about her dumb husband who apparently never washed his face in fifty-plus years until she gently nudged her bottle of Peter Thomas Roth Anti-Aging Cleansing Gel closer to his side of the sink. What kind of bathroom do they have? Are all the products locked up like at Walgreens? If my lady gets a new soap or toner and I want to try some I just . . . use it. What is this "bottle for your significant other" business? Is this how Americans are living in the heartland, just out here doubling and quadrupling up on his-'n'-hers economy-sized jugs of face wash?

Next the aesthetician starts busting out the science words that we've all heard but couldn't define if our lives depended on it (I'll wait while you tell me, without using your pocket computer, what "glycolic acid" is and does), but what hooks me is she describes the scent and feeling of the gel as "peachy clean." Is she:

- misusing the common American colloquialism "peachy keen"?
- thinking about how peaches are soft and hairy like a face and that this soap would be a good way to clean their delicate skins?
- describing the scent as both "peachy" and "clean," two things that absolutely do not go together olfactorily?

Julia describes how skin feels firmer from the first wash and this is the first cleanser of its kind (probably?) to make your skin feel firm without leaving it tight and stripped. I don't care about firmness, but I do hate that crackly dry feeling you get from washing your face with the wrong thing, but then she says that it preps your skin for your daily toner, serum, moisturizer, and eye cream, and I believe there was a time in my life when I would've tried to do all that, but now is not it. The first and last time I tried eye cream, I didn't yet know that I was supposed to apply it on my orbital bone, not to the dingy gray pocket beneath my eye, so I blinked eye cream into my eyeball, where not only was it ineffective in fighting my wrinkles and bags but also it turned my scleras neon fuchsia and I spent the rest of the day assuring rude customers at my job that I wasn't going to give them pink eye. I want to have an elaborate skincare situation, but it's so boring, and if any of it gets in or on any of your mucous membranes, it ruins your entire day. But then, as if she can hear my brain wandering, Julia says, "It's like a cleanser and moisturizer all in one!" I love multitasking. ★Adds to cart★

WHAT IT COST ME: Three Easy Payments of $13
Truly, the best part of any of these shows are the hosts, those who have to have so many factoids and adjectives crammed into their brains that it boggles my regular-person mind. Look around you, grab the nearest object, and try to describe it in a way that might make someone else want to buy it. I'll go first.

"Here we have a small Vornado fan—a personal fan that is compact and can sit on your desk or in a small area of your home and keep you cool. It has two speeds, which are controlled by a little gear under the fan. It's black. It has five blades (is that what you call them?), and the cord is long but not so long that it would be annoying. I once dropped a Diet Coke on it and it didn't break! Ummm . . . it's kind of loud, but not disruptive, unless you're sensitive to noise. It creates a lot of wind, like don't try to read a book in front of it or you will scream. I can't remember how much I paid for it, but it was pretty cheap? I think I got it at Big Lots. Anyway, it's a quality fan. I don't know that it would circulate air around a large room, but you could certainly try. Uhh, what else, what else? It's good; it does a fan's job. You should get one! If you want to buy mine, I'll throw in the layer of dust for free."

That's absolutely terrible! Now multiply that by twelve commercial-free minutes and add hand gestures and product numbers and organizing your brain to remember that "corn-flower" and "cerulean" are two different shades of blue. Do you know how much skill it takes to feign enthusiasm for something called a "foldable pet pool" for twenty minutes? I watched Carolyn do it, and she was *magnificent*. Did I ever think I'd be in the market for an "indoor restroom for pets?" I mean, I'm still not, but there's one in one of my many open tabs right now just waiting for me to get stoned and click SPEED BUY at 2:00 a.m. "Why?" you ask. Well, because a gorgeous MILF with medium-length square French-tip acrylics and a wedding-engagement ring combo the size of a megalith just told me not only does my dog need one but also there are only two hundred remaining for purchase and the clearance price is only good until the end of the day. Yes, two hundred sounds like a lot of useless doggy pools nobody actually needs, but when you think about how many ston-ers with credit cards are awake in the middle of the night ready to buy impractical shit for their pets . . . ? This might become an emergency.

Anyway, I would let any of these expertly coiffed, multitalented hosts with gleaming, fluorescent white teeth give me career advice, tell me what to eat for dinner, furnish my home, counsel me through an argument, lay out my clothes every day, raise my children, or just straight up run my life. Geniuses, all of them.

KitchenAid Nine-Cup Food Processor Plus
with Spatula & Blade Storage #K50013

EXTREMELY PERSUASIVE AND IRRESISTIBLE PRODUCT COPY: When it comes to shredding, slicing, chopping, pureeing, and even kneading, this powerful food processor does it all with precision and ease.

It's easy to use: a twist-free latched lid and one-click base make assembly quick and simple.

It's easy to clean: every part that touches food is dishwasher safe, and the base can be hand-wiped with a dishcloth.

It's easy to store: the blades and discs pack neatly inside the bowl, and a small footprint means it won't take up much space on your countertop or in a cabinet.

So take the hard work out of food prep, and chop tomatoes for salsa, shred cabbage for coleslaw, and slice cucumbers for a salad. This kitchen workhorse is an at-home chef's dream come true!

WHAT DID THE MAN IN THE VIDEO SAY?

David is on the kitchen set this evening and kicks it off by telling us that if you do all the prep work for homemade salsas and casseroles and stews and pie crusts that this food processor is going to be a *godsend* for you. I have never made a pie crust in my entire life, and yet? This is intriguing to me. As David speaks, accompanying pictures make me giggle. The salsa looks like someone bought the cheap kind from the store and just dumped it into one of those chip-and-dip combo platters you find in the seasonal section at Target. You know, when they put out stacks of neon teal beach loungers and glittery plastic Popsicle pool floaters and hang a cardboard sun from the ceiling that has a speech bubble screaming, "SUN SQUAD!!!!!!" or some nonsense like that. All that bright-colored fun shit that tricks you into thinking, for as long as it takes you to navigate your cart to the checkout line at least, that you might become the kind of person who would use something called a "backpack cooler watermelon." Oh yeah? You gonna pull up at the function with a little red backpack full of condensation-coated tall boys of Modelo? No, you're not, you're a grown man! But when you're in the store, surrounded by rainbow kiddie pools and Hula-Hoops, it seems possible. There's also a purple-cabbage-carrot-slaw situation I would totally eat. I can see how this machine could come in handy for people who hate chopping, but I am also distracted by the disembodied hand pouring some kind of viscous liquid onto the vegetables: who is that? What is that delicious sauce? Does the hand come as a free gift with the chopper???

David, who is wearing an adorable apron with his name

stitched across the top, tells us how this food processor is superior to old-school models because it doesn't require you to twist it and jiggle it to get the parts to fit together, and I feel like Ina Garten screaming, "I hate that!" while pointing my comically huge martini at the television screen. This newfangled gadget just easily clicks into place and, let me tell you, I would try to buy a fucking *spaceship* if some shellacked beauty pageant queen on TV demonstrated how easy it was to use. David walks us through the various included discs and tools and, to be honest, each one sounds better than the last. But also, when am I gonna need variations on the size of something I'm shredding? If you come over to eat my homemade coleslaw and talk some shit about the size of the carrots, I'm gonna dump the entire bowl in your lap. I want the uniform shreds, and I *need* to know that I have multiple hole sizes to choose from because I am a slut!

Okay, now David is walking us through the myriad ways QVC is saving us money on this item and, frankly, it looks too much like long division for my taste, so I'm tuning it out. But next, a treat: Tina, the 2012 national Pillsbury recipe champion and a busy wife and mom of two girls, is Skyping in from her home kitchen, where she is staring directly at the camera with a smile frozen on her red lips as she feeds the longest cucumber I have ever laid eyes on into this device that spits out uniform little discs of bright green cucumber middles.

Tina explains that she loves this KitchenAid food processor, and then she demonstrates the "feed tubes": one large that was suitable for her giant cukes, and another small, in which she is now placing a single carrot at a time, followed by a handful of radishes that will emerge perfectly sliced in the bowl. David is slicing his own carrots. Let me tell you right now that I am these advertisers' wet dream even though I don't put together crudité platters. David slides to the food processor to his immediate left and picks up a hunk of orange cheese, and when he stuffs it into what I'm assuming is the large feed tube (he doesn't specify), he refers to the resulting shreds as a "blizzard of cheese" and come on now!!!!!!!! I want cheddar in my forecast! ★Adds to cart★

WHAT IT COST ME: *Five Easy Payments of $24*

Everything should be sold this way. Let me zip up my Don Draper costume and pitch that commercials and ads shouldn't feature beautiful people sitting adjacent to the product they're selling while a plucky ukulele serenades them; ads should show real dumbasses with sausage fingers telling us how quick and painless using [something that is neither quick nor painless] is.

I could be convinced to buy anything a man in a waterproof apron who looks like my friend's dad wants to sell me. I don't necessarily need an electric pressure washer, but I could certainly be talked into buying one after watching this nice man in his sensible green polo use his to wash:

- a cobblestone path;
- gutters on his house;
- a wheelbarrow that used to have some old mulch in it;
- his garage door and his wife's car that is parked in the driveway;
- vinyl siding;
- an old deck/patio situation;

- a riding mower;
- a royal blue Ford pickup truck.

Nothing is more satisfying than watching slick, bubbling grime blasted off some lug nuts pool on the floor of this dude's garage. It's like ASMR for your eyeballs. I am transfixed by the extremely satisfying sight of dirt and bugs being power washed off every flat, nonporous surface my man can find in his ample backyard.

Bose Wave Music System IV w/ CD Player & Dual Alarm Clock #E243053

EXTREMELY PERSUASIVE AND IRRESISTIBLE PRODUCT COPY: Our Wave, your way. The Bose Wave Music System IV delivers rich, room-filling sound from a compact design that fits nearly anywhere—from your nightstand to your kitchen counter to your office space. Playing the tunes you love in the way you love them played, this sweet system boasts a CD player (yep, we know you still have 'em and love 'em), AM/FM radio tuner with twelve convenient presets, and an auxiliary port for your phone or tablet.

Dual independent alarms with rising volume provide a soothing start to your day, while the slim remote control allows for easy access to all these fabulous functions. So just sit back, relax, and let the Wave wash over you.

WHAT DID THE MAN IN THE VIDEO SAY?

Rick is on a set that looks like a patio and leads into a dining room. The first thing I notice is that there are those outdoor light bulb–looking lights strung up over the café table he has set up. I immediately navigate to the search bar to see if they have those on here. Not sure if that was the intention, but a brilliant move on QVC's part because, whaddya know, I immediately land upon Item #E355827 Mr. Beams 24′ Vintage LED String Lights for Outdoor - Edison. I'm not *not* opening a charming French bistro on the smattering of uneven stones outside my back door anytime soon, but if I were, I would buy them. They're cute as hell!

Rick does a little walk-and-talk around the circular table in this fake house's fake dining room (atop the table: one bushy artificial plant, one full water glass, one empty wineglass, one wineglass half filled with orange liquid, one wine bottle half filled with orange liquid, one fake charcuterie board with a spray of tiny purple grapes and a pale yellow wedge of cheese plus some artisanal sesame-seeded bread, one beige runner, and two Bose Wave speakers). He tells us there's a friends-and-family event going on, and I forget what that means, but I think there's some extra savings in there for me? That's lucky because Rick informs me that there's 30 percent off "hundreds of finds," including great gifts for Mom and Dad. I won't be needing those, so I decide that means I can buy a little something for myself and if anyone yells at me, I can play the orphan card without any guilt.

Rick says that he has sold one million of these CD players since Bose started selling on QVC, and that is impressive. I like knowing that other people have the same shit I do, it makes me feel validated. Every time I see another Honda Pilot on the road (with or without the dented, scratched-up passenger side from when I slid into the garage wall because the brakes went out and it was icy), I'm like "Okay, I'm not a dumbass," and I feel better about my life. What mental disorder is that? This is why I can't go outside, because I have the kind of brain that's like, "Oh, you gotta take a few hits of Flonase at this red light? No one else is in their car sniffling over the nose spray they can't live without, you weak, Snuffleupagus-ass bitch! And by the way, every car on this street is a better value and handles more smoothly than yours does." Anyway, I appreciate affirmation from people I will never meet.

Rick plays some kind of Enya-ish song on one of the Waves, and that is weird because wouldn't the quality of the device I am watching this program on affect my perception of the sound? Then he quickly pivots to talking about the QCard, QVC's very own branded credit score destroyer, and I would fast-forward through this part if I could because even though I've been trying to build my score for literal years it's still "poor," and I can't tempt fate. Imagine me fucking around and ruining my financial life because I couldn't stop charging eighty-count packs of the Perfect Gourmet Classic Potstickers to my imaginary money card! (I would.)

Rick tells us we can listen to all kinds of music on the Bose Wave: classic rock, country, Tom Jones, and Barbra Streisand are all gonna sound amazing on this sleek yet powerful machine. Um, I would like to go to a party at Rick's house. What a lineup! I am currently listening to PJ Harvey in one earbud but am strongly considering getting into Tom Jones due to Rick's charm and charisma. Hold up, Rick brought a friend. "Let's let the music do the talking," he says before introducing us to Brett, the "DJ of the day." Brett is wearing a fitted gray polo, his salt-and-pepper hair sexily tousled, and the first song he bumps is "I Can't Go for That (No Can Do)" by Hall & Oates. MY JAM????? ★Adds to motherfucking cart!!!!!!!!!★

WHAT IT COST ME: *Five Easy Payments of $67*
I may have a problem, but who cares, all this garbage I don't need is affordable. Also, it's fun to get mail. I love Quality Value Convenience!

superfan!!!!!!!

I was splitting an apartment with this chaotic old gay man and neither of us could afford HBO when *Sex and the City* premiered, so I had to do what broke bitches did in 1998: wait for it to come out on VHS and take the tapes I bought at Circuit City to my friend Jenny's apartment, where we sat on her floor and watched the entire season while sharing a Stouffer's frozen lasagna. The show reflected nothing of my life but provided something of a road map for my future, planting a tiny seed in my brain that one day after Al Gore invented a little thing called the internet (yes, I know about ARPANET, but just let this joke cook), maybe then I could write about my pussyhole on it.

More recently, my agent emailed me to say Michael Patrick King had read one of my books and called him out of the blue wanting to interview me to work on the *Sex and the City* reboot, and was I interested? I was like, "I would work as what? The sex-sweat mopper-upper?" I mean, are you allowed to work on a show like this if you only wear nine-dollar T-shirts and have no idea how many Brooklyns there are? This was my dream! During my interview I said, "Can I give Carrie diarrhea?" and I was hired immediately.

Before I figured out how to shut off my Instagram DMs, I got a handful of hilarious and stupid totally unhinged messages from batshit morons after the "Meet the Writers" article came out on *Deadline*, and also some death-adjacent threats that were less fun but entertaining nonetheless. The first one was from a dude who doesn't follow me. (I am so sorry for having to use these gross internet words, please know that I would gouge my own eyes out as penance if I had the stomach for wet work.) This dude's message read: "Hello, Miss. If you know what's good for you you will listen to this message. It has been my lifelong desire to play a boyfriend on *Sex and the City* and if you know what's good for you and don't want any trouble you'll hire me! I would be GREAT at that job." Which one, killing me or playing somebody's nameless single-episode love interest? Imagine risking prison time for the chance to play Impotent Guy or Roller-Skating Man for seven onscreen minutes. First of all, thank you, sir, for calling me "miss," I am forty-three. But also, even a cursory glance at my silly Instagram grid of shitty memes, pictures of my dog's costumed shame, and books I've read a quarter of the way through should have let homeboy know on sight that I am not the person making executive casting decisions on this iconic television program. That daunting task is reserved for my father, Mr. HBO Max.

The second message, sent by a woman with a private profile whose tortured, bleached-blond hair in her profile picture looked extremely stressed out, went something like this: "hey u fuckin bitch if u put carrie back with aiden [*sic*] and ruin my favorite show i'll fucking kill u." Um, okay? My kingdom for this murderous threat to become a reality!

I would love to die, and I especially would love to die at the hands of this deranged woman over the choices a fictional character I did not invent makes on a show that is not real regarding a man who absolutely does not exist. My funeral would be such a party, because I am a funny and likable person, plus my murder would probably be splashed across the tabloids in a sleazy John Hinckley Jr. kind of way, and people would want to be seen mourning me. Maybe Sarah Jessica Parker would come!

The internet is so gross, I wish I never had to look at anything scary or weird or mean on there, but my sincerest wish is that one day it will evolve to the point where none of its more brain-poisoned, terminally online denizens could talk to me without having to first upload their verified state-issued identification so I know exactly who I'm out here dealing with. I'll do mine! I would love to!!!!! You know why? Because I don't threaten to murder strangers online, and if the FBI needed to trace a meme I'd reposted of a repost of a repost without proper attribution back to me, that's cool and I'd happily pay the fine to Sad Kermit for my crimes.

I had to deactivate my Twitter for my sanity's sake because everyone has incurable fucking brain worms, and I saw someone whom I'd previously thought to be a very smart lady criticize a promotional photo from the forthcoming *And Just Like That . . .* series I had been working on for months in a tweet that went something like, "this show looks so bad, Miranda has a child, she would never wear white pants" and I felt my fingers start to itch as I attempted to simply scroll past as if I did not see it. I try to conduct myself decently on social media because (1) drama is boring and (2) they make you upload your driver's license to get verified and I don't know enough about how IP addresses work to feel comfortable making a burner. Also, Miranda is fifty-five and her eighteen-year-old son/man FUCKS within the first five minutes of the first episode. She can wear whatever kind of pants she pleases!

DEATH THREATS!!!!! OVER THE TUTU LADY!!!!!!!! Is this a real thing? Do people really feel this strongly about their imaginary television friends? I mean, on the one hand I get it, I have watched every episode of every season dozens and dozens of times and feel a kinship with each of these women, but on the other hand they are not people. I would not kill on their behalf, mostly because they exist only on paper and inside of my TV. Although I'm not sure that I'd consider homicide for any of my *actual* homies, the ones who can breathe my same air and talk to me, but maybe that's just supporting evidence that I'm a shitty friend. Anyway, if I had access to a time machine, here are some ways I would teleport back to my knees' best years and ruin that would-be assassin's favorite show.

SEASON ONE

Episode 1: "Sex and the City"
What if "Mister Big" was just "John the Bank Guy"? You know what I mean? Half of this dude's allure was the fact that he was all smoldering and mysterious and we had no idea what his name was. Also, he was rich and had a driver,

which definitely fills the hole where a personality was supposed to be. And, yes, Big had luxurious hair and a gorgeous jaw, but what if he's just some regular asshole withholding his attention and Carrie moves on by the middle of the season and we never think about his ass ever again?

Episode 3: "Bay of Married Pigs"

Instead of pretending to be gay for one dinner party in order to make partner at her law firm, Miranda instead dives headfirst into a full-fledged lesbian relationship with Syd, adopting several needy shelter dogs and moving into an exposed-brick apartment together two weeks after they learn each other's last names. Every episode of every future season, they get into a fight about a different lesbo one or both of them may or may not have fooled around with but never break up, ever.

Episode 5: "The Power of Female Sex"

Remember when homeboy left that envelope stuffed full of cash on that five-star-hotel nightstand for Carrie? What if she actually becomes a sex worker because having sex for free to write two-dollars-a-word newspaper columns is a fucking drag, especially when she could just get a sick apartment and all her Manolos paid for by a stream of monied, faceless businessmen who her glamorous madam Amalita sets her up with and whose names and quirks she never has to learn???

Episode 6: "Secret Sex"

Is it so bad not to meet your man's stupid-ass friends? Like, have you ever met a man's friends and felt enriched by that experience? "Oh, thank you so much for introducing me to

Tony, babe. *Love* putting a face to the name of the dude calling me a bird in the group chat!" Who are Big's friends anyway, and why is Carrie pressed to know them? I doubt that my girl is dying to talk about box scores and interest rates or whatever it is banker types talk about (LOL, COCAINE). Let's just assume he has none and get back to fucking him with a bra on.

Episode 9: "The Turtle and the Hare"

Charlotte actually marries her vibrator in a chic and tasteful commitment ceremony and all the ladies attend, dressed in the ratty old T-shirts they masturbate in. The happy couple is registered in the battery aisle at Best Buy.

Episode 11: "The Drought"

THAT FART SHOULD HAVE BEEN LOUDER. Okay, so this is one of my favorite episodes because (1) I love flatulence-related humor, (2) that whoopee cushion prank scene literally made me choke laughing, and (3) as a culture, we should really be normalizing people being together romantically but not having sex every single night, as it sets a dangerous precedent that I am too old and tired to live up to. If you are fucking every single day, congratulations to you but please don't tell me about it. My pussy has not been that active since I was in my late teens, and my decrepit living corpse has devolved to the point where if I have a fizzy water after 7:00 p.m. I will be awake and uncomfortable and not in the mood for sex for the next three weeks, minimum. Anyway, that fart should've broken the sound barrier. I'm talking a thunderous, window-rattling sonic boom that catapulted Carrie right out of Big's luxurious Frette sheets. It should've been so rancid that we could literally *see* it.

Episode 12: "Oh Come All Ye Faithful"

James's tiny penis isn't that big of a problem, if we're being honest and if he isn't intimidated by a Lelo Soraya gently buzzing against his nuts while he fucks from behind. But Carrie should've been struck by lightning for misbehaving in church! I am not a religious person, but I definitely *am* a person who was babysat every Sunday morning, and Thursday afternoon, for the first ten-plus years of my life by the father, the son, and the holy ghost; a person whose first handful of birthday parties were thrown in the basement of Fisher Memorial AME Zion Church; a person who was forced to go to a "fall celebration" with the rest of my Sunday school attendees while other kids were out trick-or-treating.

I stopped going when I was in high school because my life was falling apart, but I did dip a toe back in in my twenties, when I thought "find and marry a stable man who goes to church" was a thing that sounded good and plausible. All my years of indoctrination left one very clear mark: you don't play around in church. I mean, just in case hell is real, I don't want to have to defend, say, "cussing near the pulpit" when I present my life's worn and tattered dossier to Saint Peter. So, when Carrie leaned over the railing to get a better look at Mama Big (nosy!) I gasped, not because I was worried that she might fall, but because I was braced for a bolt of lightning to crash through the ceiling and electrocute her for misbehaving in Jesus's living room.

. . .

An aside:

IN DEFENSE OF CHARLOTTE

Why does no one ever talk about how Charlotte is the best character on this show? She's really great! Uptight? Sure, but that's not a sin, right? We all have a friend who won't join in some bullshit shenanigans they know are gonna end with us in hot water, and that person is integral to a life of good decision-making.

Mine is named Laura, and I know that if I am going to do something reckless or embarrassing to not tell her beforehand, and honestly to only tell her afterward if whatever I did was painless or successful. No, Charlotte is *not* gonna dress up like a dominatrix for the BDSM nightclub opening, but she'll be there! And with kinky hair, to boot!!

Charlotte is smart, and she has a cool job and knows a lot of shit about art; she's optimistic and hopeful, both refreshing and underrated qualities in a person. She looks good, she loves masturbating, and she keeps a beautiful apartment, which you might feel tempted to clown her for, but look around at your messy, dirty crib littered with cereal bowls and empty Tylenol bottles (just me?) and tell me you don't tip your cap to a lady whose dining room could be on the cover of *Architectural Digest* at any time.

Charlotte cooks, she survived a divorce, she knows etiquette stuff, she converted to Judaism for her man, she can tap-dance, she rides horses, she has an interesting backstory (well . . . at the very least, she has a brother and a father we've seen), and she let that weird foot guy touch her in exchange for free shoes!!!!!! She's perfect.

SEASON TWO

Episode 1: "Take Me Out to the Ballgame"
Big's gotta cuss Carrie out in the bar for fucking up his vacation, right? New Yankee or no New Yankee, if you waste however many thousands of dollars it cost for my secretary to book us a sexy Caribbean vacation getaway after throwing a tantrum about not getting to meet my boring-ass mom, I don't care who's there or what kind of date you are on, I absolutely have to call you an asshole and pour your drink on the floor. I'm sorry, but that is the law.

Episode 2: "The Awful Truth"
One thing I'm gonna go ahead and take credit for in the reboot is the return of my absolute favorite side character, Susan Sharon. I think about her at least once a week, speed-walking through that fancy shop in her cashmere, Gucci bag looped over one arm, crunching the ever-loving *shit* out of the world's largest piece of biscotti: what a dreamboat.

Okay, the thing I would change is, hold on to your butts, drumroll please . . . I would make Susan Sharon a regular member of the cast. I'm sorry, but I love her so much; she's an absolute nightmare person and would add a hilarious chaotic energy to everything the girls do. I have a couple of Susan Sharons (THAT FUCKING NAME) in my life and let me tell you: they are utterly exhausting. You know who I mean, bitches who never shut the fuck up and treat you like a cabdriver (or a hostage) as they rattle on about shit you don't know anything about? Theoretically, I love those people. They'd make for good TV!!

Also, honorable mention to this episode for teaching me one of the most important friendship lessons I have ever learned: never tell your homegirl to break up with her man, it will be your fault if she's miserable afterward. Instead, practice noncommittal yet sympathetic nodding while murmuring, "Yeah, that really stinks." It's the only way to survive with your friendship intact.

Episode 4: "They Shoot Single People, Don't They?"
Another one of my absolute favorite, most bestest ever, top-tier desert-island episodes. This is the one where Carrie is profiled for a magazine and stays out the night before the accompanying photo shoot dancing and getting wasted. She arrives late to the set and gets her photo taken while looking like shit, then the shit photo is on the cover of the magazine when it comes out and she says, "I'm all over the city looking like . . . like something that got caught in a drain," which is a line that made me cry laughing.

I had a little write-up in the *Chicago Tribune* years ago, and the dude writing it appeared to be thoroughly unimpressed by his subject, which I get! Why should this blog person be in the newspaper?!?!?! They wanted to get photos of me for the article, and rather than sending a photographer to the cute restaurant I met the reporter in, they instead decided to send him to my animal hospital job? And I was like, "Okay, sure, but you know I'm not . . . a veterinarian, right?" What were they gonna do, take a picture of me explaining what a distemper vaccine is for? Apparently yes, and when the article came out, the picture that ran alongside it was so fucking terrible, I burst out laughing and immediately thought of poor Carrie and her hungover photo shoot. I should've had a cocktail on my lunch break, maybe it would've turned out cute.

In this episode, Miranda fucks this ophthalmologist who she has to fake orgasms with, and what if instead of that she hopped out of bed, pulled out an anatomy book, and made him label all the parts of the vulva and vagina and then explained to him where his fingers should go and how?

Episode 6: "The Cheating Curve"

The power lesbians "adopt" Charlotte, despite her heterosexuality, starting a blood feud between them and Miranda and Carrie and Samantha. This is a thing I am really interested in, warring factions of adult friends, because I think it's a thing we all go through to varying degrees. I have different group chats for different things: one that I text Simu Liu thirst traps to, another for depression memes, another for internet bullshit, and so on.

It's so deliciously sticky and awkward when your work friends meet your life friends or when your married friends meet your single friends and you're stuck playing tour guide between the groups. "No, no, Miranda is the lawyer, and Samantha is in PR! And remember how I told you Carrie's not cool with that Wall Street guy anymore?" That could be so juicy.

Episode 7: "The Chicken Dance"

Another fave of mine, in particular that scene in which Sam and Miranda and Carrie are getting drunk at the bar outside the ballroom and Miranda admits to regifting the frog sculpture and Samantha lets out the world's most perfect laugh. But in my version Miranda marries Jeremy, the friend who crashed on her couch then boned her decorator, that actor who was featured in several Dick Wolf spin-offs, fresh off the plane from London and decides to become a housewife.

Episode 8: "The Man, the Myth, the Viagra"
Why was Samantha so horrified by that old man's jiggly little butt? I would have loved to see him slithering around on top of her, his teeny cheeks wiggling like a bowl of Jell-O!!!!

Episode 11: "Evolution"
Instead of bagging it up and bringing it over to her apartment, Big throws out Carrie's expensive face wash, the face wash she left behind at his apartment in an effort to subliminally stake her claim and prove that she has some permanence in his life, so she can stop carrying extra panties around in her handbag. Then Carrie gives a stirring monologue straight to the camera about the harm inflicted by the pink tax and its unfair punishment of women who just want to shave their coarse upper lip hairs off.

Also? Charlotte with the gay straight guy who maybe could've been a straight gay guy: we're *dumping* talented pastry chefs because they don't want to reach down with their precious, meringue-sculpting hands and pick up a gross, squealing, half-dead mouse stuck to a dirty, sticky glue trap? That's really what we're doing?! Not on my watch we're not!

Episode 15: "Shortcomings"
Carrie works it out with Justin Theroux the premature ejaculator, if only to keep hanging out at his family's killer apartment, eating bagels with his dope-ass mom; Samantha marries Charlotte's brother, and Charlotte has to be institutionalized as a result; Miranda does child abuse to that divorced guy's terrible son and goes to jail.

SEASON THREE

Episode 2: "Politically Erect"
Carrie love love *loves* pissing on Bill Kelley; she literally can't get enough of it and develops a gnarly UTI. She and the girls go out for drinks and they're sitting at the bar gossiping, a hot guy across the bar sends her a drink but she politely declines. Antibiotic contraindications!!!!! She sends it back, then asks the bartender for a cranberry juice instead. Hot Guy is now Mad Guy and says something shitty like, "Cranberry juice? What, are you on your period?" and Carrie waits a beat before smashing the glass into the side of his head and beating him half to death until Jack Nicholson pulls her off him then breaks her already-broken hand in the back room. (This is a reference to *The Departed*, for those of you who hate ~cinema~.)

Episode 5: "No Ifs, Ands, or Butts"
Either Carrie just flat out refuses to quit smoking *or* she teaches Aidan to love cigarettes. Whichever one is better for feminism.

Episode 8: "The Big Time"
What if Carrie immediately ran to find Aidan in that Warehouse of Credenzas™ and was like, "Big is here in a beige suit with his beige wife looking at beige couches and he's trying to bone me. FIGHT HIM TO THE DEATH"? First of all, how exciting. Imagine these two bulls locking horns next to a hulking dresser made of whatever reclaimed wood is, built by a gruff, whiskered artisan with his own two manly hands as Carrie stands by drinking a free coffee. Whoever wins gets an antique rocking chair, whoever loses dies.

Episode 9: "Easy Come, Easy Go"
This might be "easy" for me to say as a person whose ideal marriage proposal would go something like, "I have health insurance, and I also love Fritos. Should we go to the courthouse?" but I didn't think Charlotte's (forced? coercive?) proposal to Trey was all that bad? Why was she so stressed about it?! If someone took a knee in front of me, in public especially, but also even if it was just the two of us in my living room, I would pass away from humiliation. I'd start muttering, "Get up get up get up get up get up," while trying to pull them up from the ground, my palms slick with flop sweat and the food in my intestines liquefying down the inside of my pant leg. Everything is so embarrassing all the time, I don't want to add to it by forcing strangers to watch the biggest decision I'd ever have to make, on the street, or in a nice restaurant while their soup gets cold, against their will. Charlotte should've counted her blessings that a casual mention of marriage got an "Alrighty!" out of Trey, guaranteeing that there'd be no flash mob in her near future. That's a blessing!

Episode 12: "Don't Ask, Don't Tell"
Carrie shouldn't have told Aidan about Big. Maybe I'm a
big piece of shit, but telling your man that you boned your
ex-man ten minutes before serving as your best friend's maid
of honor is dumb and ruins the day for him, for you, for the
cabdriver on the way to the church, for your homegirl, for
your other friends who are wondering why you appear to
be sad crying instead of happy crying during the vows and
reception, for the wedding planner, for the photographer,
for anyone who sits near you during cocktail hour, for the
makeup artist who has to keep fixing your mascara-tracked
undereye concealer . . .

Episode 16: "Frenemies"
Carrie's man seminar is a raging success, and she continues
teaching rather than writing her column, gets boring, decides to start wearing flat shoes and uncomplicated outfits
and live a simple life.

An aside:

MY FAVORITE BOYFRIENDS
(in no particular order)

- Smith Jerrod, Samantha's Absolut™ hunk
- Richard Wright, Samantha's hotelier (hot as fuck!)
- Will Arnett, Miranda's outdoor sex freak
- Joe Starr, Carrie's hot Yankee
- Miranda's talking sandwich

- Jack Berger, Carrie's insecure-ass writer (I am a Berger apologist, more on that later)
- Arthur, Charlotte's fist-fighting WASP
- Adam Ball, Samantha's funky spunker
- Vaughn Wysel, Carrie's premature ejaculator
- Charlotte's rabbit vibrator
- Bill Kelley, Carrie's peeing politician (John Slattery, please hit me with a car!)
- Steve, Miranda's bartender
- Chivon, Samantha's "hip-hop mogul"
- Ben, Carrie's soccer-playing (non-freak) sweetie
- Dr. Robert, Miranda's Knicks doctor (Blair Underwood, my god)
- Keith, Carrie's lying LA guy (I'm sorry, but I love Vince Vaughn, okay!)
- Stephan, Charlotte's pastry chef
- Alanis Morissette, Carrie's bisexual kiss at that young-people party
- Ray King, Carrie's jazz man
- John, Carrie's "sex buddy" (the Allstate dude!!!!)
- MISTER PUSSY, Charlotte's incredible pussy eater
- Whoever Bradley Cooper played when he took Carrie home from the bar that one time
- Miranda's chocolate cake
- Harry, Charlotte's divorce lawyer (would die for him)

SEASON FOUR

Episode 3: "Defining Moments"
Miranda has no trouble using the bathroom in front of her man and takes a big shit in his toilet. YES. This is my singular agenda, and YES I absolutely will! not! rest! until we normalize beautiful people shitting on TV, so of course I would go back and put poop in this show. In this imaginary circumstance during which no one is around to say "GIRL, STOP" to me, we're starting the episode on the toilet, we're going back to the toilet in the middle, and we're finishing with a real, constipation-relieving sexual groan on the toilet at the end.

Episode 4: "What's Sex Got to Do with It?"
I fully support Miranda eating chocolate as a substitute for sex!!!!! Chocolate is reliably satisfying and easy to procure. But here's my real hate crime: I would have thrown a tantrum at the suggestion that Samantha date Maria. I mean, I like it theoretically, everyone should bathe with and then throw plates at their gay lover. BUT: Maria looked kind of nuts when, really, she was just a normal person interested in a relationship and she made the unfortunate mistake of trying to turn a fuckboy into a housewife.

If Samantha were a man, she'd be the kind of walking red flag women gossip about in the bathroom at the club: "I saw you talking to that guy near the DJ booth—don't fuck him; he's never gonna settle down; he only has time for his rock-hard penis and his bossy friends." And poor Maria was just trying to talk about her feelings and cook dinner together. Let's spare her this heartache!

Episode 7: *"Time and Punishment"*

What if when Aidan goes over to help Miranda after she falls and tweaks her neck, instead of her flipping the fuck out on Carrie (who probably/maybe couldn't have hoisted her off the floor anyway?), she's totally cool with it and lets him take care of her, and then Aidan and Miranda have sex to get back at Carrie for cheating on Aidan with Big and for Carrie sending Aidan to help Miranda in her stead?

Aidan is the best of Carrie's boyfriends—I'm sorry to break this to you but you'll live—and she was always doing him dirty! He was just a big ol' teddy bear trying to make her floors nice and drive his raggedy-ass truck in the country, and she couldn't stop being a huge bitch to him. Not me holding the fictional Aidan Shaw's water, BUT: he was cuter than Big, nicer than Big, more thoughtful than Big, more patient than Big; he (demonstrably) loved Carrie more than Big did; he was handy; he owned a cool bar; he didn't look like a carbon copy Brooks Brothers model; he somehow got even hotter (?????) when he and Carrie reconnected after their initial breakup; he was sweet; he knew shit about wood; he got his big ass in Carrie's little tub with a bunch of flowers and candles and shit; he was so nice when Carrie was being a brat about her laptop; he helped Miranda's ungrateful ass . . .

Episode 10: *"Belles of the Balls"*

Aidan should've killed Big.

Episode 13: "The Good Fight"

I'm just joking about Aidan killing Big, because honestly then this show would have to turn into *Law & Order* and we already have twelve of those. But if he *had*, then some unhinged weirdo wouldn't have tagged me in her Instagram dissertation when Big eventually *did* die, calling me—the last name on the call sheet and literal decider of nothing—a murderer.

Anyway, the cardboard baby Trey got Charlotte as a stand-in for a human one: It wasn't that bad, right? I mean, it's funny. Kind of? I would've laughed! Maybe this is where I admit I am a nightmare person to be with because I love a joke, and I cannot *stand* for the vibe to be somber for even a minute without looking around desperately for something to lighten the mood. I loved Charlotte's relationship with Trey because it illustrated the pitfalls that come with projecting a fantasy onto a real, fallible person, and ultimately, it's good that the veil was lifted from her eyes that this dude who thinks paper babies are funny is not a dude she wanted to be with, but she could've seen that while also cracking a smile. Come on. That shit was funny!

Episode 16: "Ring a Ding Ding"

CHARLOTTE SHOULD NOT HAVE GIVEN CARRIE THAT MONEY!!!!!!!!!!!! For the record, I am not a whiny "how could she buy so many $400 shoes when she earned $1.87 per article, it's so unrealistic" person, but I do think it could've been interesting (read: terrible and funny) to watch Carrie have to scramble to put together her life after being dumped out on her butt with no savings.

This is mostly fueled by my intense hatred for New York City, but let's be real. Every apartment is prohibitively expensive and owning property is for responsible people with good credit, so—*puts on writers' room invisible thinking cap*— what if Carrie was forced to sleep on her friends' couches or to be forty-year-old roommates with someone unsettling? *Imagine* Charlotte chasing after Carrie with a Dustbuster as she leaves a trail of Hershey's Kisses and cigarette butts all over her beautiful penthouse!! It would be so frustrating and hilarious and maybe they would have a compelling fistfight at the end!

SEASON FIVE

Episode 2: "Unoriginal Sin"
Is Carrie the best choice to be Brady's godmother? My favorite sub-friendship in the group was always Miranda and Samantha. They had a very sweet cackling-witches-on-the-sidelines thing going that I love. They know Carrie is ridiculous and kind of stunted as an adult, and they would be passing knowing glances as the jaded adults with mortgages in the room, and that was just so great. When Miranda succumbed to the pressure to have Brady baptized, I was like, "Okay, sure, whatever, I've been sprinkled with holy water, too." But then when she chose Carrie to be his godmother, I was like, "HUH?!" Even if Carrie and Miranda were tighter pals, let's look at this from the perspective of fiscal responsibility. (Yes, I want to throw up just from typing that, but what are godmothers for anyway?)

Samantha had a good job and plenty of money and owned her own place, if I am thinking about who takes my kid if I get run over by a city bus, I am picking the lady with a 401(k), okay? Even if Samantha didn't want to touch the kid, we know that she would hire the best nanny and send him to the ritziest boarding school. And when he came home for winter break, Miranda could rest easy knowing that he wasn't sleeping in a shoe closet. Carrie wouldn't even be mad! "Fun Aunt Who Buys Designer Toys" is much more her vibe anyway!

Episode 4: "Cover Girl"
I know people talk about how the dude Miranda met at Weight Watchers was nice and got a raw deal, but I counter that opinion with this: Miranda shouldn't have gone to Weight Watchers in the first fucking place! She should've spent the entire season eating Milky Ways and blocks of cheddar cheese or whatever it is you crave after you push a slimy, wailing football out of your body. I know that the fashion is the point, but our girl couldn't get a few months of sweatpants episodes while her vagina fused itself back together?!

Episode 5: "Plus One Is the Loneliest Number"
Man, I'm a bitch. That fancy book party Carrie had? The one with the flowers and catered snacks?! That shit is absolutely not happening. Nobody's regular-ass book tour looks like that. A color scheme? A stylist?! BAHAHAHAHA SHUT UP. No, Carrie's book event's gotta look like all the ones I've ever had: crammed in the back of an independent bookstore with a dozen disheveled people who just got off

work staring expectantly up at her as she stammers through an intro for a book those folks are definitely not gonna pay thirty bucks for; while other people mill around in the background shopping, yelling at their kids, trying to get a coffee at the in-store café, and loudly stage-whispering, "WHO IS THIS? IS HER BOOK ANY GOOD?" to a stranger at the back of the crowd.

Once during a book tour stop in San Francisco, the store I was at got fucking *robbed* while I was standing behind the lectern making my little jokes, and they told me to just . . . keep going? So yeah, I'm putting Carrie at a rickety folding table hastily set up in the story time clearing in the middle of the children's section in a suburban bookstore with a handful of old ladies who treat the bookstore like a library and shush her every time her reading gets too animated, and the three people who are paying attention give her little more than a polite chuckle. She'll retire from writing books that night.

Episode 8: "I Love a Charade"

I was not a fan of Carrie visiting Big in LA in the episode before this one, mostly because Big is such a New York guy that he just seemed like an alien out there in all that sunshine and fresh air. Listen, I loved Berger. He was funny and charming and apparently wrote a fantastic book. And watching Carrie dump all her relationship breakup baggage onto him during that impromptu picnic in the grass made my brain scream, but they were so good together, I wished they could've figured it out.

I haven't dated a writer, but I have a lot of close writer friends, and the only way to survive the menacing voice in your head that's whispering "Her book is better than your book; her book is better than your book" on a loop is to just pretend she doesn't have one. I do it all the time! I buy my friends' books, but I don't always read them, because I don't like having my deficits spread before me as I am forced to examine them. Maybe this is the self-loathing, mentally unstable personal essayist in me, but I get Berger, and he and Carrie could've been the dream couple. Also, I just hate Big so much, I can't help it. It should be a felony for a man to waste that much of a woman's time. But I love Berger and Carrie's collective wit and charm and incredible chemistry. If only he'd just taken his ass off his shoulders for five minutes and not been such a huge baby.

If Berger and I were text friends, I would gently remind him that people who publish novels and people who publish printed-out blogs are *technically* in the same category, but not really the same kind of writers, so he shouldn't worry that his girlfriend got a bigger advance than he did. She's never gonna be reviewed in the *New Yorker* or be taken seriously by anyone who earnestly uses the word "literature." And he will, just because he's a man who wrote an Important Fictional Book. Comparison is the thief of joy, and instead of moping over Carrie's big paycheck, he should've gone with her to a nice dinner while counting his lucky stars that he doesn't do the kind of writing that prompts people who have never landed a punch line in their lives to come up to him and demand his agent's contact information, because even though they aren't a writer, they "have a killer book idea that's just like mine, but way better."

. . .

An aside:

THE TOP EIGHT CARRIE OUTFITS AS VIEWED THROUGH THE LENS OF A NON-FASHION PERSON WHO KNOWS LITTLE TO NOTHING ABOUT CLOTHES AND CAN'T REMEMBER SHIT

1. THE MIXED-PRINT CROP TOP SITUATION SHE WORE TO TAKE THAT UNNECESSARY PLANT TO AIDAN'S BAR

She knew what she was doing exposing that lil slice o' midriff in the middle of the day! She was irresistible! Carrie was wearing a black-and-white-patterned skirt with a crop top and this long white jacket that had a minimalist pink-and-blue floral print on it, and she decides to go to her ex-boyfriend's new bar before it opens to drop off a congratulatory plant (WHAT?!). I cried laughing because "Remember me? Here's a present" is a trick I've unsuccessfully played, too, and also because would Aidan even *notice* this carefully crafted pattern clashing that she'd constructed for his benefit?

2. THE BIG BOW SHIRT WITH SLACKS SHE WAS WEARING WHILE MAKING A CALL ON A PAY PHONE AND TELLING MIRANDA TO MAKE A PRO AND CON LIST ABOUT STEVE

I'm doing this from memory so that it sounds as clueless about fashion as I actually am, but the girls are at the brunch where Charlotte admits she wanted to bone Dan Quayle when she was in college. Then they go their separate ways and Carrie and Miranda are walking down a side street, and my girl is serving business-casual Carrie in a pussy-bow blouse and tailored pants. She looks so elegant for having just pounded some ricotta-stuffed pancakes and fourteen sausage links! Oh, she had the sliver of quiche served with upscale spring mix and a squeeze of lemon? I guess that's why she looks so great in the pants. ★sob★

3. THE SUIT (???) WITH A T-SHIRT SHE WORE WHILE WALKING DOWN THE STREET WITH SAMANTHA AND TELLING HER ABOUT HOW BERGER GAVE HIS ANSWERING MACHINE THE DOUBLE BIRD

After spending the night at Berger's, Carrie was freaked out after he flipped off his machine while a message from his ex played, and she told Samantha about it while wearing a casual suit in the middle of the day! A suit! Just walking to brunch in a little suit!

4. THE FUZZY-COAT-TINY-DRESS LOOK FROM WHEN SHE WAS SITTING ON HER STOOP SURROUNDED BY GLAMOROUS SHOPPING BAGS

This is an episode filled with great looks that I don't know how to describe, like the short pink pants, scrunchy gold boots, and green striped sleeveless (?) tank top (??) she starts out in at the hot firefighter contest and the tight blue dress with the white feather coat (???) she's wearing at the end, but my favorite is when she's walking down her picture-perfect block in her nudish tall boots and her big furry coat carrying her $528,204 worth of splashy footwear to discover John

Slattery oozing relaxed charm all over her steps. Carrie is always sexy, but she was So Fucking Sexy sitting there with him being so dang cute. THUMBS UP.

5. THE PINK-PANTS-WHITE-TANK-PURPLE-FLOWER OUTFIT SHE WORE TO AIDAN'S STORE THE FIRST TIME

Okay, this scene is burned into my brain because it contains one of my favorite Stanford lines—"There's nothing in here but baguettes and fagettes"—but also because, if I am recalling this correctly, Carrie was just chilling in her apartment reading magazines looking ready to go and be seen by other human eyes??? Incredible!

6. THAT DEEP PURPLE FLORAL ROBE WITH THE BIG SHINY PAILLETTES ON IT THAT SHE THREW DOWN IN THE STREET TO THE AA GUY

It's truly THE MOST gorgeous article of clothing, a silky, slinky garment that was probably a dress because would you really wear something like that to just lie around the house? There's a scene in which Carrie is sitting on the side of her bed, balancing her laptop on her knees, and her hair is up in this cascading ponytail, and she's wearing the Robe, and I feel like it's my duty to tell you that I am writing this book in an orthopedic chair I had to special order on the internet with a crocheted afghan in my lap, and I'm wearing a sweatshirt with a Detroit Coney dog printed on the front and a wear-'n'-tear hole in the elbow. I'm sure there are glamorous writers who sit down to their computers in outfits they've zippered and buttoned, with flawless makeup application and enviable hair, but I don't know any!

7. THE BLUE MINI SHORTS AND OPEN-TOE HEEL SITUATION SHE CHASED A DOG THROUGH THE STREET IN

I think there was a peasant blouse involved here, too? I just remember Carrie pounding the pavement, running *for real*, for real, in little strappy high-heeled sandals with these little shorties on and thinking to myself, "There is no fucking way." This scene also reminds me of another huge nostalgia point for me while watching this show: life was so much more tricky and interesting before we all had cell phones. If I was writing that scene today, Carrie would run for half a block before coming to her senses and pulling out her phone to call someone with a car to scoop her up, but before we all had pocket computers, she was forced to run through New York City in short pants and high heels for hours in the rain. A nightmare, but she looked adorable as hell.

8. REMEMBER THAT TIME SHE WORE A RAGGEDY ROLLING STONES T-SHIRT? PLUS AN HONORABLE MENTION TO THOSE KNEE-HIGH RAINBOW GOSSIPING SOCKS

As a Fat and a Poor, the clothing on this show was not aspirational to me, which is a very freeing margin in which to exist while watching something like *Sex and the City*. I didn't ever have to worry about fitting into or being able to afford anything anyone wore at any time, so I could just let the beauty wash over me and soak into my eyeballs without feeling bad that I had no idea Barneys was the name of a store.

I'm not even a purse guy, because I have always had the kind of life and needs that require a sturdy tote bag; I'm not saving up for a vintage Fendi baguette! Where would I put my Stephen King novel and super absorbent Always overnights? I need half a dozen lipsticks and an economy-sized bottle of extra-strength Advil on my person at all times! If I leave my house with only a teeny little purse, who's gonna hold my charging brick and lightweight cardigan for when it might get cold?! That said, anytime Carrie was shown wearing something a normal person with no money could wear, I would be filled with delight, and no, I do not believe that Carrie Bradshaw has ever even heard any music let alone been so into the Stones (of all bands!!!!) that she would have, say, gotten some merch at one of their shows. That's absurd. But I do believe that she either took it as a parting gift after a one-night stand with a fifty-year-old "cool" dad, or she thought the lips logo looked interesting and grabbed it off the endcap at her local Duane Reade.

In a scene where the girls are sitting around Carrie's apartment discussing Samantha's pee-hole surgery and Charlotte's trying to turn Mister Pussy into an actual relationship candidate, Carrie is drinking wine and wearing a *very* '90s slip dress that she's paired with knee-high rainbow socks that were eerily similar to a pair I'd ordered from the Delia*s catalog a couple of years before, and while I'm sure hers were designer, seeing her in them made me feel hip for half a second, and that was nice.

SEASON SIX

Episode 1: "To Market, to Market"
This might be too spicy of a take, but what if Steve realized he was too good for Miranda and told her to fuck off into the sea forever?

Episode 3: "The Perfect Present"
What was the big deal with the white noise machine? I started sleeping with one when I started sleeping with another person every night and, let me tell you, if there's anything unrealistic about this show, it's that these women spent the night with so many men without pissing themselves or choking on their own vomit or lying awake in a panic because they smell funny and their stomachs won't stop audibly sloshing around inside them.

The thing about casual sex is that it is stressful to *literally sleep* with a stranger. What if you have restless legs or you toot in your sleep? I went out with a dude once and had diarrhea in the middle of the night, of fucking course, so I got up in the dark to go to the bathroom that shared a wall with his bedroom, and the first thing that happened was I burned my nipples on the radiator because his room was so dark. The second thing was me trying to figure out how to empty the entire contents of my bowels in earshot of a man I'd met only a week before as he slept on the other side of a postcard-thin wall in his apartment that was as silent as a fucking crypt. WHAT I WOULDN'T GIVE for some mechanical ocean waves or a chorus of croaking frogs in that moment! I ended up turning the shower on and flushing the toilet over and over, which is why I don't go anywhere overnight without my portable white noise machine. Carrie should have been grateful the dude liked to be serenaded by crickets while he slept. What if she had to fart for the second ever time in her life?!

Episode 4: "Pick-a-Little, Talk-a-Little"

Okay, I would not change a single thing about this episode, I just need to say out loud and in public that the idea of "He's Just Not That Into You" changed my fucking life. I'm not exaggerating, there was a shift in both the way I thought about and behaved within my interpersonal relationships after I watched that episode. For those of you who are unfamiliar (I can't believe you've made it this far, wow), Miranda regales the ladies and Carrie's seemingly perfect boyfriend Jack Berger with the story of a seemingly perfect date that ended with the guy not coming upstairs with her, and when the ladies chime in reassuringly ("He probably had to get up early for work!" they coo), Berger interrupts to say, nah, there's no such thing. If he was interested in her he definitely would've gone upstairs and boned her. The rest of the ladies get mad and try to shout him down, but Miranda gets it and has an epiphany.

I had that same epiphany, which was basically "If someone you're dating isn't nice to you and doesn't call you back, don't make excuses for that asshole, understand that you don't mean that much to them and move on." That is a bracing thing to hear, even if it's just from yourself, but after the initial sting wears off, it's actually kind of soothing. More soothing than writing a thriller novel in your head about why that dude who bought you a cheeseburger one time only texts you every three days at 2:00 a.m., for sure.

Episode 7: "The Post-it Always Sticks Twice"

I feel like I know too many people who in the late '90s and early 2000s took a lot of their romantic/dating cues and philosophies from this show, and the one I could never understand was, and I'm paraphrasing here, "No Proof of Girlfriends Before Me Is Allowed Anywhere, at Any Time." It's not even the show's fault; I know how TV writing works, someone someone knows is really like that and they borrowed from her life and projected it onto these characters. Unless you're fewer than, what, fourteen years old??? Whoever you bang is probably gonna have banged someone before you, and that's fine. Preferable, even!

If in 2003, when I was twenty-three years old and this final season aired, I went out with a person who informed me that they'd never had a relationship with anyone else before me (no booty call, no fuck buddy, no high school crush, no internet catfish, no nothing), I would still date them because I have a yawning chasm of emotional need inside me that only the infrequent attention from a person who doesn't care about me that much can fill. But while anxiously staring at the phone all day, willing it to ring with their call, I would say to myself, "I hope they're not a weirdo or murderer!"

Carrie didn't have to, you know, *befriend* Berger's ex-girlfriend, but she didn't have to act like a huge freak, either? Although now that I think about it, that's my new ruinous idea: Carrie becomes BFFs with Berger's ex, they get together once a week to drink cocktails and talk about how weak his dick game is. They eventually *Thelma & Louise* it off one of Manhattan's infamous cliffs after robbing a Saks.

Episode 11: "The Domino Effect"

I know Samantha's whole thing was that she liked to have uncomplicated sex, but I wish that the romantics among us could've seen her absolutely smitten, bowled over by someone truly great who actually loved her for her, just one time. She had that great relationship with daddy Richard, but it never felt like he would come undone without her, you know? He spent a lot of time leading her around by the nose, and I fucking hate that because it made it impossible for her to let her guard down all the way. Smith was so tender and was actually besotted with Samantha, and what if, for one episode, we got to see her mirror that back?!

Episode 12: "One"

There is no way on earth Miranda should have picked Steve's ass over Dr. Robert (Blair Underwood). My jaw almost shattered on the floor when Robert said, "I love you," and that made her realize that she still had feelings for Steve! I know it's a little early in the season for a Happily Ever After, but Miranda and Robert could've had one! And we could've had an awkward interracial wedding and disapproving black mother-in-law or some other cringey trope instead of that ceremony in the park Miranda and Steve had. I mean, come on, my man was a basketball doctor!!! She could've had Knicks season tickets for life!!!!!! I know that this might actually be a punishment, but in my version of the story the Knicks are good. Sorry!

Episode 14: "The Ick Factor"

Yo, I haaaaaaated Petrovsky. Just absolutely despised him. In my imaginary world, there would have been zero Petrovskys.

Episode 18: "Splat!"

If there is no Petrovsky, there certainly is no Paris. But I like the idea that Carrie would test out another city. What if she'd moved to Philly? Or Chicago?! Okay, here's the pitch: The *Chicago Reader* is starting a sex and dating advice column and they poach Carrie from her old job, wooing her with the promise of burly, corn-fed Midwestern men, an apartment that's half as expensive but double the size, and unlimited dipped beefs with a side of hot giardiniera for lunch whenever she wants. How could she say no? Chicago has most of the same shit New York has, but it's less gross and the people are nicer, and if you want to buy a car, you'll probably find someplace to park it.

Episode 20: "An American Girl in Paris, Part Deux"

If any of my show opinions warrant a threat on my life it is this: Big sucked, and Carrie was too cool for him. I know you're mad, but I'm right. Tell me about a person you chased off and on for seven years who lived up to the hype. You can't!

Big was a nicely tailored suit stuffed with noncommittal angst who toyed with this woman like a cat with that mouse Stephan wouldn't pick up, and her reward was his getting on a plane in a jealous rage to rescue her from another man? Yeah, right! In my version you find out his name because Carrie leaves a "Dear John" letter tucked into his mailbox like in *Good Will Hunting*, as she boarded a Greyhound bus to Aidan's farm. Or maybe Ben Affleck could have given her a ride!!!

★Elliott Smith song plays, fade to black★

i like to get high at night and think about whales

I have this app on my phone called White Noise, and I pay $1.99 a month for ad-free, unfettered access to dozens of sounds I can set to play for ten hours at a time if I want, sounds like "light backyard rain" or "waves crashing on rocks" or "evening bird chorus," which does not necessarily sound relaxing to me, but I am not a bird person. I downloaded it one night at a hotel in Detroit where the only available room was Rolling Stones–themed and shared a wall with the laundry room, whose water pipes screamed and groaned at a slightly intolerable pitch all day. Once the sun set and I tried to go to sleep, that pitch magnified to deafening. Now I don't leave the house without those orange foam earplugs you can get at the hardware store, but then the only buffer I had between myself and the satanic churning and howling in the adjoining room was the sound of a simulated box fan whirring inside my phone.

I follow a bunch of Instagram accounts that are just pictures and the occasional close-up video of whales doing whale shit, like drifting or feeding or surfacing or playing. And because I try to stay off the bad places on the internet, I spend a lot of time watching people argue about sports or clips of whales on BBC Earth, weeping because I get to be on the same planet as both wide receivers who can run twenty-three miles per hour and also seventy-year-old humpback whales. This is some stoner shit, for real, but have you ever just sat and thought about how there is an animal as big as a city bus and we're alive at the same time as them, and we can look at videos of them doing things? Yes, I am absolutely out of my fucking mind, but also, while you're on land reading this, there's a hundred-foot-long, 400,000-pound blue whale in the ocean *right now* about to eat forty million krill and migrate from Antarctica to the tropics probably! Isn't that amazing?

I like to take a couple gummies and, while they kick in, lie on my back in the dark with a fan blowing on my face, window open even in the winter, and remain very still with some gentle water sounds going in my headphones and imagine myself lying on a raft in the middle of the pitch-black ocean, feeling the waves created by a whale swimming six thousand feet below me. Then I imagine her swimming up and up and up until she's porpoising right alongside me. It sends a shiver up my spine and chills through my whole body because, yo, what would you freaking *do* if a whale was just cruising next to your soft human body? It makes me want to cry in both wonder and terror, eyes squeezed shut picturing a clear sky full of twinkling stars, lapping waves surrounding my body as the THC surfs my bloodstream. It's literally the scariest but also a kind of sexual (?) feeling, imagining being eye to eye with the largest creature on the planet and being completely at its mercy and it just smoothly circles your flimsy little raft. This is my favorite way to drift off to sleep. I YEARN FOR THE CHILLNESS OF WHALES.

oh, so you actually don't wanna make a show about a horny fat bitch with diarrhea? okay!

A popular basic-cable network optioned my first book, and I almost got to make it into a real TV show. ALMOST.

ACT 1

EXT. EVANSTON STREET—DAY
We open on a wide shot of a street in Evanston, Illinois, the motherland, the place of my birth, the place where I'd wait in line for a gyro from Cross-Rhodes right now if it weren't cold-ass winter. I don't know if we could've actually shot this pilot in Evanston for real because I learned from the line producer, when I learned what a line producer is, that the first thing a network has to figure out about your show is where they can shoot it the cheapest. This is a decidedly unsexy process, which hypothetically could go something like this:

SAMANTHA IRBY, EXECUTIVE PRODUCER: Since the show is about Evanston, my favorite place in the world (especially because I have not been to very many other places), I would like to shoot it there. Because I love it. And, you know, for authenticity? I watched *The Good Wife*, I can tell when a TV show is doing Fake Chicago.

VERY NICE WHITE MAN, A LINE PRODUCER I JUST MET TWO MINUTES AGO WHO IS ACTUALLY IN CHARGE OF EVERYTHING: With this budget . . . have you considered Toronto?

SAMANTHA IRBY, SEMIPROFESSIONAL MORON: Hey, I *love* a deal, but I don't speak French, and I let my passport expire in 2011. What about Iowa or Detroit? I mean, if we can't do it in Chicago, literally any town in the flattest part of the middle west would probably work?

VERY NICE WHITE MAN, PRODUCER-SLASH-GRIEF COUNSELOR: There are some great tax incentives if we shoot it in Atlanta. Would you like to go to Atlanta? They have good biscuits there! Why don't I price that out?

SAMANTHA IRBY, CRESTFALLEN HOLLYWOOD OUTSIDER: So my dream of shooting an entire series in my friend's living room while she brings us snacks is effectively dead? Shit, I gotta text everybody I told they "could maybe be an extra" and tell them to go jump in the lake instead.

During the cold open of this show, the fictional SAM (*description*: FAT, BLACK, GLASSES, RED LIPSTICK) is walking along a busy rush-hour sidewalk, listening to ear-buds with the cord. I'm sorry, but even the television version of me is practical and would never risk losing an AirPod she can't afford to replace!!!!!!!!!!! She is on her way to her morning shift at the fancy bakery where she works. The real bakery where I used to work was all right. It had tiled floors and glass-topped café tables and neat rows of cupcakes and Danish in the display case, but my TV bakery would obviously look like something out of a Nancy Meyers movie, which may be a played-out reference, but what can I say, I don't watch a lot of designer-kitchen movies.

Let's talk about the most awkward thing I have ever been forced to do in my life: WATCH PEOPLE PRETEND TO BE ME WHILE SAYING JOKES THAT I WROTE TO MY FACE. Flea, the casting director, is an incredibly nice and bubbly woman who doesn't pull a single punch, and she warned me that casting "Sam" was gonna feel like being awake during surgery, but she promised that she would make it "fun." I, a person who does not know how to have fun, immediately broke into a full-body sweat. I assumed it was gonna be like looking through a book of mug shots to find a person whose crime was being funny and looking a little like me. But the way it actually works is Flea and her team look at hundreds of photos and self-tapes and then they compile the best ones into a little demo reel and email it to all the producers. Then you watch the tapes alone in the dark while attempting to fold yourself into an invisible ball, itching with embarrassment. Or maybe that was just me?

We were auditioning actors over Zoom, and as a person

who is intrigued by all the unimportant minutiae of some-one else's life, it was incredible to see inside the bedrooms and kitchens and at least one hall closet of these women. They'd be reading my shitty jokes to the camera, and I'd be on the other end squinting at the screen like, "Where is that bedspread from, Anthropologie? What kind of face lotion does she have on her dresser? Would it be inappropriate for me to send an email asking how on earth she can keep so many plants alive?" I promise you it's not glamorous to lis-ten to people introduce themselves in their normal voices before slipping into the impression of you they perfected after watching a bunch of YouTube videos. *Oh man, she's really killing that weird shit I do with my hands when I talk. Hold up, how noticeable is my lisp for real? Wait, is she choking on a lungful of mucus, or do I actually sound like that?* It's like a fun-house mirror but without the fun.

We decided that TV Sam was gonna be twenty-seven-ish, not as old as I am now (literally every scene would be about knee pain) but also not "young," because I have zero inter-est in trying to figure out how young people talk now. This show was going to be based on my first book, *Meaty* (You've read that, right?), which came out when I was in my early thirties and is basically about all the years leading up to that. When I wrote that book, it was kind of a joke, you know? Like, "Okay, guys, you can glue together some printed-out blogs and sell them at the merch tables outside shows," and I definitely didn't think I would ever write anything again! At this point who fucking cares, but if I'd known then that I was gonna write more books, I maybe would've spaced the shit out better. Far be it from me to make a plan, but if I had even a scrap of foresight or ambition I would've spent a lot more time writing about my Cypress Hill cassette and the pink Kmart board shorts I wore to that one eighth-grade dance.

INT. PHARMACY—DAY

I feel like I need to make it clear that I don't think I am so extraordinary that I deserve to have a television show made about my life. For starters, I'm still alive, and that makes it weird. Not only am I alive, but in my current incarnation, I am relatively boring, at least in terms of the standards set by prime-time television. BUT, when you write a book and people adjacent to Hollywood read that book, you will inevitably be told by many of those people that you should attempt to make it into something, and that feels like the kind of thing you just gotta *try*, right? While I love to slam the door in the face of an opportunity, this was one that, at the very least, if it failed, I'd have a little money and experience, and if it worked out I'd get to, oh, I don't know . . . Instagram behind-the-scenes photos from the set? Drink lots of Diet Cokes that Viacom has to pay for? Convince Forest Whitaker to play my season–two love interest?!

Okay, so Sam isn't going to work, she's actually going to the pharmacy to get some prescriptions. As Sam walks inside, we hear the voice mails playing on her phone as she listens to them:

1. **A BANK REP:** The bank is calling to remind our heroine that her account is overdrawn due to a seventy-eight-dollar charge at McDonald's. This is a ludicrous amount of money that isn't reasonably possible to spend at that fine purveyor of fast foods (imagine, if

you will, me stuffing seventy-eight cheeseburgers into a Ford Escort), but that is how you know this show is a comedy.

2. **JENNY:** Sam's best friend, Jenny, has called to ask about going to the mall, which Sam obviously can't afford to do because she owes First Bank & Trust of Evanston upward of a hundred dollars (the fees!!!), but Jenny clearly knows her friend and offers to pay for everything. This is something my real Jenny would absolutely do, and I was compelled to immortalize it so that she'll keep doing it, okay.

3. **KATHLEEN:** I didn't really make any friends in that old boardinghouse I lived in, but since that's where TV Sam was gonna live, we decided to invent one: a spacey weirdo who is basically an amalgamation of every person I used to run into in the halls on the way to the communal bathroom. Kathleen has called to let Sam know that their building, which had been recently evacuated, is ready for habitation.

Sam gets in line to talk to the pharmacist and turns to speak directly to the camera. She says, "The last few days have been stupid as hell," and let's talk about how hard it is to translate what I do on the internet (cry and complain) onto basic cable, a place where watching a lady type on a computer is boring as hell.

It's so funny because imagining how cool it would be to put some of my stories on TV is a fun daydream, but trying to figure out a device that incorporates my writing without every episode involving a minimum twenty minutes of fake me staring blankly at an empty computer screen is daunting. How do you realistically portray a "writer" on TV, especially when said writer spends eleven hours a day bagging apple fritters and writing up cake orders before locking herself in the upstairs office for the evening to type her sad lil jokes into her boss's computer?

We could take the Hannah Horvath route and just have Sam talk a lot about being a writer without doing much of it on-screen, or there was the Carrie Bradshaw option: watch Sam type one sentence and read it aloud, then just smoke a ciggy and go to bed or whatever. I figured that every episode would feature Sam in a different place—at the bus stop, in a gas station bathroom, trapped in quicksand—telling the camera a story: "So the other day I had sex with an off-duty circus clown/paid for my drinks at the club with laundry quarters/watched a guy get open-heart surgery in the middle of the street . . ." Then you'd get to watch the action interspersed between the story beats.

For example:

After listening to her voice mail at the pharmacy, Sam grabs a bag of Combos (originally this was meant to be Cool Ranch Doritos, but another thing I learned during this process is that every product you see on television must be cleared by the entity that manufactures said product, and Mister Dorito was like, "Wow, no thank you," but the Combos people were cool!). She starts eating them in the pharmacy line (I would never actually do this, but TV Sam is brave and Real-Life Sam doesn't want to be called a pig in the middle of Walgreens) and says, "Where was I? . . . Oh yeah, my shitty life."

INT. ROOMING HOUSE / SAM'S BEDROOM—
NIGHT

The night before! Sam is in her bedroom with a woman I named HOT BABE because I haven't gotten good at the character-naming part of this whole thing. Sam and Hot Babe stumble into Sam's room, wasted and groping each other through their sparkly party clothes from the club, then Hot Babe throws Sam onto the bed, pushing aside a pile of books and dirty laundry, of course, and starts to voraciously eat her out (this is feminism, baby!) while Sam chugs Neon Pink Stomach Upset Relief straight from the bottle. Needless to say, Misters Pepto and Bismol were not on board with our using their fine product in this depraved way.

INT. SAM'S BEDROOM AND HALLWAY—
CONTINUOUS

When I was young and kind of homeless, the internet did not exist, but I have zero interest in making an ancient historical period piece, so this Sam is young *right now* and has a special Instagram Corner set up in the least grimy, most presentable area of her dilapidated rented room. Okay, listen, I didn't get an email address until after my senior year of high school, back in the days when you damn near had to learn to code just to open some spammy chain mail from your friend's mom. But if me then was alive now, what in the world would she have in her apartment? What would she listen to music on? How would she call people? Do people still make calls?

I met my coolest ex-boyfriend—no no, not you—at an MF DOOM show (RIP). This guy wouldn't stop staring at me and so I went up to him and asked if it was because the men's slacks I was wearing, which I'd gotten at the Salvation Army earlier that day, looked weird (they did), but because he was handsome *and* he lied and said, "No . . . ?" I decided I liked him. He asked if the dude I was with was my boyfriend and when I said, "Well, we've had sex two times, but he says not to call him too much since it's 'casual,' haha," he bought me a drink and we stood awkwardly in the middle of the dance floor shout-talking because it's impossible to dance to rap music.

At the end of the night as the lights came on and everyone scuttled into the street like roaches, he pulled out his phone to get my number, and my stomach fell out of my butt because I'd forgotten until that exact moment that my phone was shut off because my friend's dad had kicked me off their family plan, and I had forgotten to pay my grossly overdue phone bill myself, i.e., I'd just drank all of Sprint's money. Luckily for me at the time I had a roommate who'd insisted on keeping a house phone, but unluckily for me I had to stammer, "Uhh, my number is 773-743-XXXX, but please don't call after ten p.m. or leave any lewd messages on the machine if that's your thing because that's not only my number" under the punishing glare of an emergency floodlight in the middle of a silent disco. I know how that looks and how humiliating it feels but what I *don't* know is the technologically appropriate equivalent today. A prepaid phone? A prepaid phone with no money on it? A prepaid phone with a busted screen that freezes every time you try to watch a TikTok??? In the show, the next morning, Sam guides Hot Babe through the hallways of her house, which is loosely modeled after this squalid dump I lived in when I was an orphaned teen and where everyone had to use a communal kitchen and bathrooms. One time, after payday,

I was alone in the kitchen carefully labeling my bounty of recently purchased Aldi cereals, and one of my housemates walked in and rolled his eyes like "Yeah, don't worry about that getting stolen." But it was cheap and didn't require a credit check, and that was my single requirement.

Fictional Sam leads this beautiful woman, who just went down on her before spending the night in sheets that, frankly, probably could use a washing, through this near-condemnation rooming house from hell. They pass a sleeping bum sprawled across the hallway floor and a list of handwritten rules tacked to the wall ("no ferrets or rap music") and make their way to the kitchen, where they encounter another one of Sam's housemates, a disheveled weirdo named KATHLEEN, who informs Sam that the building was ruled uninhabitable, again, and they have to evacuate for at least two days while black mold is cleaned out.

INT. CTA BUS—LATER THAT MORNING
Sam's on the bus on the way to her job at the bakery, still sticky from wasted Hot Babe sex the night before. Now is probably a good time to loudly and proudly declare myself a Bus Person. I know that logically there is a stronger case to be made for the elevated train in terms of efficiency and ease of use, but there's also something to be said for riding in a vehicle that the person driving can hear you being stabbed on.

Sam sits crammed near the front, half-asleep. Her phone continues to buzz, and she rolls her eyes at it. An OLD MAN (*description*: OLD) across from her is eating a pile of onions and lettuce disguised as a salad (this is a real thing that happened), and Sam says, "This is worse than if he'd just pulled his fucking nuts out" to the person next to her (a not-real thing that never happened. I would never speak to anyone about anything, especially an innocent stranger on the bus). Then Sam shakes a bunch of Imodium into her coffee, and Onion Guy gives her a look, and she's like, "Fuck you! It's medicine!"

In real life I would worry that a man brazen enough to eat a stinky onion salad on a public bus at seven in the morning would have no fucking problem murdering me on the spot, so I would avoid eye contact and busy myself with my phone, but this takes place in a magical television universe where my fictional counterpart gets to be loud and brave with zero consequences!

INT. BAKERY KITCHEN / FRONT COUNTER—
MOMENTS LATER
Sam walks into the bakery through the kitchen and greets all her coworkers, who are positively delighted to see her, which is my way of getting revenge on everyone who worked at Judy's who was mean to me or never talked to me or made a face when I walked into work. The TV bakery is called Amy's, because I don't want actual Judy, who is hopefully enjoying her life and riding a horse with an American flag saddle somewhere on the West Coast, to sue me.

One of the weirder things about writing an autobiographical show is that I had to populate the world with people who felt like real people but weren't the actual people I knew. Sam goes to the front counter where her work friend FERNANDO is organizing the pastry case. I never worked with anyone named Fernando, but in my real life one of my best friends is a hot and hilarious Mexican advertising executive named Fernando, so I kinda squeezed him in here, reimagined as a tattooed pastry chef who is flirty and funny, and also a poet?

Fernando asks Sam to try some of the tarte tatin he just made, but Sam's like, "Ooh no, my guts," and then they banter for a little bit, so you get that they're close enough to fuck with each other in a salty way but also that there's love there. Writing scripts is fucking weird, and writing a pilot script is the weirdest weird of all, because unless you're writing a show about a bunch of infants who meet each other on the day they are born—wait, should I write that show?—you have to figure out how to make people talk to each other in a way that feels both real and accurate, but also isn't pure exposition.

I have written nine hundred versions of this episode, and one of the (many, humiliating) notes I got on the very first one I turned in was: "Real people don't talk to each other like this." I had written, basically, biting, hilarious quip after biting, hilarious quip, volleyed back and forth between people in the guise of their having a normal conversation, and one particular exec's reaction was, "Hey, some people are boring and unfunny." In my life? Never. But, I don't know, unless you're writing *Veep* or whatever, there has to be someone who just says "yes" and "okay," and doesn't speak in punch lines. Sam tries Fernando's tarte tatin. I mean, come on. She chases it with another swig of "pink bismuth digestive relief," and Fernando is like, "Dude, that stuff is not supposed to be used long-term," but Sam waves him off. Then he reminds her that he has a show that evening that she should come to, oh and also their boss, AMY (*description*: WHITE, 40S, BOUNCY BLOND PONYTAIL, COMMERCIAL

GOOD LOOKS), is looking for her. Sam makes an outdated *Gone Girl* joke, and Fernando tells her to get upstairs before she "sees us on the security cameras and thinks we're doing reverse racism." That joke is fucking funny.

INT. PHARMACY—DAY

We cut back to the pharmacy, where Fake Sam tells us the story of how she got this job, which is a truncated version of how Real Sam got that bakery job: my boss had to pee during the job interview, her tiny baby started crying in the crib in her office, I went and picked him up, and he immediately stopped crying, she came out of the bathroom and hired me on the spot. I didn't know a scone from a macaron, but I *did* have many years of babysitting pissed-off white babies under my belt and clearly my shhing and rocking technique was enough to convince her that I could be trusted to take care of cupcakes, too.

INT. BAKERY OFFICE UPSTAIRS—CONTINUOUS

> AMY
> If you could tell me how to ship pecan
> sandies to Kansas without breaking a few,
> Bob, I'd love to hear it!

The bakery I worked at was both a retail and commercial business, serving your standard bakery needs like wedding cakes and fondant-dipped cookies and assemble-your-own gingerbread house kits at Christmas, but we also did event catering and made cookies for Starbucks and dozens of loaves of bread for Northwestern's cafeteria every day. Judy is a bad bitch. She is literally a gorgeous model who put herself through business school and opened her own bakery that she ran with an iron fist, and because that's my girl (and she's still alive) I wanted her fictional counterpart to be the exact same.

I always worked the later shift because getting to work at 5:00 a.m. isn't my ministry, but the downside of the late shift is that the tone for the day has already been set. Orders are already running late, and people are already mad, and you're essentially walking into a tornado that stops for a second while everyone turns to you like: OKAY, GREAT, BILL PAXTON, GET IN HERE AND FIX THIS. So, Sam clocks in, and Amy pauses her call to give Sam the option to either change the baby or walk the dog. Celluloid Sam chooses the dog even though Human Sam would absolutely choose the baby, because I'd rather change a dirty diaper than go outside. Sam leashes the dog (I named him "Wrigley" to make fun of every single person in the Chicagoland area who has a goddamned dog named "Wrigley," aka approximately 98.7 percent of all registered Cook County dog owners) and throws a pack of wipes in Amy's direction, accidentally smacking her in the face, because it was absolutely important to me to make the kind of fun, slapstick show where people fall down and get cream pies in the face.

EXT. SUBURBAN STREET—MOMENTS LATER
Sam's out absentmindedly yanking Wrigley, a rancid ottoman, down the street while texting. Just as she's picking

up his poop (how to make fake TV dog poop: use a nutty chocolate protein bar and shape it using a hair dryer on a low setting), a hot dude bends down to pet him. As she does that thing where you have to turn the bag inside out so you don't get any of the shit on your hand, she sees the hot dude and registers that it's BRANDON (*description*: 20S, TALL, BLACK, MUSCULAR, and uhhhhhh, HOT). Sam stares up at him for too long without saying anything, which is exactly what I do: become fully paralyzed while in the proximity of a handsome person. But the hot dude isn't important, he's basically in here as an avatar for every single one of my high school classmates who I'd run into while they were home from college to passively remind me of my ongoing failure to fully realize my potential.

Sam asks Brandon what he's doing on this sad, regular-person street, and he goes into a whole thing about college, but here's the main point of this Brandon character: to introduce the idea that Sam is a "writer" into the show. I really wrestled with the idea of my writing being a part of this show, and if it were up to just me, I don't know that it would be. I mean, practically speaking, writing is boring.

On the one hand, the only writing I was doing when I worked at the bakery was at night, after we closed, on the little computer in the upstairs office while the overnight crew was down in the kitchen making Danish and bread for the morning rush. I didn't write anything of consequence, just elaborate romantic fantasies written as short stories featuring thinly veiled versions of myself. On the other, if you tune into a show about me (in hindsight, an absolute nightmare possibility!), you're probably doing so because you've read something I've written, and it would be super weird if the writing went unacknowledged on the show. We reached a kind of compromise that is hard to explain, please bear with me as I struggle through the vision: TV Sam would be a mixture of nineteen-, twenty-five-, and thirty-two-year-old Actual Sam, working nineteen-year-old Sam's job and boning twenty-five-year-old Sam's sex partners and having thirty-two-year-old Sam's burgeoning writing/performing career. Does that makes sense?

I shudder thinking about walking people who've actually lived this life with me through their real-time fact-checking of all the events I creatively maneuvered into this show: "Dude, we were twenty-five at the same time and I know for a fact you did not [*verb*] [*human male name*] in the back of [*type of vehicle*] while wearing [*unflattering article of clothing*] after we left [*nightclub name*] high on [*street drug*]! Why are you lying on basic cable?"

INT. PHARMACY—DAY

Do you remember that old show *Herman's Head*? As a kid I was obsessed with it, and as an old kid, I'm still fascinated by people's interior monologues, all the little shit that runs through your mind as you go about your day. I thought it would be fun, especially in this moment when Sam is trying desperately to impress this hot person Brandon, to see Sam in the pharmacy contradict literally everything she says.

BRANDON

Are you writing a lot these days? Pretty sure
I still have a copy of your zine somewhere in
my room.

PHARMACY SAM (*to camera*)

I'm not.

SAM ON THE STREET

I am! I've been writing some things, you
know, on the internet . . . ?

BRANDON

Oh you mean like a blog?

SAM ON THE STREET

Yes, like a blog! I, uhh, have a blog!

PHARMACY SAM (*to camera*)

I do not know what a blog is.

The dog looks at Sam like, "Bitch, you do??" Sam shoots
him a "Shut up" look in return, and I'm not sure how we
were gonna teach a dog face-acting but never let anyone tell
you I'm not delusional enough to try.

I never had a zine in high school, but I *did* once write a
monologue called "Boxes" for this play my friends Ebony
and Allen performed, and our friend Matt told me it was
"really excellent, man" afterward, but that's kind of a lot to
be explaining in a twenty-two-minute show.

ACT 2

INT. DIVE BAR—THAT NIGHT

Sam sits with JENNY (*description*: MID-20S, BLACK, GLAMOROUS), who's home from grad school. One thing I should probably unpack with a new therapist is this massive inferiority complex I still have over never having finished, or even really started, college. Until we get to it, I'm gonna keep trying to work it out in public, which is obviously going really well. But, in the scene, a storytelling open-mic show is happening in the background. A distracted Sam texts as she talks to Jenny about how much the show sucks, Jenny looks annoyed because it's fucking annoying when you're trying to have a conversation with an asshole who won't put down her dumb phone.

In this show Sam and Jenny were gonna do a lot of shit my real friend Jenny and I did when we were young and fun and mentally ill with zero regard for our safety, like party every night and get into fights and sleep with losers. My real friend Jenny has a degree in art history and once invited me to a gallery show where I got wasted on free wine and started singing Stereolab's "Hallucinex" too loudly until she kicked me out for embarrassing her. But the Jenny in this show is still in school and fighting with Sam for hanging out with her mother and sleeping in her childhood bedroom when she's not around.

So yeah, I used to hang with my friends' parents and it made shit weird sometimes, but who cares. It's a perfect situation to mine for comedy:

Sam and Jenny have a fight in the bar because Sam is texting Jenny's mom, which Jenny hates. Sam pivots to asking

Jenny if she thinks anyone would pay attention if she started writing again while carefully avoiding that impressing their old friend Brandon is the impetus for this inquiry. Jenny brushes her off.

They argue for a few beats, and then Fernando comes over because he is hosting this open-mic storytelling show called *Guts and Glory*, because that's the name of the show my friend Keith and I used to host once a month in the upstairs bar at Schubas. Fernando starts flirting with Jenny while Sam gets mad, and I only wrote this one episode, but maybe that was gonna develop into an actual crush or something legitimate later in the season? We'll literally never know!

INT. DIVE BAR—SAME
Jenny chastises Sam some more for hanging with her mother and Fernando tries to break the tension by offering to buy them a round of drinks. I love picking up the tab, I love other people who pick up the tab. Nothing feels fancier or more special than drinking a cocktail somebody else bought for you. Jenny gladly accepts the offer, while Sam violently shakes her head.

SAM
I can't get drunk tonight, dude. I feel like a
Toyota Camry is driving through my small
intestine.

A thing I had to learn about writing television scripts was making sure that moods, feelings, and events all tracked throughout an episode. I also learned that Hollywood people love to say the word *track*, and in this pilot we needed to track all this shit:

- Sam is kind of a loser.
- Sam is kind of a loser who also needs a place to stay for a few days, because her building is gonna be condemned or whatever.
- Sam is an exasperating friend?
- Sam is okay, but not great, at her job.
- Something, although we're not quite sure what, is happening with Sam's intestines.

Jenny asks Sam what's going on, and Fernando does a thing that happens to me when I tell a new person I have irritable bowel disease: offers an unprompted, uneducated suggestion for how to treat an illness I haven't specified and that they have no expertise in treating. Sometimes it's well-intentioned, other times it's condescending, and in this case, Fernando suggests that Sam try being a pescatarian, which is a thing many people have told me (unsolicited) to try, sadly none of them are a gastroenterologist or even able to spell the word *pescatarian*.

INT. DIVE BAR—LATER
The bar is now packed, and Sam sits with Jenny, who's clearly tipsy and less uptight. Sam is sober and has procured a banana, and she takes tiny bites, which is funny because where the hell do you get a banana in a fucking bar? We get some more riffing between Sam and Jenny, arguing about mom texts and writing careers, interspersed with scenes

of Fernando on the stage, wrestling the mic away from a woman who's crying and dragging on too long: "Babe, this isn't the Moth."

As the future star of a Humira or Stelara or Entyvio commercial coming soon to interrupt the YouTube video you're deeply invested in at its most climactic moment, it was important to me to show the twenty-seven people who were gonna tune into this show that people with chronic illness do more than excuse ourselves from social gatherings while clutching our midsections and grimacing. We ride the bus! We walk our bosses' dogs! We shovel Tums in our mouths while we belly up to a bar! Jenny asks Sam if she's actually feeling okay, no joking around, and Sam responds by shaking her bottle of Imodium in Jenny's face.

SAM

I've got it under control, thanks. I don't need
a second opinion.

JENNY

Bitch, you need a first opinion!

Casting every character other than Sam was deliriously fun for me because I didn't feel the pressure to perform the character of Sam for the women tasked with playing her (me?), and the people we got for Jenny and Fernando were so damn good it almost makes me mad that I won't get to write extremely detailed sex scenes for future them. Sam begs Fernando to let her stay the night at his place in front of the girl he's trying to convince to go home with him, which is a terribly awkward and cock-blocky thing the real me would never do because I'm not a hater, but he forcibly moves Sam out of his way, telling her to go fart on Jenny's couch all night because he's, you know, gonna be "busy."

INT. BAKERY KITCHEN—THE NEXT MORNING
Sam (wrinkled, disheveled, fresh off what was clearly a long night with a drunk moron) is doubled over, actively vomiting into an industrial garbage can as Amy walks in.

> AMY
> Jesus, that sounds medical. We're short-
> staffed, and I've got errands to run, so I'm
> gonna need you and Dennis to do this
> wedding cake delivery to the Woman's Club
> today.

Sam continues vomiting without looking up or acknowledging Amy in any way.

> AMY
> Great! The cake is boxed up in the walk-in,
> all the venue info is next to the order phone,
> the van keys are on the hook. You've driven
> it before, right?

Sam starts to stand, feels a fresh wave of nausea, puts her head into the garbage can, and retches.

> AMY
> Okay, good talk. Remember that this is the
> most important day in someone's life, so

try to not fuck it up. Maybe tuck in your
goddamn shirt.

Amy walks away, to go file invoices or something, and
Sam dusts herself off and starts for the door but immediately
has to turn around and hurl again. You know, this was gonna
be my one shot to get a realistic vomiting scene on prime-
time television, and it's shit like *that* that bums me out about
not making this show. I don't care about vital storytelling
or whatever *jerkoff motion*. I care about eye-bulging,
capillary-bursting thunder puke.

I don't need a show about me and my stupid-ass friends,
at all, ever, but I *do* want to right the biggest and most con-
sistent wrong in TV and movies today: that weird little spit-
up "oopsies, I puked" vomiting that everyone does. That
"obviously just spitting out a mouthful of oatmeal" fake-ass
vomiting is infuriating to me. I'm supposed to fully immerse
myself in the story of someone who just dribbles a little
chunky soup out of the side of their mouth and passes that
off as vomiting? I can't! Every time I throw up, I shatter all
the blood vessels in my eyes and face, salty tears pour from
my eyes like a waterfall and mix with a river of snot, and I
expend so much violent energy I have to go lie down afterward to recover; what is this delicate puke-burping we see
all over television? I hate it.

We were gonna make a *spectacular* vomiting scene. A deep-
from-the-pit-of-her-belly upheaval of the entire contents of
her stomach, complete with realistic sound effects, in stereo.
I wanted you to have to pause the TV in disgust after hearing that shit. I was very explicit in my desire to go down in
television history for unleashing the most realistic vomiting

on the American public, and maybe that is the reason the people with the money wouldn't give me millions of dollars to make that happen. I get it.

EXT. BAKERY PARKING LOT—LATER
Three months after I started at Judy's real bakery, I was promoted to working in the office for much of the week, but tapping on a calculator and printing accounts receivable reports on a dot matrix printer does not for exciting television make, so, for the pilot, we decided that I was going to tag along on deliveries, trying to keep platters of assorted petit fours and other fancy sweets cool and level in a sweltering, airless van with bad shocks.

EXT. BAKERY PARKING LOT—CONTINUOUS
Sam is not too good or proper to roll around in the back of a van while trying to hold an anniversary tier level, and DENNIS, who she is accompanying on this delivery and who in real life was shy and quiet but loved to talk shit with a caustic wit, is like "Sure, whatever, but if we fuck this up, it's gonna be my black ass that gets fired."

The actor we cast to play Dennis was so sexy that I wanted to choose him based on his picture alone, but I was told that's not how it works. We needed to make sure he had acting skills (huh?) and comedic timing (what??). I don't need ~thespians~ for the stuff I write; I need someone who will work for hot dogs and doesn't mind puking during a sex scene. Someone who isn't gonna worry about a black mark (or, at the very least, a questionable one) on their future storied career.

Anyway, dude was my ideal kind of man: burly, hefty,

doughy, gruff, bald with a goatee that's going gray, very funny but also kind of mean. The kind of man where you can't tell if he wants to fuck you or fight you. Dennis and Sam have the kind of banter that could be interpreted either as flirting or arguing depending on how horny yelling makes you. Then they get in the van and drive off.

INT./EXT. WEDDING VENUE—AFTERNOON
We ended up shooting a "pilot presentation," which is a fancy way of saying "twelve-odd pages of a script." My original script was thirty-two-ish pages, which had to be whittled down because we didn't get thirty-two pages' worth of money to make a full pilot. It's hilarious—and I mean that, I really do—to look at a thing I spent seven years trying to perfect for several networks and dozens of pitch meetings, and when it was *finally* up to Hollywood standards, when *at long last* we got the "It's perfect!" email, it was immediately followed by: "Here's five dollars. Now make a short version that is just as good as the long one."

I gotta be honest and tell you that I don't want *anything* this badly. Literally nothing. I don't even want to work this long and fruitlessly to stay alive. Here is an abbreviated list of things I did over the seven years I was getting jerked around while trying to make this show that apparently nobody wants:

- sold, wrote, and published a book
- got married
- leased my very first niceish car
- quit the job I worked at for fourteen years
- moved to southwest Michigan

- wrote a lot of "freelance articles" because I was broke
- buried my cat Helen Keller
- read 9,836 books
- had a uterine ablation
- went on two book tours for two different books
- lived in Martha Plimpton's house for a summer
- wrote the "Pool" episode of *Shrill*
- sold, wrote, and published another book
- flew to Dallas to interview Lizzo for the cover of *Time*'s Person of the Year issue
- worked on someone else's show
- stayed in quarantine for a full calendar year
- got a horrible dog
- attended my stepkid's seventh, eighth, ninth, tenth, eleventh, twelfth, and thirteenth birthday parties
- worked on another person's show
- had many, many meetings, during which people asked, "What's up with your show?"
- watched approximately 77,243 hours of television
- leased a different niceish car because my first lease expired
- got E. coli
- ruined the *Sex and the City* reboot with piss and jokes about osteoarthritis

Here's the thing: you don't get paid for the work you do on your optioned project. At first I just stared at the wall waiting for something to happen. Then, after months of that, I took some other jobs because I needed money and a distraction and crossed my fingers that we wouldn't get the picked-up-straight-to-series call before my contract was up, but eventually I was just taking every single call and doing every staffing interview because . . . well, why not? My green light call obviously wasn't coming. At the very least I could learn something new or use my brain in a different way while I was waiting. Plus, the same old material (my stupid self, YUCK) doesn't get *more* inspiring the longer I work on it. As more years passed, the more I started to feel gross and weird about putting a fictionalized version of my life on television.

People always ask if my friends are nervous to end up in a book, and the truth is, no one cares because people don't read. (Except you. You are handsome and literate with excellent taste in reading material.) But we all *love* watching TV. At the beginning of this process, I was so floored by the idea that someone would want to see my diarrhea stories on television that of course I wanted to pursue it, especially because that felt like my only shot to make more than the fifteen dollars an hour I was making at the time. Who am I to shit on an opportunity? Imagine my being so bold! But I didn't really, let's say, think about the long-term implications. I didn't think about, you know, the possibility of snarky critics panning my actual life in the newspaper or internet people trying to figure out who Brandon might have been based on—it's my friend Mark Wellington, if you must know.

We tried our best. The top dog at the network declared the original version of the script "too niche." And that's fine. Thanks for reading, pal, time for me to take my ball and go home, sitting in the passenger seat of Kirsten's freezing car in a Wendy's drive-thru at midnight after we'd taken her kids to Grand Rapids to see Janet Jackson. I read that "niche" as "too horny and shitty." But one thing about these Holly-wood types is that they never tell you the actual *why*, leaving you to interminably circle the drain of self-doubt, picking at flaws that might not even be flaws, until you eventually throw your script and your dreams in the Vitamix and switch to a career in shoe sales or something.

We moved on to a bunch of meetings, for the second time, at all the networks we hadn't had meetings with the first time around, and let me tell you: each meeting was better than the last. I wish I could say that I walked out of a single conference room covered in framed movie posters and outfitted with an overwhelming number of too-small chairs and felt anything other than soaring optimism. I would love to talk to someone who's had a bad pitch meeting, someone who had a breakdown in the Hulu guest bathroom after being laughed out of the office, because I've had a dozen of these awkward blind dates, and I left every single one think-ing, "That was so great! They really liked it! We're gonna make a show!" only to get a text a couple of hours later from my agent saying, "Sorry, they passed."

That fucks me up, not because I don't understand a net-work not wanting to spend literally millions of dollars on a single-camera comedy that can be summed up as "diarrhea and crying," but because it forces me to question my judg-ment and perception and pretty much makes me feel insane. Am I delusional or does "we can't wait to work with you" not mean what I think it means? It feels like when you're desperately in love with someone who says, "YOU'RE AMAZING, YOU ARE WONDERFUL, SO WITTY AND CHARMING AND A JOY TO BE AROUND, I CAN'T GET ENOUGH OF YOU," and then you're like, "Okay, can we kiss, then?" and they hit you with the "No <3." And, as you melt into the floor, your brain's helpful response is to replay every interaction you've ever had with them, searching for clues you might have missed or overtures you misunderstood, over and over again until you die. Shopping a show is exactly like that, multiplied by the number of networks your agent has a good relationship with and who'd be willing to spend fifteen minutes listening to you grasping for example shows they already know and like to compare yours to ("Umm, okay, wait, uhhh, it's like *Insecure* meets *Hoarders* meets *Mystery Diagnosis*?") because they skimmed the script you sent over weeks ago five minutes before they met you.

With every pass, I felt more and more relieved. Who the hell am I to have a show anyway, a thick-skinned marble slab of a woman with chromium insides and no feelings? No! I have depression and rude friends! My frazzled nerves wouldn't make it past the first *Variety* announcement, let alone the eventual weeks of bad reviews and tweets. It's good not to have your own show. It's good to be staff on a show already in production and not made by a loser; the stakes are lower, the insults and cruel memes feel (slightly) less personal, you don't have to worry about sounding dumb at the costume meeting. Mental health–wise, this across-the-board rejection of my life as I've lived it could actually be a blessing?

Anyway, back to the pilot. In this scene, Sam and Dennis argue while unloading the cake at a palatial mansion and in front of a harried wedding planner who is pissed they are late, and Sam vomits into a planter before screaming that she's gonna shit her pants and runs into the venue, doing that increasingly urgent hybrid yell-sob that only comes out when you really gotta poop, run-walking past conference rooms and trying every locked door lining the hallways, dodging men in suits and fancy ladies in tasteful daytime formal.

INT. WEDDING VENUE HALLWAY
AND BATHROOM—MOMENTS LATER

The camera toggles between Sam stumbling through the hallways of this very posh wedding venue, dry-swallowing chalky diarrhea pills and sweating through her clothes; Sam in the pharmacy, head hung in shame at what's about to transpire. Meanwhile, Pharmacy Sam doesn't even speak. She just shakes her head, like "Oh no, here it comes." In my mind and out my butt, I imagined this being at the Woman's Club of Evanston, a place where I once delivered a bunch of opera tortes for some gala or something while actively trying not to shit on myself, because weddings and expensive parties are the most humiliating place to take a gross poo, and I say this as a person who's been forced to shit in the street. The juxtaposition of a wild-eyed woman leaking feces through a $500-per-person wedding??? Hilarious! And, also terrible.

Sam bursts into a bathroom to find it completely empty. Phew! She slams into a stall and struggles to get her pants down and apron off. After a beat, EMILY, the bride, and three bridesmaids pour in, circling in the lounge area right in front of Sam's stall. I'm not even sure what we told the casting director to look for other than "EXCEPTIONALLY

PRETTY," because its common knowledge that beautiful women don't take shits and are horrified when ugly peasants do.

They don't know Sam's in there, and they start gushing about how beautiful Emily looks and how handsome MATT (the groom; *description*: A HUMAN MALE, IT DOESN'T MATTER) is and how the wedding is gonna be great. In my perfect world, because I love mess, one of the bridesmaids would've been like, "Sorry to tell you this before your big day, babe, but I sucked Matt's dick three years ago," but you can't be that kind of chaos agent with glorified extras when making an actual show.

Sam is sitting there sweating and bracing herself against the walls of the stall, trying to clench every hole in her body shut, when there's a KNOCK on the bathroom door. Oh no! Matt wants to have a special greeting-card-commercial moment with his almost wife! Present-Day Sam is dissociating in the pharmacy as Matt and Emily share a tender moment right at Sam's stall.

At this point they lean in and have a romantic soft-focus kiss, the camera lingering on their lips. Then Sam, forgotten for a moment in the soap-operatic fog of nearly wedded bliss, rips a huge fart and unleashes a torrent of wetly spluttering diarrhea. I wish you could've heard the noise we chose. It was so loud and gross-sounding. If someone was shitting like that in a public bathroom you were in, you'd call an ambulance for them. It had just the most perfect full-evacuation-of-bowels sound effect I have ever had the pleasure of hearing. This wasn't a delicate "toot," it was a hurricane blown through a tuba, and I *loved* it.

Matt and Emily pull apart, faces frozen in horror, as Sam

calls out in a pained you-just-heard-me-shoot-partially-
digested-chili-out-of-the-cannon-of-my-butthole voice.

> SAM
>
> Hey, guys? I am really happy for you, and I'm
> so sorry to be asking this on your wedding
> day, but could you do me a favor and come
> in here and take a look at something?

ACT 3

INT. HOSPITAL ER—EVENING
Sam is in a partitioned room in a hospital gown with an NG
tube up her nose; it clicks softly as it sucks bile out of her
stomach and deposits it into a collection cup. DR. MEHTA
(*description*: 50S, GREAT-LOOKING, CHEERFUL) pulls
back the curtain with a WHOOSH.

Dr. Mehta is my real-life doctor's name, and I don't know
if we could have legally gotten away with using it, but it
doesn't matter now, so let's let it cook. He's the absolute
best. I don't even live close enough to see him anymore, but
I keep talking about him because he's dope, but also because
he's still practicing. So if you live in Chicagoland and you
need a guy, I got one.

The morning I first met him, I was delirious after having lain awake all night due to the tube going from my nose
down the back of my throat and into my stomach being, oh,
I don't know, a wee bit uncomfortable? He walked in like a
joy mirage in a happiness desert, funny and handsome and
talking to me about a CT scan and [*science words*] and steroids

and [*collections agency words*], and all I could think was: "Is this brick shithouse gonna be the one who looks inside my butt?"

If we'd sold the show to a network that allows full-frontal and ass play, this would be the time where we flash-forward to a fantasy scene in which Future Sam is lying on her side in the outpatient surgery wing, drowsy on propofol, and the camera pans over her hospital gown to the back where it hangs open. Then we'd watch the doctor lift one moist, heavy-ass cheek in slow motion (*the sound effect*: hot, sticky summer skin peeling off a plastic deck chair) to insert the scope into her anus. But we didn't, so instead, Sam gives the doctor a rundown, and the doctor leaves to order blood-work. Sam asks if he knows if there's a payment plan.

INT. HOSPITAL ER—LATER

Sam is lying in bed, smiling peacefully and watching *Judge Mathis*, which I still can't believe we almost got to digitally insert into the show. The doctor returns, and Sam mutes the television, and they have a long conversation that would probably be both boring for you to read and annoying for me to copy and paste.

Dr. Mehta goes through a partial, yet still terrifying, list of illnesses and disorders Sam could be experiencing, including: ulcerative colitis, a bowel obstruction, celiac disease, diverticulitis, Crohn's disease, bacterial infection, and polyps, although Sam can't get the thought that this happened because she tried a goop cleanse out of her mind. I wanted the list to be comically long, maybe even slowed down, chopped and screwed style, because that's what it feels like when you're on morphine and a medical professional is rattling off all the things they have to rule out in the limited amount of time you have until someone figures out your insurance is expired.

I remember lying there wanting to laugh because if he'd known that the only test I could afford for him to run was an imaginary one, he would've snatched all those tubes out of my various holes and wheelchaired me out to the parking lot. But this Sam doesn't know how much endoscopies cost, so she nods gratefully as the doctor tells her it's gonna be a few days for them to get her sorted out.

> SAM
> So, what you're saying is . . . I should stay
> at the hospital . . . overnight . . . for a few
> nights?

The doctor nods: unfortunately, yes. Sam looks around and takes in the large flat-screen TV mounted on the wall, thinking about the dude passed out outside her padlocked room. She sees the large private bathroom while thinking about standing in line outside the communal one at her place. She glances at the pitcher full of fresh ice chips on the table and smooths the soft, clean blankets over her legs. Finally, she looks back at the doctor.

> SAM
> If you say so, I guess I have to? I mean, if it's
> for my health.

INT. HOSPITAL ROOM—LATE NIGHT

Sam has a bulky oxygen monitor clamped on her finger, is hooked up to an IV, the nose tube taped dramatically across her face, as she sloppily tries to type on her old-ass phone in the dark. She's typing "how many irritable bowel diseases are there?" into Google when a text pops up on her screen from Brandon. His text reads: "Hey Sam, I'm here until Sunday, let me know if you're around. Don't forget to send me your writing!" Sam looks up: OH SHIT, I SOMEHOW FORGOT ABOUT THAT DICK I WANNA SUCK. She then goes back to the Google home screen and erases everything in the search bar except "how" and finishes the sentence with "do you start a blog?"

INT. PHARMACY—STILL THAT SAME DAMN DAY

Sam is walking away from the pharmacy counter with an armload of prescriptions. The worst thing about getting out of the hospital when you don't have a mom to come pick you up is that you then have to drag your tender, vulnerable, poked-up hospital body all by yourself to a building teeming with germs and bacteria. Then you have to stand in line for either five minutes or five hours, imagining invisible little protozoa slithering into your blood-draw needle holes waiting for medicine that might cost $9 or $900. The only thing that could possibly make that torture go down easy is fantasizing about the hilarious story you can write for your reignited crush about it, which you can then post on your new blog.

TAG

(Or, the little bit after the final commercial break that may or may not have credits running over it.)

EXT. CHICAGO STREET—DAY
Sam navigates her way down a busy sidewalk, earbuds in, playing the voice mails she got while laid up in the hospital.

> ANN (O.S., which means "off-screen")
> Hey, hon, it's your second mom. Are you
> mad at me? Why haven't you returned
> any of my texts? Should I message you on
> Facebook?

Sam clicks on the next voice mail.

> FERNANDO (O.S.)
> Listen, you never told me whether or
> not you'd be into joining this intramural
> badminton league with me, and I gotta
> let the dude know by tomorrow. Hit me
> back.

Sam rolls her eyes like, "Yeah right," and clicks Next as we PULL OUT.

> AMY (O.S.)
> Samantha, it's Amy, your boss. Dennis left,
> frankly, a rather incoherent message on the

bakery machine? Something about the van
being stolen? Should I—

JENNY (O.S.)

Jenny again. Are we in a fight? Did that guy
from the bar murder you? Also, would you
mind blocking my mom on Facebook?

HOT BABE (O.S.)

Hey, sorry about leaving so fast. But I think
I forgot my wallet at your place? Oh, by the
way, this is—

Sam deletes this last message, and we PULL UP IN A
SLOW CRANE SHOT and watch her continue shuffling
along the sidewalk.

DENNIS (O.S.)

Sam! You shit at these white people's
wedding and then left me here without a
ride? This is why I told you I don't trust your
sneaky ass. And did you steal the fucking van?
Sam! Sammm! Boss lady is gonna kill me,
Sam!!

END OF EPISODE

what if i died like elvis

A reason I don't do too much superficial maintenance is that it is hard to sustain. Maybe it's depression, although it also could be apathy or possibly even extreme boredom, but the idea of regularly dragging my lumpy, smelly body into a harshly lit salon to pay for someone, who is wondering what I'm even doing this for, to spread hot sugar wax on my face, and use a little piece of cloth to rip the hairs out of it, feels the same to me as imagining myself waking up bright and early one morning and strapping a pair of hiking boots on to go climb a mountain. I have just taken my first sip of water today at 2:57 p.m., I cannot be a person who reliably gets treatments done to herself.

I don't like the nail salon because in my daily life, I am trying to apologize less for simply existing, and that's impossible to do in a place where a stranger you've known for thirty seconds acts personally insulted by the ragged state of your cuticles. I hate being attended to, even when I'm paying and tipping 25 percent for it, because not only do I not deserve it, but I will also never maintain it. As soon as

I'm ushered into the chair (after circling the parking lot for five minutes, and after getting water all up my sleeves during the pre-manicure compulsory handwashing), I automatically begin my well-rehearsed atonement for my weak nails and lack of exfoliation as the nail technician tsks loudly at all the work ahead of her.

I don't even get anything fancy, I just pick whatever deep purplish shade I land on first on the nail polish color wheel while pretending to understand the difference between dip and gel and shellac. Then I sit in humiliated silence until it's over, and I can overpay and leave. But, of course, not without some effusive apologizing for oozing nail blood all over the gloved fingers of the person who caused them to bleed in the first place.

I got my nails done a few weeks ago because I was gonna see people I haven't seen in years and there is a disease in my brain that rationalized: "Maybe if your nails are tidy and dark and shiny, they will distract from the fact that the rest of you looks like a melted pillar candle." My regular brain knows that no one is clocking your nails when you have, you know, a head and tits and a face, but it's never the real mind that causes me agony, now is it? Diseased Brain is louder and meaner—and, if we're being honest, funnier—than Regular Brain, and the only tool I have to shout it down is one I developed called "Wedding Guest," which mostly involves repeating "You are not the bride" over and over to myself when I get overwhelmed about being seen by other human eyes and only having greasy sweatshirts at my disposal to present myself in.

Wedding Guest was borne out of a "What the fuck am I gonna wear to this ceremony?" panic attack two hours before my friend's little sister's wedding, for which I'd purchased no new clothes in the hopes that it would force me to be chill and relaxed as I casually "threw something on" when it was time to go. As if I could ever be chill!!!!!!!! Being perceived is excruciating, especially if you can't go person to person explaining why you look like that. I'd go to a lot more stuff if I knew I could take each person aside and explain to them why I look and dress the way I do.

Anyway, the night of my friend's little sister's wedding, I'm slick with sweat even though I'm fresh out the shower, tearing garments off hangers and throwing them straight into a donation pile because I only buy aspirational clothing that looks like someone else is supposed to wear it until, like a cool breeze blowing through the tenth circle of hell, a revelation came to me: You're not the one getting married, who the hell gives a shit what you are wearing? You are background filler! You're an extra without a speaking part!

And it's true. If you go to a thing that's not your specific thing and you can manage to avoid people's stupid camera phones the whole time, then it absolutely does not matter what you are wearing or if you are even there. It works, man. Every time I start wringing myself dry because someone I like invited me to something that requires a bra, the only way to pull myself out of the shame tornado is to stop and say, "WEDDING GUEST," and that resets my brain for at least the amount of time it takes to get myself into a pair of daytime pajamas and on my way to whatever the event is.

I went to the *Sex and the City* reboot premiere in a hoodie and wide-legged Adidas track pants, and no one on the red carpet gave even half a shit because I write fart jokes and am not pretty or famous. Sarah Jessica Parker is the bride, and I am the homely third cousin who only got an invite because someone more important couldn't attend, and it would never matter to anyone if my lipstick was smeared or my eyebrows were uneven, and reminding myself of that was better than a deep tissue massage. I went from "Oh no, Boris Kodjoe is gonna see that I look like microwaved dog vomit" to "He won't even register my presence," and you know what? I was fucking right. The assembled paparazzi literally put their cameras away when the luxurious black car HBO sent for me pulled up outside MoMA, and my scuffed FitFlop hit the red carpet. No one cares about the wedding guest!

Except this time, I wasn't going to a party, or even a fancy premiere. I was going to a weekend at a snowy lodge on Lake Michigan with six people who might actually notice my dishevelment and grow concerned. So to keep them from calling an ambulance as soon as they laid eyes upon me, I paid $60 to run my fingers through a meat grinder and have them come out the other side polished and gleaming. The application process is more complicated than surgery; after you wash your hands and inadvertently wet up your whole shirt, then you get your nails shaped and filed and your cuticles cut and pushed back, then there's basecoat, two coats of color, a topcoat, and then you roast your hands under an eighty-watt UV light until the nail polish has cured and hardened to an indestructible veneer that is guaranteed to last from fourteen to twenty-one days, which is a horrifyingly long time for a person for whom personal upkeep is an arduous chore.

I will admit the nails looked very nice, even after a week of chopping vegetables and writing blogs, and even though I had already begun to regret getting them. The week after *that* week, they started looking kinda gross, but only if you inspected them closely; I found them borderline intolerable since I can't stand to type with anything on or near my hands, so I made them even more disgusting by taking a big toenail clipper and chomping through the many layers of shellac to make the infant-sized nails I prefer when tapping out my lil feelings. That was a good temporary solution but not good enough, so after a few more days I really started losing my shit about my thick, craggy, heavy-as-concrete nails, and so late on that chilly Sunday night two plus weeks after not a single person at that cabin noticed the trouble I'd put my hands through for their benefit, I decided I needed to figure out how to get them off at home. Because even though you're legally required (I think? Let me check my contract.) to have them removed at a salon by a trained professional, I could not wait another second.

Google instructed me to "gently buff over the tops of your gel polish with a nail file, then soak a piece of cotton wool in acetone and place onto the nail and secure this on the nail by wrapping a foil square around it and leaving it to soak for fifteen minutes." Aha! I could do that! I keep a box of brand-new, coarse-grit nail files under the downstairs bathroom sink, because sawing my nails to dust on the toilet is a relaxing way to pass a boring evening, plus we had nail polish remover upstairs! I was ecstatic because I usually never have the tools I need to do the thing I decided to undertake on a whim in the middle of the night! I thought it was gonna tell me to run out and buy a fucking Dremel or some shit.

I finished watching the NFC championship game, and as Kirsten headed up to bed, I looked down at Plumful #81 with grim determination, like the hero in a "he's too small to be the starting quarterback" inspirational Christian movie. (The manicurist told me this color would look "classy," which, of course, sent me down a "Do I visibly lack class?" spiral that was immediately replaced by a "Why do I care what this stranger thinks?" spiral that I am *still* spiraling through because I do, inexplicably, care!)

Anyway, I went into the bathroom and found the box of files in my emergency downstairs bathroom kit, whose contents also include: nail clippers, two unopened Reach Crystal Clean firm-bristle toothbrushes (I hate slimy-sweater teeth, and if I could use sandpaper to grind them down to immaculate little stumps I would, so I have to order these mouth-sized Brillo pads off the internet because Rite Aid wants me to keep my tooth enamel, I guess), a dollar pack of Epielle makeup cleansing tissues from Big Lots, a bottle of Aleve with the red arthritis cap, liquid bandage, saline nasal spray, patchouli oil, and a bottle of Eco-Dent baking soda tooth powder, which tastes pretty yucky but is abrasive in just the way I like. I grabbed a fresh file and very ungently started grating at the shellac on my fingernails, mesmerized as they rained purple-tinted dandruff down into the waste-basket at my feet.

For those of you who've never tortured yourselves in this particular way, this stuff is designed to cling to your nails no matter what; tsunami, plague of frogs, or nuclear fall-out: if you've had polymer baked onto your nails under a blistering ultraviolet lamp, that shit is never coming off. I went through six nail files, and it was still valiantly hanging on, dulled some but going strong. I knew we had acetone upstairs, so I gathered up my supplies and emotionally girded myself for battle. I started to feel a little sick as I was walking through the kitchen. Nothing severe, just a little warning gurgle that sometime during the night I would be awakened by a sharp abdominal pain and be forced to hobble to the toilet wearing the one slipper I could locate in the dark while trying not to shit on the bedroom floor.

Cosplaying as the thoughtful spouse, I stopped to wash the dishes in the sink so they wouldn't grow new life overnight. Other good husband cosplay ideas I currently use to cheat-sheet my way through marriage, for those of you who might need help not getting divorced:

- Make the bed every morning or whenever it is you finally get out of it. I don't always fluff the pillows, knock a few points off for that, but it's a nice thing to do for your person, but also for yourself because truly nothing beats sliding into a made bed at the end of yet another day in which you've cheated death.

- Cook dinner a lot. If you don't have a real job, like me, you should be doing this. There's no reason if I am in a blessedly empty house at 10:00 a.m. on a Tuesday that I cannot be making a roux for homemade clam chowder while enjoying my other solitary-at-home activities like listening to embarrassing podcasts or wondering how many people I've never met are mad at me.

- Keep track of your own personal garbage. I am a Trash Nomad, which means that I like to scurry around the house like a little shitgoblin toting a trash bag, a trash bag I use for stuff like bills I want to pretend don't exist, packaging from irresponsible shit I couldn't resist purchasing and don't want to have a conversation about, Starbucks cups from $7 oat milk lattes I drank three days ago, etc. Then, rather than adding it to the communal can and risking someone adding up my coffee cups as they collect the garbage on Wednesdays, I put it in the outside bin when no one is looking, thus sparing my wife the shame of knowing that she lives with an animal.

· Buy things for your person that could also be for you. This is my favorite trick. You look so considerate, like, "Hey, I got you a heated blanket," and then you get to bask in a shower of smooches and glowing praise because you are so kind and thoughtful. When they forget about it in three days, you can commandeer that gift and have your very own brand-new heated blanket, which you bought in the color that most appealed to *you*, because you wanted it to be *yours* in the first place. It's genius, really.

In any case, as I was soaping a saucepan with Palmolive, I spotted a container of probiotics standing sentinel among the shorter vitamin bottles clustered around the sink, vitamins that the healthy people in this house are ostensibly taking even though I've never seen them do it and the bottles are never moved or replaced. My guts lurched another time, once more with feeling, and I looked at the probiotics bottle and thought, "Maybe I should take those, it might help smooth out an otherwise turbulent intestinal night ahead." That is a thought I have never had before, but this is the danger of being the only one awake in the house. You start doing shit you'd otherwise never do because there's no one in the next room hollering, "Don't [*ill-advised action verb*] my [*food item, usually*]!"

I opened the bottle and shook a couple into my palm and thoroughly chewed those tough, squidgy gummies (to release the nutrients, was my thinking), then drank a full glass of water before dragging myself upstairs to finish my nail project so I could sink into a deep, restful sleep with the unblemished hands of a lady in a lotion commercial.

I sat on the toilet (lid down) and put *Project Runway* on the iPad and started tearing the sheet of foil I'd brought with me into jagged, uneven strips. I found a half-empty bottle of acetone and some cotton pads and cursed myself for being so insecure that I did a thing I don't even like, something that has nothing to do with my personality, just to trick people who already know me into thinking that I've become a better version of myself. Then I soaked a pad in acetone and stuck it to my gross, scratched-up forefinger and tried to wrap a jagged strip of foil securely around it to hold it in place for the fifteen minutes the internet promised me it would take for the polish to "lift effortlessly from the nail."

It took me a thousand years to get one hand done. The bathroom was hot, and I was getting a little light-headed from the fumes, but I soldiered on, dutifully applying acetone pads to my right hand using my left one, whose fingertips were covered with clumps of awkward-to-maneuver dripping-wet foils. Once I got all ten of them precariously secured, I sat very still, which isn't a requirement but felt necessary in the moment considering how hard I'd worked and how each foil threatened to fall off every time I exhaled, watching my little stories on the iPad I'd balanced on this decorative bench we got because the bathroom is too big and when spaces are too big, it is important to fill them with dumb shit you don't need, and then I started feeling really hot. Like *really* hot.

I don't get my period anymore, and sometimes I forget about perimenopause. Cut to: me wide awake at 4:30 a.m., nightgown damp with sweat, howling "WHAT THE FUCK IS THIS?" at the ceiling. But as I broke into a full sweat in the bathroom, I remembered how old my uterus is, and I wrote off the fire creeping up my cheeks as "old-lady disease." Once the timer chimed, I started carefully peeling off the foils, expecting to find clean, pristine nailbeds beneath. Well, that shit didn't really work. It mostly just succeeded in making my hands look like I'd been digging around inside a corpse, so I threw a small, manageable tantrum and started scratching and picking at the polish in a rage, when all of a sudden my head started filling with blood.

Or at least that's what it felt like? Inside my skull it sounded like the ocean crashing over and over against rocks, except those rocks were my brain. There was this overwhelming roar that beat in time with my pulse, then it hit me that I was gonna shit myself, and I flipped the toilet lid up while trying not to lose my balance due to the blood pounding behind my eyes. I assumed I was having a stroke, because anything other than chest pain is obviously a stroke, right? And then I felt like someone was pouring warm liquid jelly inside my face, pooling it inside my nose and lips. I touched my mouth and I could feel my lips spreading, like those old Ball Park hot dog commercials where you watch a bunch of sweaty wieners plumping up from the heat of the grill.

I finished my diarrhea (Is it ever finished, really?) and stood up to look in the mirror and almost laughed at the person looking back at me. My cheeks were splotched with neon pink wheals, my left eye was swelling shut while both of my eyes looked as if I'd splashed cranberry juice in them, and my lower face was serving 1989 Joe Camel at the race-track smoking a celebratory cigarette after coming in first place.

I have one serious voice that I almost never use. I can't even control when it comes out, but when you hear it, you know something is UP. I put all of my wet cotton and shred-ded foils into my personal bag of trash and went into the bedroom, where Kirsten and the dog were sleeping, then my serious voice took over when I said, "Kirsten. Wake up. Something is happening to me."

I turned and went back into the bathroom because my diarrhea truly is never! fucking! finished! She jumped up and ran in after me, and watching her face register my face was so absurd, I almost started laughing again. I could see her mentally dialing a divorce attorney!!

I get weird allergic reactions to shit sometimes, and I keep Zyrtec and Zantac in my Dopp kit, because that works when I have hives. I'm not a doctor, so please don't try this or blame me if you do. I would never survive in jail, I have too many allergies. I asked Kirsten to grab it. She returned with the pills and a bottle of water and her phone, saying, "I'm gonna call the nurse hotline," as I tried to choke the two tiny pills down my throat, which was suddenly made of razor blades.

She went back in the bedroom, and I barely heard her muffled voice over my raspy wheezing, a new symptom that had erupted in the previous ten seconds. Kirsten came back into the bathroom with the nurse hotline on speaker and told me they needed my consent for her to talk about me.

I opened my mouth to confirm my identity to the nurse on the phone but all that came out was Charlie-Brown-teacher-trombone voice because my tongue had doubled in size, making it impossible for me to speak clearly.

"I AM GOING TO ASK YOU A SERIES OF YES OR NO QUESTIONS," the nurse shouted, cutting me off, impatient with my mush-mouthed rambling. "DO YOU UNDERSTAND?"

ME (*with maxi pad tongue*): Yuth.

HOTLINE NURSE: Is your face swollen?

ME (*my lips the size of an inner tube*): Yuth.

HOTLINE NURSE: Are you having trouble swallowing?

ME (*struggling to inhale*): Yuth.

HOTLINE NURSE: Is your tongue swollen?

ME (*tongue growing too large for my mouth to properly contain*): Yuthhh.

HOTLINE NURSE: Samantha, I need you to hang up the phone right now and dial 911. Will you do that?

I scoffed. Surely she was overreacting? Or maybe covering her ass so we couldn't sue Blue Cross when I passed away atop a toilet I probably should've bleached a few days ago? Surely, I just touched or inhaled something weird and eventually the medicine was gonna kick in and I'd be fine. I am one million years old, and a piece of shellfish hasn't murdered me yet. This was gonna be like the time I washed my clothes with Gain because it's all they had at the corner store, and I spent a couple hours covered in hives until the Benadryl did its job. I didn't need a fucking ambulance, come on. I mean . . . . right?

HOTLINE NURSE: Samantha, will you end this call and dial 911?

ME (*trombone farting*): I can drive.

HOTLINE NURSE: I cannot recommend you drive yourself to the emergency room. You need to be taken in an ambulance so that EMTs can PERFORM LIFE-SAVING TREATMENTS ON THE WAY.

Well that sucked all the oxygen (I'm sorry!) out of the goddamn room.

Haha, okay, so I was dying. Possibly dying? Probably dying! I looked down through my one open (and rapidly swelling shut) eye at my underwear. I was going to die in a bathroom on a toilet full of floating diarrhea next to the fake grass mat the dog pees on, wearing underwear with a rip near the leg hole, with fucked-up, disgusting bloody-looking carnage at the ends of my bright red sausage fingers. I could hear Kirsten scrambling to get her clothes on in the other room, and I told the nurse I would call an ambulance and hung up so I could do some mental calculations.

It was midnight on a snowy Sunday at the end of January in a town with one post office, and calling an ambulance would've taken the same time as waiting for a spaceship, maybe longer, so I put the hoodie I had yanked off when I thought I was having heatstroke back on and dragged my wheezing near corpse down the stairs. What would you grab if your airways were swelling shut and your brain was boiling and you were about to croak? I hope you never find out, because I grabbed my phone with 1 percent battery, a huge charger brick I had to unearth from under a pile of junk on my desk that I wasn't even sure was charged, a lip balm (?????), and my wallet, shoving them into a backpack as I staggered to the back door.

Kirsten flew out the door ahead of me into the pitch-black night, jumping off the deck and sprinting through the snow to heave the manual garage door up as I tried not to slip and fall down the stairs. She found her keys in her jacket pocket and started toward her car. Leaning against the grab bar on the deck I mustered whatever strength I had left in my body to choke out, "No! (*wheeze*) No, no! (*cough*) Please (*gasp*) my car!" Imagine me, breathing my very last earthly breath and pulling up to the morgue in a fucking canary-yellow Honda Fit??? You can't!

As she was racing through the slick, deserted streets (in my shiny black SUV, whose lease I would no longer be responsible for if I died in it—a silver lining), all I could think about was how I was gonna die with only a quarter of a finished manuscript that wasn't good enough for posthumous publication—like how fucking typical that this would happen when my book is overdue and I hate its current fragments and, wow, what a nightmare, the meeting my agent and publisher would have! ("What order is this in? Is there a theme? Did this bitch even know how to read? Can we sell . . . twenty thousand unpunctuated nonsense words?")

I put on my KF94 mask as we pulled into the circular drive outside the emergency room and walked in alone, because during Covid times, if you are not a child, you gotta go in and die by yourself. And even though a licensed Blue Cross Blue Shield professional emergency telephone nurse had told me my death was imminent, I am so ashamed of myself and so averse to making a scene or doing anything that might bring negative attention to me, that I *stood in fucking line and patiently waited to check in.*

There was a lady with a crying baby who, from what I could overhear, had already been seen but wanted to lodge a complaint about their visit? Behind her was an older gentleman asking for directions to the other hospital across town, and behind him was a young tweaker who, once he got to the window, screamed that he needed to use a phone so loudly that security came over to see what was going on. They started arguing. My one good eye is like a millimeter from sealing itself shut, and even then I didn't tap the security guard on the shoulder to ask if they could move their shouting match a smidge to the left so I could, you know, get the help I needed? On second thought, maybe I *don't* deserve to breathe air.

Standing there sounding like Bane and watching a pointless disagreement between two people I'd probably never see again because what, I didn't want anyone to call me rude? That is diseased! When I got to the window, I politely wheezed (it was more like the bray of a sick donkey) my name and date of birth at the hole in the plexiglass the receptionist sat behind, and after she found me in the system and printed my identification bracelet, I slid to my left over to the triage nurse who, without looking up from her computer screen, asked me to please describe my symptoms.

"Well, ma'am (HEE HAW), I am having (HEE HAW) a pretty bad (HEE HAW) allergic reaction to something (HEE HAW), I think?" She finally looked up, eyes widening as she asked me to move my mask away from my face and when I did, she flew back in her chair like she'd just seen Ghostface and his butcher knife.

"Ashley!!!!" the triage nurse screamed over her shoulder. "Get triage one ready!"

I closed my eyes because I felt woozy and fanned the stale air around me because I was still so fucking hot, and the nurse came running around the desk like, "Whoa, whoa, whoa, you don't get to faint!" and hustled me back to the triage room so they could get my vitals. I slumped in the chair, my breath sounding like a tin can full of glass shards rolling down a mountain made of ball bearings, as Ashley appeared and clamped an oxygen monitor onto my finger.

"I think (HEE HAW) it feels like (HEE HAW) strep?" I said as that sharp, tacky streptococcus feeling suddenly crept up my esophagus and into my throat. I reached up and touched my burning-hot neck, filling with the overflow lava from my pulsating blood-head, with fingers, I hadn't noticed until that very moment, that had swelled up like balloon animals.

Ashley looked away from the monitors and down at me and said, "Ahh, fuck this," and left the room, returning seconds later with a wheelchair. "Prep Trauma A!" she shouted into the little walkie-talkie affixed to her collar while patting the wheelchair seat. I stood up and said whatever "No worries, I can walk!" sounds like when your tongue is the size and thickness of a pack of wool socks and you are steadily losing oxygen. Imagine being such a fucking sicko that even though your eyes are two bruised fists, and your mouth has tripled in size, you're worried about imposing on the woman trying to save your life.

"In situations like this," she said gravely, "it is against hospital policy to let you walk anywhere. You gotta sit."

So I sat in the wheelchair, and Ashley took off running.

I've been in the hospital a whole lot of times, and I gotta tell ya: I never had better, faster service than this, including the time I walked into an ER and projectile-vomited all over the intake lady. This whole part of the story, save my idiotic waiting around, took three, maybe four minutes! At the end of an impossibly long hallway, Ashley turned the corner into a shockingly bright room: three surgical lights were mounted above a table with oxygen tanks and a crash cart pushed next to it, plus six people in the middle of doing . . . I don't know what, but they all seemed very busy.

I'm a loser, so my first thought was "Wow, all this for me?!" and when I stood up to get on the table, I was sheepishly like, "Hi, guys," as if I was the last person to arrive for a dinner reservation they couldn't get seated for without me and not a person who was about to lose consciousness. They all turned at once and bum-rushed me, stripping me out of my clothes in less than a second and throwing a gown over me as I climbed up on the table. On my right side, I heard a woman's voice say, "BIG POKE," as she stuck me to put an IV port into the crook of my arm, and then a woman next to her said, "ANOTHER POKE," as she jammed an EpiPen into my thigh. A nurse behind my head was reaching over me to affix a bunch of heart-monitoring electrodes to my chest. On my left side was a doctor in black scrubs (fancy!) who was trying to look in my eyes with a penlight and a doctor in green scrubs with a clipboard who kept repeating, "What did you take? What did you take? What did you take?" while I tried to choke out the word "Zyrtec" in a way he could understand around my enormous tongue.

Black Scrubs instructed me to "scooch [my] butt down and open [my] mouth as wide as possible," and I tried to make a joke like "(HEE HAW) sure but (gasp) you gotta take me (HEE HAW) to dinner first (gasp)," and Black Scrubs looked at me with such kind pity that it broke my heart.

He very solemnly said, "Samantha, you are funny, but you are also in anaphylactic shock. I am trying to clear your airway, please stop joking and tilt your head back."

That was not my first time being booed offstage, but it was certainly the most jarring, especially since he didn't even give me a chance to workshop the one about how my throat was tighter than new leather shoes, so he should use his meat tube to intubate me.

"Clear my airway"? "Anaphylactic shock"? Those are death sentences!

I think the most upsetting realization I had that night was that when faced with imminent doom, these-could-be-the-last-few-snorting-breaths-you-ever-take kind of doom, I naturally defaulted to joking. I will die, eventually, being a fucking clown. A clown who is desperate to coax even a *hint* of a smile from the very serious people tasked with making sure she lives to honk her big red nose another day.

I think about dying all the time; I wonder when it's gonna happen and what embarrassing thing I'll be wearing when it does, and if anyone is gonna see me dying and think I look stupid. I started thinking about death so much that when the pandemic hit and every news report was like, "Bye, fat people!" I added Kirsten to my bank account, which is a thing I never thought I'd do because what if she decides to get cute? I don't even like sharing popcorn with her at the movies, but if someone coughed into my mouth and I died from it, I didn't want her to be tasked with that olden-times gay shit where she has to go through a bunch of headachy paperwork just to withdraw whatever money I have to cremate me before she moves on to her new nonfat wife who loves nonfat lattes and also being alive. Sob. But never in all my fatalistic daydreaming did it ever occur to me that I would go down to hell doing a dumb-ass bit.

I am very good in an emergency. One of the things that made me so good at my animal hospital job is that I am unflappable in a crisis, which is a quality I didn't even know I possessed until the first time someone ran in screaming with an injured, bloody pet, and instead of crawling under the desk to tremble and cry, I took the shrieking dog from its owner and ran it back for a doctor to start working on it. I sat at the front desk, literally the first semi-friendly face people would see (you gotta withhold the exuberant friendliness until you gauge whether the client approaching the desk is cool or an asshole), and I can't count how many times over fourteen years someone was shoving a wounded half-dead (or sometimes fully dead) animal at my face while screaming "HELP ME" in all caps. I never freaked out or got scared. I just assessed what was going on as quickly as I could (hit by car, attacked at the dog park, consumed a pan of weed brownies) and did whatever was supposed to happen next without falling apart.

I mean, who does that help? Maybe that's why I was so cool and relaxed in the face of my own demise? Either the doctors were gonna fix me or not, no use panicking and wailing about it, may as well try to have a good time while gasping out these final jokes. If only I could apply that to my living life.

My airway was clear enough not to need intubation, so I laid there with my eyes shut and tried not to say anything as the doctors and nurses went about their business of injecting me with antihistamines and Pepcid and enough prednisone to knock down a horse. I opened my eyes a crack to watch the doctor make marks on my hands to track the swelling, and even though it would've been the perfect time to make that Ball Park hot dog joke, I didn't.

Green Scrubs switched places with Black Scrubs and asked, "What have you eaten today?" and I braced myself for whatever judgment was gonna come for my answer. But here's what's actually nuts: for the first time maybe since I was an infant with no cookie-grabbing motor skills, I hadn't had any snacks since dinner, which I'd eaten at a very responsible 5:00 p.m.

Maybe there *is* a God who is watching over me because had it been literally any other night in my life, I'd be forced to (1) admit I was high and (2) recount a long list of bad gastroenterological choices and potential murderers: "Well I walked by a slice of cold pizza someone left on the counter and took a bite without asking what was in it; then I drank a glass of water with lemon that had been on my desk for either two hours or two days, I don't remember; my knee was hurting so I took a pain pill that I found loose in my bag that I hope was tramadol; I had seventeen stale M&M's; then for dinner we had a stew made from milk, eggs, soy, tree nuts, shellfish, wheat, and peanut butter, and afterward I let a bunch of bees sting me."

I hadn't had any food for seven hours, but in the madness of, you know, trying to catch my breath, I completely spaced on the probiotics. They just *poof* disappeared from my brain. All I could remember was the nail polish remover and the foil squares and *Project Runway*. Green Scrubs told Black Scrubs about something called "acetone poisoning" and they put their heads together to have An Important Conversation, while I couldn't resist wheezing, "But, you guys, I didn't *drink* it," which prompted a quick (humorless) science lesson about inhalants and skin absorption that I absolutely deserved.

When all the doctors and nurses were satisfied that my eyes had begun deflating down to their normal size and my cheeks were "less red," they gave me my phone and told me I could text Kirsten and invite her to watch me lie on a bed for several hours. I sent her that "I lived, bitch" meme of that dude in the hospital, and told her she could come keep me company in the trauma ward if she wouldn't rather go back to our warm house with its assortment of pillows and lightning-fast internet and refrigerator filled with a variety of fizzy water selections. She chose to come in because she's a nice lady, and she slept upright in a padded folding chair with a mask covering most of her face while I watched *American Gangster* (edited and with commercials) on a dusty television set hanging from the ceiling, with strict instructions to call the nurse if literally any twitch or pain or feeling occurred while they were out of the room.

I was lying there fantasizing about my real life, in which Denzel Washington and I live together in a cozy ranch house with a couple of cats and lots of motivational wall art that says shit like "Fall asleep with a dream, wake up with a purpose," when a bell went off in my shrinking head: PROBIOTICS. How could I have forgotten that handful of bacteria I'd tossed back before going upstairs?! I pressed the call button and shuddered at the sight of my half-unpolished fingernails. The nurse came in and asked if I was okay, and I told her, with considerably less rattling and wheezing coming from my chest, thank goodness, that I remembered that I had taken some probiotics twenty minutes or so before my head and bowels erupted in tandem and that was the likely cause of my bloated fingers and itchy wheals. Maybe it didn't really matter but, just in case, if I didn't make it, I absolutely did not want "acetone poisoning" to be listed as my cause of death. Imagine some dumb bitch at my funeral like, "LOL THAT ASSHOLE DRANK ACETONE ON THE TOILET? Rest in piss, I guess!"

When you go into anaphylactic shock, they have to keep you for four hours, because, apparently, when the epinephrine wears off, the symptoms can come back. Life is hell. Every time I learn new shit about the human body, it makes me yearn for the grave. So I lay in the trauma room until 5:00 a.m., wired on prednisone and adrenaline, and when at the final check-in, my face and hands had shown satisfactory improvement, Fancy Black Scrubs cleared me to go home.

"Wait a minute, I think you forgot something, don't you need to yell at me about my weight before I go?"

But he didn't; he just asked to which pharmacy in town they should send a prescription for an EpiPen. Oh no, am I gonna spend the rest of my life as an EpiPen guy?

I used to work with this dude who had an EpiPen, and I swear to God every time you said anything he'd find an excuse to bring it up. Like, I'm asking everyone what they need from the bulk office-supply spot and here he comes talking about "Remember, I carry an EpiPen," and, yeah, sure, I fucking remember, but also I'm ordering wet wipes and printer paper, not roasted peanuts.

Is "how to be an insufferable twat" in that thick pamphlet of instructions and contraindications Walgreens staples to your little prescription baggie when you get your allergy meds, or is that just a choice homeboy was making? I picked up my three-hundred-dollar lifesavers and tossed the papers without reading them just in case they were like, *Welcome to your new life of pissing off everyone around you!*, and then I called to make an appointment with the allergist I was referred to. After a two-week abstention from antihistamines (for me, a two-Benadryl-a-day kind of guy, rawdogging my everyday allergies and sinus sensitivities was torture), I went to the doctor and let her touch the eczema I haven't dealt with in a decade and listen to my low-grade permanent wheeze and educate me on why my nose seals itself shut every time someone wearing a strong fragrance enters the room I'm in.

Then she looked up the probiotics' ingredients on the

computer in the exam room and told me that the coloring agent they used to make them orange was probably the culprit behind my near-death experience. And I laughed internally because, WHAT???? Uh, everything I used to destroy my teeth with has some toxic combination of artificial colors and/or flavors! Favorite slushie? The blue kind! Favorite Laffy Taffy? The green kind! Was I really about to be relegated to a life of beige foods?!

I girded my perpetually itchy, irritated loins for a lecture on the dangers of doing my grocery shopping at the gas station, but I didn't get one, she just sent an order for my new steroid skin cream to the pharmacy, and then she sent a different order to the lab for a bunch of blood work she wanted me to get so she could figure out what my dang problem is. She's a doctor, not a magician, I know, I know. Until the results come back, I'll just be over here swapping out all my gorgeous and fancy-scented soaps and lotions for deeply unsexy fragrance-free Dial and many other unscented, uninspiring products with labels that have phrases like "sensitive skin" and "for adult babies who might die from smelling a flower."

The doctor offered to write me a note I could photocopy to hand out to people in my life when I ask them not to light candles or wear fragrances around me, an offer I politely refused. The roasting I would receive behind my back from my rude-ass friends would destroy me, so I'd rather suffer in silence. Or let my tombstone read "Died Because Jessie Would Not Stop Wearing Floral Perfumes." I'm never getting my nails done ever again no matter what or consuming any products that come in colors not found in nature, and I should probably invest in a bunch of bars of plain soap to stash in my bags and glove box. Maybe I could just walk around in a stylish gas mask? Anyway, RIP to the fun and sexy olfactory parts of being a person. Next time you are enjoying a crisp, extra-large neon teal Baja Blast, pour a little out for your girl.

shit happens

I caused a public toilet clog. I can just ghost, right?
Have you ever had to reach into the toilet to break up a
turd? It's a horrifying feeling. What about fishing around in
murky piss-water to loosen a wad of toilet paper you mistakenly thought would swoosh right through to wherever
poop goes? Is it so much worse than, say, using a disintegrating newspaper sleeve to pick up a hot turd fresh out of
your dog's butt? I don't know, but it sucks. You're a human
being who probably doesn't have a job in which you have
to encounter another human being's literal shit, so maybe it
hasn't occurred to you yet that some real person whom you
have never met is gonna happen upon that clog and have to
deal with it, probably for less money than they deserve.

When I walk into a public bathroom stall, the first thing
I do is flush the toilet, especially if I have to poop. You only
need the shock of unfamiliar lukewarm sewage water rising
to gently kiss your butt cheeks one time to learn the hard
way that some asshole—probably you—clogged it before
you unsuspectingly got there and plopped down to get to

work. If the toilet doesn't flush or feels weak, I move on to a less potentially humiliating toilet bowl, so this nightmare doesn't happen to me.

BUT IF IT DID: the first thing I would do is look around to see if there were any tools to help me undo my damage. I peed in my local Trader Joe's a few mornings ago (I am trying something my rheumatologist suggested called "remaining hydrated," which mostly means driving to different places and hoping I don't piss my pants there), and they had a full bathroom situation with a changing table—handy if you need to fully disrobe in order to take a huge, messy shit, but don't want to get any on your dress and also don't want to put your outfit on a ground people urinate on. Anyway, they also had multiple soaps, a hand dryer, *and* paper towels, in case you hate Earth, and both a plunger and a bowl-cleaning brush. If you look around and see those, use them.

Yes, that wet *squashsquashsquash*-lactation-slash-grunting noise the plunger makes as you try to suck your shit out of the toilet's throat is embarrassing, but not more than thinking about another person looking at your stool! If there's no plunger, but there is a cleaning brush or any other sticklike implement, you could (and I have) try to break it up into manageable, flushable pieces? But then you're left with the dilemma of what to do with a plastic wand with poop on it, which I would try to clean with hand sanitizer, but I understand that that is absolutely unhinged behavior and a consequence of my prison brain.

Okay, so, I guess my answer is plunge if you can, break it up if you can figure out how to do so without splattering shit everywhere, and failing either of those, you gotta walk out of there saying, "DON'T USE THAT STALL, I

AM VERY HEALTHY AND CONSUME A LOT OF
BEANS, SOMEONE PLEASE ALERT THE CUSTO-
DIAN WHILE I WAIT HERE AND STAND GUARD"
at the top of your lungs. So, basically, the opposite of ghost-
ing. You literally have to enter holy matrimony with that
poor toilet.

*If you are staying in someone's home and using their shower,
what products can you use from their shower?*
I feel like everything is fair game here. If the person hosting you is me, then I have already mentally walked through
123 scenarios for how your stay in my house might get
fucked up by me, by my terrible pets, or by the items I've
stocked—or failed to, an even worse nightmare. My regular-
ass bathroom is nicely appointed and stocked well enough
to accommodate a C-list celebrity on vacation: Aesop hand
soap and toothpaste on the sink, Aveda shampoos in the
shower, Kiehl's body products on the big block thing with
the spare towels and washcloths in it (What is that called? A
credenza? A toilet cupboard?? A washroom dresser???), and
everything smells good and looks expensive and has an air
of fancy, but not *fancy* fancy? It's "the nice mall with good
air-conditioning" fancy. "The chain restaurant with a valet
stand" fancy. MIDWEST FANCY.

This year, I had to switch to a more, uhh, utilitarian
grooming regimen to manage my allergies and whatnots,
but even if you wanted to use my unscented, non-lathering
soap with the waterlogged prescription label hanging on by
the one remaining drop of adhesive, I would be okay with
that! You would be bored and depressed, but at least you

wouldn't be breaking out in hives. I would still go out and get something nice for you to use in my shower if steroid body wash isn't really your ministry, and you should use as much of it as you want, especially since it's only in there so you will think I love myself and have good taste.

My boss and I walk into the bathroom together.
Am I supposed to carry on the conversation?
No, as soon as you reach the door and you discover that she's not headed to the coffee room, or wherever you thought she was going, you are supposed to pretend you forgot some essential bathroom item at your desk (cell phone? tampon? rocket launcher?!), and bang the heel of your hand against your forehead the way people do in cartoons and excuse yourself, clenching your butthole and bladder as tightly as you possibly can while peering around the wall of your cubicle to clock her walking back to her office, then squeeze every muscle below your belly button taut as you painfully waddle back to the bathroom to relieve yourself in peace.

Can I keep talking on my cell phone in the restroom?
WHY DO PEOPLE DO THIS?! Who in the world are you talking to who doesn't immediately clap their flip phone shut the minute they hear your voice echoing off the metal stalls of a public bathroom? What do you have to say that can't wait thirty seconds, or thirty minutes? Is a child lost? Has a dam broken? Did your car burst into flames? Have two celebrities whose happiness you are deeply invested in

decided to get married?! Please tell me, what is the emergency that is so fucking dire you must subject a lady who is just trying to have discreet burrito diarrhea in a shopping mall to a conversation you could easily resume after you've done your business?

I don't want to talk to you while you're sitting very still in a dark, air-conditioned room where no one's privates are exposed, let alone when there is a chorus of other people's farts providing musical accompaniment. No one ever says anything important, ever. And, even if they did, no one ever says anything that can't just wait six minutes!!!!

Is it rude to squat over a toilet so my precious butt cheeks don't have to make contact with the seat?
Yes, it's rude, and you know it's fucking rude because you've turned around to flush, with your filthy shoe, I presume, and noticed that the toilet other people have to use looks like it's been run through a fucking car wash. No one with piss control does this, it's always the person with a deluge sprinkler installed where their urinary system should be splattering every available hard surface with droplets of pee. It's especially galling when they've covered the seat with toilet paper ostensibly as a protective measure, proceeded to liberally spray-paint said toilet paper ring with Pantone #FFF9B3 Portofino, then walk out without cleaning up any of the actively dissolving pissed-soaked tissue clumps. What is the point of this, to spare yourself from the microscopic germs you will never absorb through your butt skin?

I have a friend who does this, constructs an elaborate toilet theater in every public bathroom stall into which she enters, and what kills me is I have seen this bitch eat food with her unwashed hands after handling bus poles and gas pumps and revolving doors. There's more shit particulate on your phone right now than on a toilet at the bus station, just sit the fuck down already, we live in a society!!!!!!!!!!!!!!!

Should you tip the bathroom attendant?

Many years ago, when I was still an optimistic young thing trying to find her way in the adult world, I got a makeover at a cosmetics counter in a suburban Nordstrom. First of all, this was in the '90s, before there was a wide range of makeup shades for ~diverse skin tones~ or whatever marketing girlies are calling black and brown people now. Second, I didn't know—and still don't, honestly—how to advocate for myself. Specifically, I didn't know that you are allowed to say no when someone is slathering wet putty two shades lighter than your face across your chin in an attempt to "sculpt" it. I was only there in the first place to pick up an elusive bottle of Chanel Vamp nail polish for this rich lady, someone I was working for part-time as a personal assistant, to take to her manicurist.

"They don't have nail polish there?" said me, a dumb sack of potatoes stuffed into an ill-fitting buffalo plaid flannel and scuffed Doc Martens, fiddling nervously with the constrictive velvet choker cinched around my neck as my boss counted hundred-dollar bills into my other palm.

"Of course they do, but it isn't *Chanel*." Her, disgusted.

"Do you need anything else?" I asked, already dreaming about how I was going to waste all that leftover change.

"Grab me a jar of [*Swiss neck cream that costs more than my rent at the time*], and hurry back. I have a nail appointment at six," she snipped, shoving a homeless man into the oven for her dinner.

I bought the nail polish and the neck cream, and as I was lurching my way toward the exit, a lady who thought I was rich waved me over to her counter and offered to "refresh [my] look." I don't know how to put on eyeshadow or what to do with highlighter, so of course I said yes. I had literally never had anyone even touch my face before, let alone carve cheekbones into it. I climbed up onto one of those awkward square stool-seats with the little lip that does absolutely nothing in terms of lumbar support, and my feet didn't reach the footrest that is meant to help stabilize your body as you tremble atop what is essentially a pogo stick. So I clenched my body tight to keep from tipping over as this liberally perfumed stranger made observations like, "Wow, this is a lot of blackheads," and "You've never heard of exfoliation, huh?" while pressing her fingers into the skin around my nose.

After twenty minutes of painting and poking and manip-ulating my post-puberty oil-slicked T zone, she held me at arm's length and chirped, "You look great! Anything else besides the foundation, setting powder, bronzer, eye shadow quad, and lip pencil for you today?" I felt around the cluttered countertop for my glasses, then put them on and squinted at my reflection in the mirror. I looked seventy-five years old, and that's being generous. I looked like I'd tripped and fallen face-first into a child's crusty fingerpaints they haven't used in a year. I looked like I had been embalmed and the mor-tician fell asleep in the middle of doing my makeup, then woke up five minutes before my funeral and did a rush job on me before wheeling me out. It was horrifying?????

I found a bathroom upstairs, tucked inside one of those chic department store sections with realistic-looking mannequins who audibly snickered at me as I speed-walked past with my head down, making a beeline for the bathroom. I panicked when I saw there was a bathroom attendant, because I'd definitely been planning to take my shirt off and wedge my entire skull under the faucet to try to scrape the layers of modeling clay off my poor face. She gave me a once-over and said, "I have makeup wipes," and I could've wept with relief. I sat on a toilet, with my shirt off, and used half the pack to get my face clean. Then I exited the stall and gave the attendant most of that rich lady's change* because (1) she was nice to me and (2) her job is to wear a satin-lined vest and listen to rich ladies shit out caviar all day and fetch them tampons. Tip the attendant!!!!!

Women like to socialize in restrooms. In what part of the restroom is it appropriate to casually chat?
THE AREA TEN FEET AWAY FROM THE OUT-SIDE OF THE DOOR. Pretend your conversation is a cigarette and move it away from the room where I am trying to squeeze every last drop of moisture out of my body so I won't have to pull the car over whenever I leave this fictional place we are all at. Also is "women like to socialize in

---

* I bought the foundation. I am powerless in the face of a person who has scolded my unruly eyebrows.

restrooms" a thing? Is anyone actually "casually chatting" in close proximity to where other people are trying to dislodge their constipated stool? Have I been talking to my friends wrong my whole adult life?

If you're in a clear standoff for some poop privacy, how do you determine who should leave first?

I went on a cross-country tour a couple of books ago. Let me immediately disabuse you of the notion that this is a glamorous endeavor. I was supposed to be gone for two months; in theory, that is very exciting. In practice, how am I going to have enough clean underwear? How do I keep my outside clothes from looking like I've . . . worn them outside? Why don't hotels have washing machines? I would kill for a vegetable served on an actual plate. Where did my charger and my extra travel charger and the charger I packed just in case I misplaced the other two chargers go? People can smell that I don't have access to my regular toiletries, right?

The thing that I was most worried about was the thing I am *always* the most worried about, i.e., WHERE AM I GONNA POOP? I'm not the one booking the flights, and I'm not in charge of the planes, and, sure, I'm mostly eating Gatorade and Hudson News pretzels, but that doesn't mean my bowels are gonna cooperate or be predictable! As a matter of fact, they often choose to do the opposite! Most of the days were formatted like this:

- Flight in the morning; arrive at unfamiliar airport stressed and disheveled after trying to figure out the best way to get a cab in a town that doesn't have Uber.

- Land in next tour stop; if it's too early to check into hotel (call hotel to ask whether it's too early to check in), collapse in a chair near baggage claim and watch people wrestle their suitcases out of the conveyor until it's time to check in.
- Dread the awkward game the front-desk person is gonna make me play while trying to soak in [Denver/Portland/Boston] from the back seat of a speeding car.
- Arrive at hotel, try not to sound like an asshole while explaining that I'm "On book tour, you know? So my publisher booked the room? You should have a credit card on file from them? I know you need a card to hold for incidentals, but mine will literally catch fire if you insert it into your machine right now? Hold on, let me find the emergency number they put on my itinerary. . . ."
- Lie down in dark, temperature-controlled hotel room and burn with shame.
- Put on least-dirty dirty outfit for event, have a lovely time at event, get back to hotel room, and try to do some intestinal math to determine whether I should attempt to eat a real meal that may or may not give me in-air diarrhea the next day depending on whether God has chosen to smite me.
- Lather, rinse, repeat for two months!

Even if I could shit on a schedule this would be tough, and even though I tried to time my BMs so that I could enjoy them alone in the sanctity of my private bathroom at the Omaha Marriott, it rarely worked according to plan, which meant that I had to get good at going in bookstores, restaurants, coffee shops, supermarkets, and train stations, often without the luxury of time to wait for whoever else was in there to get over their shyness and get out so I could go in peace. But I can't be fucking around missing a plane somebody with a corporate card paid for because I didn't want strangers to hear me poop, so here is a surefire trick from me, an expert, on how to take a big steaming public shit: put on headphones and play your music loud enough to drown out both your rectal noise and that intermittent throat clearing from the woman a few stalls down who is doing, what, her taxes? Why has she been in here so long?!

You can't conjure a single-stall bathroom in the middle of the Detroit Metro Airport, but you *can* build your own isolation chamber in the middle of a sea of stalls by putting your little earbuds in, blasting your favorite Girl Talk or Anita Baker track at a skull-shattering volume, then letting your butt do its thing where everyone else but you can hear it. I don't know why it works, but it does.

One of my coworkers, who unfortunately has colitis, does not use the air freshener at all when doing her business. In order to not single her out (she is not the only culprit), I would like to put up a polite sign in the restroom to ask that people use the spray when necessary. What kind of wording would you recommend for this task? I can't really find any suggestions for this type of situation.

Damn, the lady with *colitis* can't get a fucking break??? Instead of sniffing farts, maybe you should do some fucking work!

I'm hosting a couple of friends from out of town.
What products and amenities should I make sure
I have in the bathroom?

Pooping in other people's bathrooms presents such a conundrum. Especially when you have to come out and talk to them as the stench of your waste permeates the air. I don't want to make brunch plans when you just listened to me evacuating my bowels. I want to flush the toilet so many times you wonder if I'm waterboarding someone in your bathroom then walk past where you're cringing on the couch directly into the sea, never to be heard from ever again.

This is what I have in my bathroom:

1. An ADA toilet

   Okay, so, some shit just can't be helped, especially if you live in an apartment, but there's a tall handicapped toilet on the Lowe's website (where I conduct all my most important research) right now for $160, and why would you ever stoop to use a miniature toilet when you could just not? Nothing is worse than walking into a bathroom to discover you have to do a deep-squat yoga pose just to have a little poo. It's like going to kindergarten conferences and the teacher expects you to dislocate your knees in order to crouch down into a child-sized chair so she can yell at you about your naughty kid. No one wants to poop like that!

2. Good toilet paper

   We can argue about what this means as long as we acknowledge that I am right: if you don't use Charmin Ultra Strong with diamond weave technology, you should not invite anyone else to use your bathroom. Cottonelle makes a good super-strong toilet tissue, too, but they didn't have that at Target when I went the other day and, who are we kidding, I am a sucker for branding, and those shitting Charmin bears are very good salesmen. Nothing is worse than having toilet paper disintegrate in your hand as you're scrubbing around in your asshole. Second worst? Having to unwind ten feet of re-recycled paper that turns into pulp the second it comes into contact with even one drop of moisture. Don't force your guests to get shit on their fingers!

3. Antibacterial soap

In case they get shit on their fingers.

4. Something that smells nice, or, if "nice" isn't possible, we'll take "smells better or at the very least different from human excrement"

I can't tolerate a lot of scents and perfumes, especially the stuff that's in air fresheners and car fresheners and most colognes and flowery candles and, and, and, but my bathroom is stocked with matchbooks and incense cones and Poo-Pourri, because even though we all know what shit smells like, and we know that smell will dissipate eventually, no one wants to be the one who stunk up the function and makes everyone uncomfortable. In a perfect world, in *my* perfect world, no one would react at all, but since we live in hell, maybe you should leave a discreet bottle of something on the back of the can so instead of shit you can smell like shit in a flower shop.

5. PILLS

I find sleeping in other people's non-hotel houses too stressful and will never do it, because I have too many requirements and am too self-conscious to be able to relax when I think someone down the hall is wondering why I've gotten up so many times or I think they are mad because I got in bed to watch *A Few Good Men* on my iPad at 7:30 p.m. rather than stay in the living room to listen to them talking. No one's guest bed is ever tall enough, and their houses are never cold enough. And you can't call me a bitch for thinking that if I'm up the road at the Comfort Inn.

No one down at the Radisson is counting the number of minutes I spend in the shower. But the worst thing about staying with someone is risking their being the kind of person who doesn't have a well-stocked medicine cabinet. Did you know some people put essential oils on their forehead when they have a headache instead of washing down a handful of ibuprofen with an iced espresso like a normal person? ASK ME HOW I FOUND THAT OUT. I don't want a hot compress when my [*any body part, name one*] hurts. I want something from Walgreens to make it stop.

Hotels at least keep a few packets of Benadryl at the concierge stand, or they can get some delivered; I was hungover at a fancy SoHo hotel a year ago, and with a few taps on my mobile device, a brown paper bag stuffed with diet Gatorades, quarts of matzo ball soup, and a bottle of Tylenol magically appeared outside my room door. I didn't even have to put on pants! No one wants to be the bitch with a tummy ache rifling through her friend's expired UTI medicine looking for a couple of Tums??? So take your ass to Rite Aid and just clear an entire shelf into your cart. Your friends will be so grateful!

Let's say there are three stalls in the restroom and the third one is occupied. Which should you choose?
This is not a real question, unless you are a monster. Come on, man, do your number two in number one! Ugh!! Maybe they should go back to letting us not be outside.

food fight

Okay, we all know the traditional marriage vows: better and worse, sickness and health, having and holding. When I got married in 2016, standing on the deck of the crumbling farmhouse I had already filled with half my earthly belongings, I was fully prepared to love and cherish my rich or poor wife until death parted us and all the other fine print love forces you to submit yourself to when deciding to legally bind yourself to another person until you both die clutching the deed to a house you couldn't pay off, suffocated under a pile of overdue credit card bills and scratch-off lottery tickets.

Kirsten and I didn't do premarital counseling because, honestly, I prefer to be emotionally reckless and irresponsible but also? We're fine. We are a combined 173 years old! We're both women!! What could truly go wrong? Besides, what do they talk to you about in therapy? Managing joint finances? Setting goals? Whether to buy a human child if the urge to procreate ever arises? Those things, I can navigate. No one ever sits you down to soberly talk to you about sharing your grown-up kitchen with another person!

I lived in blissful solitude for a long time. From eighteen to thirty-five, and you learn a lot about yourself and what you require for life when it's just you that you have to think about. You don't have to pretend to love soaking nuts and beans or dragging butternut squashes up three flights of stairs at the end of a long workday and then trying to figure out how to turn them into something resembling a delicious dinner. You can buy frozen fish sticks and eat them directly from the cookie sheet you never really scrub all the way clean while sitting six inches from a television tuned to whatever the fuck you want that is turned all the way up. It doesn't matter if the tartar sauce makes it back to its shelf, because no one else is gonna see it.

When my lady and I met, my kitchen was that of a feral teen, stocked equally with things you're not supposed to buy as a responsible, bill-paying adult and with ingredients I'd purchased to make one specific dish at some point in history but then never found another way to use again. Packs of ramen noodles jostled for real estate against half-flattened tubes of herb paste that I'd used one squeeze of in some long-forgotten recipe, once and never again. My single-person refrigerator was a gleaming beacon of order: one carton of broth, a few bottles of good beer in case someone came over, maybe a jar of fancy mustard, and possibly a lone slice of left-over pizza.

I bought things as I needed them. I used the precise amount the recipe called for, then I left the refrigerator mostly empty so that there would always be room for the next thing. I was a busy single person who did most of my food shopping at a place where the cigarettes were next to the ice cream. There was no need for me to crowd my precious shelf space with softening pears no one was around to eat.

One morning not long ago, on a normal day, not the day we're having a party or the day out-of-town guests are coming for a weekend or the day an entire group of missionaries has decided to set up camp in our sunroom, I opened my new refrigerator—my first-ever major appliance purchase after the one that came with the house collapsed in on itself—in search of a Diet Coke. This is what I encountered:

- fish sauce
- oyster sauce
- sriracha
- sambal oelek
- harissa
- homemade preserved lemons
- gochujang
- four? five? kinds of mustard
- catsup (not to be confused with ketchup, which is actually good)
- Heinz chili sauce
- horseradish
- soy sauce
- tamari
- hoisin sauce
- dark soy sauce
- a bottle of white wine
- Herdez green salsa
- mayo (Hellmann's, always)
- congealed bacon grease in a Ball jar

- black and green olives (both disgusting)
- capers
- labneh
- Better Than Bouillon (both chicken *and* vegetarian)
- plain Greek yogurt
- tahini
- homemade strawberry jam (ew)
- homemade apple butter (eww)
- grape and strawberry jams, from the store, WHICH IS HOW I LIKE THEM
- A1 steak sauce
- many squeeze tubes: garlic, ginger, chili, lemongrass, tomato paste, anchovy paste
- minced garlic
- miso paste
- two dozen eggs
- oat milk
- buttermilk
- half-and-half
- so much wilted produce (a lot of it dead and inedible to me, a person who won't touch veggie slime)
- loose jalapeños
- loose lemons
- a cucumber that might be a zucchini or vice versa
- American cheese slices
- Gouda cheese
- Swiss cheese
- Havarti cheese
- fancy shaved Parmesan from the health food store
- Feta cheese
- a bin of lunch meat

- definitely expired fresh hummus from the falafel spot
- water with a charcoal stick
- many kombuchas
- many sparkling waters
- four mason jars filled with assorted homemade pickles
- assorted dressings, store-bought and homemade
- homemade peanut sauce that was all wrong but my wife is reluctant to toss
- assorted Blue Apron ingredients we never used but she is, again, loathe to throw out
- leftovers in various stages of decomposition

How could I, a regular person who is not an archaeologist, be expected to locate the single can of Diet Coke I like to have first thing in the morning amid all this ridiculous nonsense? Why didn't the person at the county clerk's office warn me that my bride-to-be and I needed to have similar views on condiment storage before we signed our names on a marriage certificate? Why didn't our minister, who is also our neighbor and lawyer, ask if we'd ever discussed how many types of milk two people need to keep on hand at all times? I'm lactose intolerant; I can't even process all the milks we have crowding out all the things I might actually be able to eat, which are huddling in a corner behind all of these kombuchas and shit.

My wife and I also bought a car together, which is another point of contention because I don't believe that the most expensive thing I've ever owned should also double as a rolling reusable tote bag and spilled granola dispensary, but we do not *even* have time to start getting into that. The refrigerator is the only thing we're forced to share that we have drastically different views on how to use. And I'm not sure how you turn a person who insists on pickling her own carrots into a person who doesn't also feel entitled to stack jars of them eight deep on the highest shelf where the leftover take-out should go. But this is the person I ended up married to. Has anyone ever gotten divorced citing "too many assorted milks"? Is this the "for worse" to which I am resigned???

o brother, where art thou?

One thing I have never had to think about, literally ever, as a person who has neither sired nor birthed an heir is: What is my child, that person who shares so much of my DNA, who is made up of most of the same scientific stuff that made me, doing right now? What is half of my gene pool doing out there in the world?

I had a deadbeat father, for sure, and one thing that has fascinated me both in general and about Bad Dad specifically is his ability to walk away from someone who was at least half-comprised of his actual blood and other genetic materials. And I don't mean in a "How can you ignore this financial obligation?" way, although, duh, yes that too. I would have loved to have the much-needed shoes or clothes he could have helped to provide, but what I mean is, how can you complete your stupid little daily tasks and cook your dumb meals while disconnected cells from your body are in a different part of the country doing their stupid little homework and having unrequited crushes and misunderstanding Tori Amos lyrics? I can't run to the farmers market without standing at the foraged greens and ground cherry stall wondering what my cat Carrots is doing back at home.

I have a sister I don't speak to, or who doesn't speak to me, because we can't talk to each other anymore. It really is that simple. I didn't grow up with my sisters, because they were all practically adults by the time I was born, and our relationship continues, to this day, to exist in this awkward place. They don't see me as a peer, but I don't see them as maternal or elder or any of those words that connote that they are matriarchs deserving of my automatic deference and respect. It wasn't important to the ragtag constellation of legal guardians and state officials who were responsible for us that we be close as siblings. Our rearing was much more "blood is thicker than water, but water tastes better" than "I got all my sisters and me."

It's been sevenish years, and I don't think I even have my sisters' current phone numbers, and that's okay. One of my sisters and I tried to have a relationship for a long time and amicably split when it was clear it wasn't going to work out. Which feels a little weird, but also I have a general idea of where she is and what she's doing, so it's fine. We should teach seminars on how to break up!

When my mom was dying—and I mean, when my mom's fragile-bird body lay in a hospital bed in the ICU surrounded by beeping metal boxes, spiderwebs of tubes snaking in and around her brittle frame, when she was *dying* dying—her doctor gathered all of us girls outside of the room and told us that the pneumonia she'd developed while in hospice was so advanced that her death was imminent. They were going to put her on a morphine drip so she could ride a wave of narcotics into the afterlife. He told us that she would probably lose consciousness soon, and that each of us (me, my sisters, and my mother's mother) would each be allotted thirty seconds to say goodbye, or whatever we needed to say to her, before she slipped into an incommunicative state. I had turned eighteen almost four months to the day before this moment; I had been working at a bakery for most of the summer, my first non-babysitting job, and earlier that day, I had clocked out early and asked my best friend, Sarah, to drive me to see my mom at the nursing home at Touhy and Western, where she'd lived since I was thirteen.

It's so . . . *funny* is the wrong word to use, but it's the only one I can come up with that captures it—weird? strange?? absolutely fucked-up and absurd???—to think about what it must have been like to be my friend back then, for those kids with nice clothes and limitless futures and phone numbers and Volvos in their driveways, to be friends with someone who sometimes didn't have a place to live, whose parents were not ever coming to school for conferences, who needed to be picked up from her mom's nursing home to go to the movies.

For me it just felt normal, right? Because that was just my reality. No one fell from grace or was otherwise derailed by illness or injury from a promising life; we started bad and hovered right above bad for many years until sliding incrementally into worse before landing in godawful. But I wonder what that was like for *other* people, people whose lives had so far been untouched by terrible shit, not knowing what kind of shape I was gonna show up in or where I was coming from or where I was going and what I'd be facing once I got there. I like to think that I hid the turmoil well. And it's comforting to think that no one clocked how bad my situation was, but I'm sure I didn't.

I got to the nursing home that day, and my mom started gasping for breath as soon as we walked into the room. The hospice nurse told me she'd been trying to stay alive until I could get there, which is an unreal thing to hear that I could not have processed in the moment. They shooed me out of the room, telling me which hospital to go to, and I could hear someone down a hallway on a phone requesting an ambulance transfer and mentioning something about "making arrangements." I had known for years that she was going to die, but in that moment, I knew she was going to die *that day*—a surreal thing to realize—and it was almost inconceivable to turn to the friend I'd met two years before in high school gym class and ask if she wouldn't mind dropping me off on her way to hang out with her boyfriend, so I could watch my mom die.

My mom's wish was to die in Evanston Hospital, the same hospital in which she'd spent many years working as a nurse, the same hospital in which she'd given birth to me and all my sisters, who were in various stages of crabby bitchiness as we listened to the doctor giving us quick instructions about how to conduct ourselves during our thirty seconds of individual goodbye time. I wondered what would be the best thing to say, like would she want me to keep it light? Should I tell some jokes, send her out with a laugh? I didn't want to cry or make her feel bad, but also, I was mad at her, for having a baby when her ob-gyn had specifically told her to abort me, because the last thing a forty-year-old woman with multiple sclerosis in 1980 should have been doing was giving birth to a human child. I was also mad at her for telling me that fucking story. I mean how fucked-up was that?!

I zoned out, sitting on the floor with tears leaking down my face, wondering what my sisters were gonna say and chastising myself for not having thought of something good and poetic in the last five fucking years I'd had to prepare something. I tuned back in as they started squabbling over the order in which we'd get to go in and talk to her. I assumed we'd just go in birth order, which was perfect because it would give me more time to think of something brilliant and touching, and also I'd be batting cleanup and could send my mom on her way with something better than anything any of my sisters had said. It was decided that Carmen would go first, and I would follow, which I didn't love, but I could tell the doctor was already exasperated by our collective bickering, so I decided to just be cool. Carmen had her thirty seconds, and I went into the room and gestured for her to leave; I could not *imagine* being overheard during those thirty . . . twenty-nine . . . twenty-eight . . . twenty-seven . . .

My sister was still sitting in the fucking corner. I was like, "Dude, get the fuck out, I want to be alone with Mom," but she just kept sitting in the chair at the head of the bed, holding Mom's hand, and—

Twenty-four . . . twenty-three . . . twenty-two . . . twenty-one . . .

"You sat on the floor in white pants?" she asked. I looked down at my bakery pants, which were kinda grayish in spots from sitting in a lake of invisible disease in the hallway.

"You bitches took all the chairs?" I asked back, like are we really talking about my pants right now as morphine is dripping into our mother's arm? And then BOOM, we're fighting, yelling at each other over her lifeless body about I don't even know what, how life is miserable and unfair, and I am never presentable, as if there's a way you're supposed to look on the worst day of your life.

"Get out!" I screamed, and I could feel everyone in the hall turn to look at us. "You had your turn, now get the fuck out!"

She got up and moved slowly in the direction of the door—

Ten . . . nine . . . eight . . .

And I sat gingerly on the side of the bed, trying to avoid Mom's spindly legs. I said something like, "This is the worst, I'm gonna miss you for the rest of my life, and I love you so so much."

She reached up with her long, skinny hand and pulled the oxygen mask away from her gaunt face. I didn't even know she had that left in her, but, of course, she was going to say something to me, her favorite child. Probably dispense some sage wisdom or finally admit that the reason she'd had me was because she was disappointed in her other children and wanted to take one last shot at having a good one.

"I really love you, Mom," I said.

She held the mask away from her mouth, looked at me, looked over at my sister, opened her toothless mouth, and croaked, her voice soaked in predeath and bitterness, "Are you sure?"

EXCUSE ME, MA'AM, BUT I'M SORRY, WHAT THE FUCK DID YOU JUST SAY?

Mom let the mask snap dramatically back over her mouth, and I burst out laughing, incredulous. I'm sorry, but what a bitch??? The doctor poked his head in like "Time's up," and

I could see my other sister, Jane, gathering herself to come in and say her final piece, so I stood up and looked down at my mother for one last living time and said, "I am going to think about this for the rest of my life."

She didn't respond.

The repast after the funeral was in the basement of the church, because no one in our family had a house nice enough to invite a bunch of crying people over to eat potato salad in, and I remember nothing of that day. I'm sure I ate fried chicken, consoled people who hadn't seen my mother in over a decade while letting them cry on my nice black dress, and gossiped about who was wearing what with my nieces, but I cannot recall who or when or if it was a spicy wing or a thigh. Except I remember one thing: as I walked past the kitchen on my way out of the bathroom, I had a small heart attack when I ran smack into my father, a man who had died four months earlier.

I took a step back, mouth hanging open, then looked around to see if anyone else was seeing a ghost standing in the middle of the room holding a plate of catfish and greens and macaroni and cheese. No one seemed to notice the poltergeist other than me, and when he said, "Hey, baby, I'm so sorry about your mom," it hit me: MY BROTHER.

My jaw hit the floor. "Cedric?!"

He nodded, and smiled, and I noticed that one of his front teeth turned just a little bit, just like our father's. He also had his same exact hands, which are also my same exact hands. I hadn't seen Cedric in years, since I'd slept in the passenger seat of our dad's old Cadillac as he drove down to Memphis for a visit, and the only memories I'd retained from that trip was the McDonald's riddled with bullet holes in the drive-thru glass—someone mad about a nonfunctioning ice cream machine, perhaps?—and the navy-and-yellow entertainment room in Elvis's house with its wraparound couch and three built-in TVs, the height of luxury.

I don't remember what happened next, or who else was there, or how the evening ended. I can't remember whether I talked to him again. I don't think so. It was twenty-five years ago, which is insane to me, that my parents have been dead for twenty-five years! That's a generation!! Generation orphan!!! I don't feel old enough to have parents who've been gone for that long, which is hilarious, because somehow I *do* feel old enough to move into assisted living, which I would do immediately if I could. I can tell you what didn't happen, though: no one thought to get Cedric's address or contact information—was email invented in 1998?—so that was the end of that.

The grief I live with feels like when you suddenly remember a famous person you like is dead. An episode of *Sanford and Son* comes on and you're like, "Aw, Redd Foxx, I really loved him," except it's me hearing an old clip from *The Tom Joyner Morning Show* and thinking, "Aww, my mom, she loved that guy." It's been such a long time, and I knew my parents for so few years, and some of those years my brain was nothing more than a little clump of lukewarm oatmeal . . . is it bad that I don't miss them? Am I still supposed to keep a candle burning for someone whose voice I cannot recall?

Sometimes, when I want to both feel sad and punish myself for not feeling sad, I'll project an idealized version of my parents and bum myself out thinking about a life that never could have been. Brain, picture my mom, Grace, laughing and carefree with no multiple sclerosis and Sam, with no wartime PTSD, or alcoholism, and not punching me in the face for washing the dishes wrong, then add a duplex in a nice neighborhood and a steady source of income, cool? Okay, good job, I'm crying. But, in general, to me they represent two fleshy bullets dodged. It sounds so callous, and maybe I'm a fucked-up sociopath, but imagine if I was forty-three and still actively distressed about this. Would anyone care? No, because they're busy scouting nursing homes they can barely afford for their own parents!

It took me eleven years to get my dad's ashes, and even then I couldn't do it; my sister Carmen went to the funeral home and collected the dusty box and "dropped by" my job to give it to me. I thought I should try to find my brothers, my dad's two sons from his first wife, to see if they wanted his cremains before I dumped them out in front of a run-down liquor store or in the front row at an Al Green concert, but so much time had passed and our extended family has maybe eight people in it, and no one knew how to get ahold of them. Plus, they're old-school, not the kind of guys to put shit on the internet—or even deal with the internet at all—and my weeks of searching every name I could think of to try to find one of them yielded nothing.

So one spring Kirsten and I drove to Nashville (I'd already been to Memphis enough times, I mean how many times does a person need to stand in Elvis Presley's kitchen, Nashville was close enough), and I essentially threw his ashes in my own face as I tried to empty the container into a lake on a golf course. And then that was it. No fanfare. I felt unburdened. I could officially move past having a dad. Maybe brothers, too.

. . .

A year ago, I got a message on Instagram. I am wary of DMs, even from people I know, so I almost didn't open it. I'm not even sure why I eventually did, probably some gross combination of guilt and morbid curiosity. The message was from a young, gorgeous black woman whose name I didn't recognize. It said something like, "Hi is Samuel Irby your dad? I think you might be *my* dad's sister."

First of all, I'm not gonna lie, my dad was the kind of person you might not readily admit to knowing, let alone being the offspring of. Once, when I was in high school, a giant man in a sanitation uniform accosted me in the corner store, grabbing my arm like, "IS SAM IRBY YOUR DADDY?" and I started sweating and opened my mouth, but no sound came out, and dude continued, "Unh-huh, you look just like him."

I sighed, and I don't know what, curtsied? Literally anything to get out of that situation. And as I was leaving the store with my two-for-a-dollar Honey Buns he called out, "That motherfucker owes me thirty-five hunnid! When you see him let him know James is looking for his ass!"

I did tell my dad eventually, when I next saw him, and his mystified response was along the lines of "Wow, and he let you live?" This tells you everything you need to know about my father: he was bad at gambling and always on the run from the consequences of his actions, and he would've absolutely sold me to a loan shark for $3,500!

This woman on Instagram told me she'd seen my book in an airport bookstore and thought the coincidence seemed too good to be true, and I wanted to say I hoped that she hadn't bought it, but my niece (???) didn't deserve to have my anxieties vomited all over her, so I just thanked her and asked about her dad. I wanted to ask if he would be mad that I dumped our dad's ashes on a golf course, or if he would be weirded out that I'm married to a woman, or if he had any memories of what I was like as a little kid that would make me cringe to death, but I didn't. I just said, "Is your dad doing okay?" When she responded with his phone number, I had to laugh, I mean, of course, I should just call and ask him myself. I'm a grown-up—am I?—and he's my brother. I gave her my number so he wouldn't be weirded out by an unfamiliar area code and told her I'd call him soon. Easy.

Except I hadn't seen Cedric since my mom's funeral, and even then, it's not like I knew him that well. I knew a few things about my father's two sons, but they were much older and lived far away in Memphis, and had a different mother I had never met, so they loomed large as mythical figures in my mind, characters in bedtime stories from times I couldn't remember. I was nervous about being rejected, for how I looked or how I talked or what I was interested in. I worried it might be weird between us because of how differently we'd been brought up. My brothers, my sisters, and I were all raised by a loose network of the same overlapping people, but each circumstance turned out to be wildly different.

My mom was in high school when my two oldest sisters were born and forty when she had me, the lady who birthed us looked the same, but she was two different people. My dad is not my sisters' dad, but he came into their lives when they were in elementary school, shortly after he'd split from my brothers' mother. And the man who was a glowering, erratic figure in 1968 was both different, yet somehow better, than the one who made me get out of a car in the middle of the road to teach me a lesson in 1992. What was I gonna say? "How much of a psycho was Daddy when you knew him? Want to compare our parallel traumas?"

I let many, many weeks go by. I mean, when was even a good time to call a person whose schedule you don't have access to? What if they worked on the weekends and had random days off during the week? What if they worked the night shift and are asleep during the day? What if they worked the day shift and went to bed unusually early at night? What if they hate talking during their commute? Or they like to talk first thing in the morning? More important than that, people hate talking on the fucking phone! I love it, of course, but I am a monster. Is it appropriate to text someone saying, "hey idk if this is u but hi im ur sister"? I could spin out and ask a hundred more completely plausible questions like these. The longer I stalled, the more I psyched myself out. What if this was a joke? The internet is weird, man. People do fucked-up shit like this all the time, and I'm not so arrogant that I'd think it could never happen to me or that I'm so smart I'd be able to sniff out a scam.

But I'm trying to be less fucking cynical all the time. I decided I would call, just to see. I told people I was gonna call, so they'd hold me accountable and follow up. I even sat on a couch next to my friend Megan and spent an hour working out a plan for what to say when I *did* call, like two girls hanging out after school plotting what to say when they prank call the house of the boy they think is cute. It became bigger than a catch-up phone call; suddenly, in my mind, it was going to be a referendum on my entire life and my choices. I kept inventing more and more reasons he wouldn't like me or ways in which I wouldn't live up to his expectations. Imagine me practicing my opening argument: "Hello, one of my dad's other children! How have you been for the last twenty-five years but also your whole life, because I don't really know anything about you? First of all, please don't read my books or literally anything I have ever written anywhere at any point in my life. Now that that's out of the way, what shows do you watch?"

One Sunday, I was at home watching the Kansas City game and doing the crossword on my phone when the screen lit up with a call from a number I didn't recognize. I jumped like I'd been caught doing something naughty, which is how I always feel when the phone rings while it's in my hand. "Can they see me right now????" This is me hiding from the ringing phone in my hand. I answered it because it seemed like bad manners to ignore someone on a Sunday afternoon—maybe it was God calling!—in favor of a puzzle I was never going to correctly solve, and was surprised, delighted, elated even when the smooth baritone on the other end of the line said, "Is this Samantha? Hey, baby, this is your brother."

how to look cool in front of teens?

**Do not try to engage or bond with
them over anything young people like.**

I have a TikTok account, and its sole purpose is for watching TikToks that other people send me; I will never be partici-pating in a single challenge or posting a video of myself of any kind. I know to leave that to the experts: beautiful high schoolers with no screen-time restrictions. I did download the app because I don't wanna be the old guy watching Tik-Toks on a browser, especially since I was *already* an old guy looking at tweets on a damn browser, and my friends bru-tally roasted me for doing both, which I deserved.

I watch YouTube for cooking videos and clips from *Inside the NBA* I've already seen dozens of times, but that's it; I don't go on young-person YouTube, I have no idea what they're doing over there! I'm sure there are other platforms kids use that I have no idea even *exist* and I like it that way. They should have their shit and I should not have to learn new shit. Some local teens follow my Instagram, and when I was alerted to this disconcerting fact I didn't think, "I'm dope, the kids love me." I thought, "Oh no, why? To make fun of my memes?" I'll never know the answer to that question and am fine with the assumption that they're cooking my ass in the group chat, because the worst thing you could ever do is try to talk to an old child about their social media activity.

Let me save you from the heartbreak caused by the withering look on your nephew's face when you attempt to make small talk about anything invented in the last ten years: don't.

Never earnestly ask for their opinions on literally anything you enjoy.

Have you ever been watching, like, the most incredible show of your life? The kind of show where you're saying to yourself, "I can't believe they made this show that's fuckin' perfect for me, I love it so much, how did I get so lucky." You call your best friend about it, and you text your crush about it so they start watching it and give you an excuse to keep talking to them, and for a time you make this show your entire personality because that's how exhilarated you feel about it, and then a kid walks by the television and glances at it for a millisecond, then goes, "Ew, what are you watching? Haha, dude, it looks like it sucksssssss," and you suddenly feel like you just took a shotgun blast to the chest? Yeah, me neither.

**Do not mention their body ever, in any capacity,
and try not to notice that they even have a body.**

Bodies are an off-limit subject for me in general because if I have to talk to *you* about *your* body, then you're gonna very courteously ask *me* about *my* body, and then I have to watch you struggle to be polite as I launch into a laundry list of my physiological issues while you try not to say "Have you considered dying?" to my face.

Yes, teenagers need to bathe, but don't tell 'em that. Also, they know their hair looks like that. Don't say shit about it, because the look they will give you in response could melt steel, just know that they know and they're choosing for it to be that way. I can pretty easily access my most hurt teenage feelings, and I remember my aunt telling me once that I looked terrible and needed to "pick my titties up." That quote tells you everything you need to know about both my aunt and my teenage style and body.

The last thing that will endear you to a kid is pointing out how wrecked their shit looks. The way they dress is supposed to be confusing and upsetting to you, and the only way to deal with it is to pretend they're a hologram or standing behind one of those carnival cutout things until life forces them into a middle management job and flat-front khaki pants while you shut up and wait for it to happen for real.

Let them drive your car.

I mean, not . . . *my* car? But *your* hypothetical car is the perfect thing to hand over to a large child who rolls their eyes at everything else you suggest if you want that kid to think you're cool. Wow, the way their immature little eyes light up! I put in a few hours as the designated driver's ed instructor for the driving-age teenage boy in my house last summer, and let me tell you something: I hated it. Mostly because I had no idea I even knew the phrase "keep pace with the flow of traffic" until I heard my disembodied voice saying it, sternly, to a child who kept fucking with the radio stations when he should've had his eyes on the goddamn road.

All that cool stepmom shit flew right out the window as soon as he made a left without signaling (!!!!!!!!!!) and I said, "Sir?? Hello???????" I was like, OH NOOOOO, I'M MY OWN DAD AND I GOTTA GET OUT OF THIS CAR WHILE I STILL HAVE AN OUNCE OF YOUNG-NESS, but that didn't stop the words "why are you speeding up to a yellow light" from coming out of my mouth. His response, of course, was "*you* do it," and then I had to do another awful old-person thing, which is to say, "I've been driving for twentysomething [*redacted*] years," then ask him, "Who pays the note on this [*redacted*] car" as he laughed and offered to get me some Metamucil since we were right by Walgreens.

Talk about smoking weed, but never let them see evidence that you smoke weed just in case you need some plausible deniability.

One of my friends' dumb-ass kids got busted with fake edibles, and I cried laughing when he told me the story. Imagine looking into a kitchen cluttered with primary-colored Hasbro beakers and a Disney-branded microscope with supersized heart eyes like, "Aww, Lil Blobbo has a passion for science just like his dada," as you watch your kid melting boba or whatever and then finding out he bagged the results and tried to sell them on the playground like Nino Brown. I would cough up my esophagus laughing!!!!!!!!!!!! How do you even navigate that as a parent? On the one hand, selling drugs is bad, I guess, but on the other? I applaud that entrepreneurial spirit! The thing about a kid committing a crime is that they always gotta find someone over twenty-one to serve the time for it, which is why I love getting high, but I've also never seen marijuana in my life.

Act like you don't care that they think your clothes are bad.

I dress like a garbage man, and I do care what people think sometimes, but I'm also honest enough with myself to admit that there isn't much I'm willing to do about it. But if I ever attempt to look less *Mad Max*–ish and want some validation for that effort, the last person I would try to squeeze a compliment out of is a dopey kid wearing a two-dollar Shein bodysuit because they absolutely will not give it to me!!!!!

Middle-aged people get ragged on for our clothes, and,

yes, it's funny, but also: What can you do? If you try to wear youthful outfits, you look like a fucking asshole, and if you wear what you actually *want* to wear (e.g., the matching pastel pink sweatshirt and -pants with iron-on kitten decals I saw somebody's grandmother rocking during the Olive Garden lunch rush last week), your friends will put you in a home. So that leaves you with no other choice than the standard-issue wrinkle-resistant floral cropped palazzo pants (with slimming technology™) and the cotton-blend popover with three-quarter sleeves and shark-bite hem they ship to your house the morning of your fortieth birthday. "Dress it UP or dress it DOWN, suitable for DAYTIME or EVENING," screams the ad copy. "Versatility is key when your arthritis makes changing into a 4:00 p.m. dinner shirt too cumbersome!"

It's not my fault I look like this after I get dressed. My body is very cold but also very hot, and my knees don't bend, and my breasts need to be hoisted up but also welded to my sternum, and the pants gotta be easy to yank down because I no longer have bladder control. What else am I supposed to wear other than this stupid-ass shit? Yeah, man, I don't love head-to-toe fleece, either, AND YET: that is what my targeted ads show to me, therefore that is what I am putting on. So, no, I don't want to go into H&M so you can try to find me "a different shirt that's cooler." My rayon tunic and I are just fine eating our Sbarro in the food court.

Repress your need to argue and/or be right.

They will never submit. You will never make your point. They will never concede your victory. They will write off your arguments as old-fashioned and claim that everything you know came from a textbook written in 1950, even though you just learned it five minutes ago from a pastel-colored social justice infographic your most earnest friend shared. Their information is FRESH and CURRENT and their ideas are NEW and HOT and come courtesy of a young man on YouTube YOU DON'T EVEN KNOW ABOUT BUT HE'S THE TRUTH.

Reconcile yourself to this now: all the ways you do things and everything you believe is old and wrong, and your best year was 1997, before they were even born, so hang it up and let them lead the way. Teenagers have endless amounts of energy, especially the ones with no real problems. I'm not gonna yell myself hoarse trying to convince someone with a belly full of my food standing in a house whose deed has my name on it of some political point that, if we're being honest, I don't really care about that much. What I *am* gonna do is walk away and remind myself that my outdated public school education is perfectly fine before screaming into a pillow about "the olden days." (More on that in a sec.)

Do not invite them to watch your preferred television programs.

They'll fucking ruin it. It'll feel good at first, to have your decisions endorsed by someone whose smooth, uncalloused fingers are on the cultural pulse that just slipped through your desiccated, liver-spotted hands. They'll sit down next to you on the couch, dig their grimy paws into your TV snack, and you'll be stoked that this young person, who would otherwise step over your flaming corpse to get to a pair of AirPods, is showing interest in a thing that is interesting to you. Until ten minutes (if you're lucky) into it, when they start workshopping their new open-mic set, cracking wise (but not funny) every time someone on-screen so much as pauses to take a breath.

Even if the teen in question is marginally amusing, the shit's irritating. But since most of them don't have the lifetime of discouragement and misery you need to truly develop a good sense of humor, it becomes an exercise in how hard you can grind your teeth and grip the remote until they all shatter from the pressure. Because a child who mainlined seven seasons of *The Office* in one sitting won't stop saying "That's what she said" during the climax of that austere Icelandic crime drama you've been watching. So just don't even bother inviting them to watch with you. By default, everyone will think you have a mysterious secret show you don't want them to know about, which is fucking cool, and you won't have to worry about cruel mockery or rejection.

"Taco Bell? Sure why not!!!"

JUST SAY THAT.

Pretend you are not bothered by noise.

I just bought these fancy earplugs that are "discreet" and claim to reduce noise by twenty-five to twenty-seven decibels. And no I don't know what those words mean, but the science doesn't even matter, I just need to hear *less*.

Less punching, less arguing, less *Bob's Burgers*, less starting hybrid punk electronica bands, less begging, less shriek-ing, less "Mom?"-ing, less door slamming, less *King of the Hill*, less barking-ass dogs, less fighting-ass cats, less ring-ing phones, less text messages, less people at the door, less *Scream 4*, less street traffic, less slime-making, less "Can we get boba?," less basement karaoke, less crying over home-work, less children chasing a ball outside, less human life in general, LESS EVERYTHING. Unless it's something I wanna hear, like a door closing when people leave.

Okay, but here is my advice: yes, I have tried noise-canceling headphones, and I have a couple of pairs of the good ones that actually work, but the thing about them is if people see them on your head they're like, "Oh, she's just lis-tening to some dumb nineties metal song. It's fine to inter-rupt." I am definitely listening to Faith No More on repeat but, no, it's not fine to interrupt because I am very busy fantasizing that you don't exist. Sometimes I think teenagers have a Pavlovian response to the sight of the headphones themselves, like no one was gonna say anything to me until they visually registered that I was shutting them out of my headspace, and they became overcome by the overwhelm-ing urge to stop in front of my chair and furiously motion for me to remove my fancy quiet-makers only to ask, "Hey, whatcha doing?" PRETENDING I AM DEAD is what I wanna say, but I never do because I want to be scary but not scary like *that*.

The key is, even if you want to stab your own ears out, you gotta play it smooth because if you stand in the middle of whatever room you're in and dig down deep to the bot-tom of your diaphragm and holler "EVERYBODY SHUT

UP" as loud and hard as you can, it won't work. They'll stop
for one millisecond to give you the "Wow, she's unhinged!"
eyes and go right back to banging a tambourine against the
wall, and your only choice will be to bury yourself alive,
which no one will notice, because they're too busy cater-
wauling for no good fucking reason while they laugh at your
pain. That's why I've spent $4,873,245 on earplugs in the last
few years. So that I could sit unbothered through an actual
hurricane if need be while looking like I don't have a care
in the world, especially if that hurricane is named: "We just
got surround sound speakers."

Do not give them any books or ask if they read books.

You will be disappointed every single time. Even if you hand
a teenager a book that's called *Juul Pod Pizza Rolls* or whatever shit kids care about, they will look at you as if you're
offering them a steaming pile of your own excrement and
say, "Thanks . . . ?" in a way that will devastate your ego.
Maybe this has been my experience because the teenagers I
know are all popular and well-adjusted. When *I* was fourteen, I would've taken a book a grown-up gave me and carried it around like a talisman until it disintegrated in my
hands but this was in the time before cellular phones, no
one knew what binge-watching was yet, and *Ricki Lake* was
only an hour long, which left me with a lot of unoccupied
late-afternoon hours.

**Make an appointment with an allergist
to help you deal with all the smells.**

I have "I spent the entire eighties blowing rails" interior nasal cartilage, and it's due to one thing: a potent combination of Bath & Body Works body mist and Old Spice Wolfpenis—that's one of the scents, right?—that hangs like a fog over every communal living space in my house. My mom used to lose her voice anytime someone sprayed air freshener in the room she was in (cut to: child me lugging an enormous pink can of strawberry Money House Blessing and just straight up *saturating* the air with that shit), and she would get so mad while I laughed and laughed. And now my karmic punishment is that I live with several walking clouds of clashing smells.

I'm all for kids having choices until they choose to live their lives surrounded by a Pigpen-style smog of a mall fragrance called something like "Hawaiian Breeze Sunshine Coconut Kiss," and yeah, I'm a hypocrite. I spent many high school days gagging everyone around me with the cloying smell of Victoria's Secret Pear Glacé, whose accented *e* made me feel extremely worldly and special. Which is why I don't say anything. I just grimace to myself while purchasing Flonase by the case, and leave a window cracked even in the winter. As a result I appear to be chill and relaxed even though inside my head I am screaming.

Do not expect thanks for literally any kindness you show them.

If a tree falls on a teenage boy and you walk by and lift it off him, saving his life, just walk away without saying a word and buy yourself a beer, because the acknowledgment or gratitude you might expect will never come, and if you stand towering over him, and ask for it, you will look like a groveling simp. Cool people don't need supplication from a little bitch who can't vote and smells like milk!!!!!!!!!

Get control over the reactive muscles in your face that want to twist into an agonized internal scream as you watch your own terrible adolescent behaviors demonstrated by someone else's child.

For the rest of my life, I will never, ever forget the day my mother and I stood inside a Lane Bryant that's now a Chipotle in downtown Evanston, and I threw a tantrum because she didn't have money to give me to buy something at the Barnes & Noble that turned into a Pret a Manger that's now a T-Mobile and also to buy me new jeans that didn't have a friction hole in the crotch. I very dramatically stormed out and walked around downtown looking in store windows at stuff I couldn't afford (everything!) before ending up at the library looking at (free) books for a few hours before walking all the way home, because I didn't have the kind of mom who would wait for me or even look for me to make sure I hadn't been murdered—a fate I would've deserved.

I can't remember whether I apologized for embarrassing her or humiliating myself over twenty bucks, but I am very sorry to my current self for having to relive this cringeworthy memory at least once a week, which is clearly me at my *most* mentally ill, because I'm spiraling at the memory of something only a dead person knows I did. What a freak. I do not think of fun childhood birthday parties or warm Christmas memories. When I get sad about my mom my brain is like, "Hey, dude, remember that time you fully melted down in front of a rack of Venezia medium-wash five-pocket button-fly average-rise stretch bootcut jeans?" If you don't get that joke—congratulations!

Anyway, it's an exercise in . . . *something* trying to keep your face neutral while witnessing a high schooler doing a thing that's gonna haunt them at 3:00 a.m. every night for eternity, but just know that if you intercede, you'll be dismissed, so don't even worry about it. Go cringe in another room while your mom's ghost laughs at you from the spirit realm.

Don't talk to their friends!

Unless they talk to you first. I asked one of my in-home teens if they enjoy talking to adults, and the answer was a resounding NO. That gave me such a gratifying feeling, knowing that my silence and gentle hostility was a welcome reprieve from all the "HEY, HOW'S SCHOOL THIS SEMESTER?" conversations forced on them by other adults. The neighborhood kids were eating breakfast here one morning after a sleepover, and I heard one tell the other in a hushed, reverential voice, "Don't be so loud, Sam is in a bad mood." I don't think I'd said more than hello to this kid in weeks and yet: deference and respect for my tight-lipped, hateful exterior.

Swallow that story about how "it used to be."

The most surprising thing I have learned about myself in my current life as the Reanimated Corpse of Al Bundy is how quickly I find the phrase "when I was a kid" trying to claw its way from between my anxiously clenched teeth. I know that when your parents hit you with the "back in my day . . ." your eyes would roll up to your brain and your ears would seal themselves shut, and you swore that once you were an adult, you would never even *think* about saying something like that to an impressionable youth, but I'm gonna come to your poor mother's defense and say that a kid will look you dead in your fucking face in a room that you work a soul-deadening job you fucking *hate* to keep warm, wearing the third pair of sneakers you bought so far this year, and tell you that you couldn't possibly understand how hard their life is.

"Oh, okay, sure, we had to do our grocery shopping on the bus, but please, by all means, tell me and my fucked-up childhood poverty teeth how hard it is to be shuttled to the orthodontist." At least that's what I think, but I don't say that, because you know what? They don't care and it's fine. That trauma is meant to ruin the rest of *my* life, not some innocent's, so why waste my breath recounting the torment of trying to do division longhand or getting caught talking shit on a muted three-way call when I could just go talk to some food about it??????

Watch horror movies.

This is a thing I discovered by accident. One afternoon when I was sitting in the sunroom (in broad daylight, because I get too scared!) watching *Orphan*, a kid walked by and said, "Wow, you're into horror? Cool," as they passed through on their way to open six different cans of LaCroix and take one sip from each before leaving each of them precariously placed next to different expensive things that shouldn't get water spilled on them. Yes I covered my eyes through most of it, but who cares! I got the approval of a child!!

Buy them dumb shit their mom won't?

It doesn't even have to be anything good or expensive, just know that if Mommy said no and Aunt Sammy says yes, then that kid is not only gonna think you're fucking cool, they're gonna think you're cooler than their dumb mom, and you can use that leverage in your friendship should you need to shut Mommy's ass up real quick. Example (but don't do this): "I know you think you know everything, but your kid likes me more than you, so who wins now?!"

Also, it helps to satisfy the urge to buy shit (the *click-click-click*ing heals me, I swear) without having more stuff piling up in your crib, waiting for you to find a place for it. I get a crumb of serotonin from adding something I don't need to a virtual shopping cart, my friends' kids get a frivolous thing their cruel parents would never waste money on, and then the kids think I'm thoughtful and awesome without any substantial proof!

Act like you're doing incredibly interesting stuff on your phone.

This is what I do on my phone: (1) Look at Instagram. Seven hundred times a goddamn day, I just mindlessly scroll past a lot of faces I don't even actually know, watching their stories and admiring their restaurant choices and wondering how they have so many interesting-looking friends. (2) Check my credit score. Life was infinitely better before you could just . . . check your life's worth any old time you felt like it. When my credit score was zero, I literally had no idea, and it didn't impact my mental health or emotional well-being in any tangible way, and now that I get emails from the bank imploring me to log on and find out just how risky some imaginary bank might find their potential association with me, I can ruin my day with just one click? I am powerless against it. (3) Play *Best Fiends*. I wish this was sponsored, because I spend so much real (fake, credit card) money on this match three puzzle game that was probably invented for third graders that if I ever accidentally saw *how* much, I would throw my phone in the garbage.

I also spend an embarrassing amount of my daily allotted screen hours using this one coloring app, whose creations have become a real source of pride for me. I say all this to say: no one has to know that whatever you like is weird or dumb, and if you do your phone stuff silently in a corner of the room, everyone assumes you're reading about foreign policy in the *New Yorker* and not blowing up slugs with bugs in your cartoon garden.

Play your music loud in the car.

Play whatever it is you like listening to at a skull-fracturing volume, especially if the parents of the kids you're shuffling between lacrosse practice and the mall are hushed-NPR-voices-in-the-car people. I always feel so much pressure in a quiet news car, like okay, we're just gonna sit at this red light pretending we care about the deficit? No way, brother, turn that easy listening up. Even bumping your soft shit at the *very least* makes you cooler than the people your age who don't. I'm not kidding, you could pull up to the Girls Scouts meeting blasting Sara Bareilles and the kids will stare at your rattling minivan in awe like, "FUCK!!!!!!!!"

GET TATTOOS.

No easier way to look like a fucking Son of Anarchy than to cover yourself in skulls and tombstones and other garbage that makes you look like you don't care if you live or die, which, I'm sorry, babe, automatically makes you cool as hell. I'm not sure how many tattoos I have, either 42 or 297. Who can say, but all of them are so stupid and even the meaningful ones mean something in the dumbest possible way; I have an enormous, hilarious joke tattoo making fun of a guy I don't even talk to that much who has no idea he has inspired me in this way, but nobody has to know that. They just need to know that I'm carefree and reckless and willing to destroy my future employment prospects for a laugh.

Have you ever met some uptight bozo but then found out that they have some ugly, moronic tattoo, and that makes you want to be their best friend? That's the power of randomly picking a piece of shitty body art off a wall and having it stabbed into your skin, where it will remain for the rest of your life: you can make friends, terrify your enemies, and one day overhear a seventh grader say, "She won't make eye contact with me or listen when I talk, but she looks really scary and cool."

we used to get dressed up to go to red lobster

We waited three-plus hours for diet salad.

I went to the fancy mall fifty-three miles away, ostensibly for a bar of fancy soap. I mean, it wasn't about the soap as much as it was about needing an excuse to spend a Saturday morning any place other than my house. But an overpriced chunk of glycerin was as good a reason as any.

I dragged my friend Emily with me because looking at stuff I can't afford alone makes me depressed. When we got there, the mall parking lot was surprisingly packed for a non-last-minute-holiday-shopping day, and I cursed my poor planning as I was forced to park several miles away from the closest door. I locked the car and was nearly mowed down by a horde of people rushing toward the gleaming mall doors— dozens and dozens of people clawing at and climbing over one another to get to the entrance first, tearing at each other's clothes, teeth gnashing and dripping with thick saliva. I stopped a man as he threatened to knock the walker out of a frail woman's hands and said, "Dude? What in the world is going on here today?"

He looked at me as if I'd suddenly sprouted a second head, then dove to his left to avoid a pair of sprinting college kids whose shoes pounded the ground so hard sparks shot out from beneath them. "We finally got a Cheesecake Factory!" he shouted. "And today is the grand opening!"

A freshly constructed Cheesecake Factory, the uncontested ruler of the reheated, prepackaged mall chains, opening only an hourlong car ride and a half a tank of gas away from where I live? And I just so happened to want a block of twig-and-berries natural soap on the day of its grand opening? My karma was obviously right. I fought my way through the throngs of people in sensible gym shoes clustered around the door, dragging Emily's tiny limp body behind me, and made my way to the host, who informed me that there could be a wait of "several hours" between me and a plate of Roadside Sliders.

I watched frustrated packs of tweens sighing and grimacing at their watches, angrily punching orders like "mom get me NOW, k?" into their phones as they stormed away in a huff. Adults pressed their impatient faces against the brand-new cold cases housing the "more than thirty legendary cheesecakes" as their toddlers wailed and tugged at their pant legs, begging them to just feed them the bag of Cheerios they'd left behind in the car. Was I really going to waste three-plus hours in the middle of a perfectly acceptable weekend outside a restaurant entrance crammed next to a cell-phone-case kiosk with your aunts and uncles, waiting to get food I'd already eaten before? YES, I WAS.

Good fortune such as this simply doesn't happen to me. And now, all of a sudden, I'd accidentally stumbled across the grand opening of the luxurious, wicker-chaired faux-Egyptian-mall-restaurant fantasy of my dreams. There was absolutely no way Emily and I weren't going to put our names in. Where else can you get an entire bucket of soup for six dollars?

My love affair with the Cheesecake Factory had begun much like everyone else's: a girl in my suburban high school took me there for my seventeenth birthday. It was the most glamorous, luxurious place I had ever been, and I was genuinely in awe of the seventy-two-page menu. I couldn't believe they would bring you a literal goblet of ice water and refill it every thirty seconds. Ten out of ten, would go again. And I did. Dozens of times. And, okay, maybe I exaggerated the number of menu pages, but you could easily go there once a week for the rest of your life and never get the same thing twice. Try to beat that. You can't!

Nestled inside a booth the size of a mid-priced sedan, backs and knees sore from pacing in front of Ann Taylor and the North Face while trying not to think about the unhinged ridiculousness of spending an entire day waiting to order something called a SkinnyLicious Caesar Salad, we clinked the bucket-sized glasses of our margaritas, then sipped them and sighed. It was worth the wait.

My older sister used to manage a McDonald's.

When I turned ten, I had a sleepover, which is humiliating to think about now because we lived in this terrible courtyard apartment that had mice and only one toilet just off the living room where everybody was going to sleep. My big plan for the evening was to rent the New Kids on the Block *No More Games* pay-per-view concert and eat snacks until we threw up. But the cable box was broken, and the screen kept cutting out, which was devastating both as the party host, but also as a person who would have taken a bullet for Jonathan, Jordan, Joey, Donnie, or Danny. In that order.

I saved every issue of *Bop* and *The Big Bopper* magazine I could get my sticky Laffy Taffy hands on, and I would obsessively read every article multiple times before carefully dissecting each poster and picture from the magazines and taping them in a giant collage on the wall of the room I shared with my mom. LOL, she had to go to bed every single night under the watchful eye of Donnie Wahlberg. I'm screaming!!

Anyway, I was wrecked that I wouldn't be able to perform the choreographed dance moves I had prepared to sing along with "You Got It (The Right Stuff)" and "Please Don't Go Girl," and my mom was mad that she'd wasted $49.95. The fuzzy green screen and eardrum-shattering beep screaming out from our old TV set were probably karmic retribution for my having gotten our house phone shut off by racking up literal *hundreds* of dollars' worth of bills for taking the phone into the bathroom to call 1-900-909-5KIDS several times a day and listening to recordings from the boys that I thought were tailored specifically to me. Those calls cost two dollars a minute, which seemed like a bargain for access to Jordan Knight's most secret thoughts and feelings.

That sleepover, we ended up watching a video of *Earth Girls Are Easy*, which was maybe not the coolest thing to screen for a bunch of fifth-grade girls, but it was the only tape we had in the house, then collectively slept the fitful sleep of the extremely disappointed.

The next morning, I woke up before everyone else and found my mom in the kitchen drinking Folgers instant coffee crystals and chain-smoking cigarettes. I was about to ask her if she'd bought good (read: sugary) cereal to serve for breakfast, my only hope for rectifying the events of the night before. I spotted the canister of grits next to the stove and steeled myself. I would have to explain to the sleeping girls in the other room what those were, and why we were expected to eat them, but then the front door opened and in walked my sister Jane, a recent graduate of Hamburger University, carrying boxes stuffed with Egg McMuffins and stacks of Styrofoam hotcakes clamshells. It was like if Santa Claus was a black woman with a dyed-blond mushroom cut in a red-and-white-striped shirt and one of those ribbon-looking lady neckties they had to wear in the nineties. She saved my whole stupid party! Everybody loves McDonald's breakfast, and I was a legend at school the next day, for approximately seven minutes, but who cares. Thank goodness for that degree in Hamburgerology (this is real), the only college diploma between the four of us. Our mother was so proud.

What is your Starbucks order?

I like to listen to people's complicated coffee orders, because walking a person through the seventeen steps it takes to make your optimal morning coffee while a line of pissed-off people who are already late for work doubles in on itself before wrapping around an entire city block takes the kind of bravery I have never and will never possess. It is remarkable to me. Thrilling, really. I live every single day in fear that a stranger might yell at me for some normal community thing I am doing wrong, like pulling up to the gas pump at a weird angle or exiting out of the wrong door. So, I cannot imagine being brave enough to take my time giving explicit instructions about my latte while people who are close enough to touch me get mad at me. All that hot, concentrated rage aimed at my back? During the morning rush?? Absolutely not, babe!

Sometimes in the drive-thru I'll roll down my window and listen in total amazement to the person ahead of me rattle off all the modifications they want for their drink, because how do they even know all that stuff? How did you know to say "blended-in java chips"? As in, "Can I get a grande strawberry cream Frappuccino with no classic syrup, one pump caramel, one and a half pumps toffee nut, one pump hazelnut, and java chips blended in?" I only know that's a real thing you can order because I texted it to myself as two high school cheerleaders driving their mom's Chrysler Pacifica shouted it over Olivia Rodrigo turned all the way up into the intercom. Who told them to say that? Did you know there's such a thing as "toffee nut syrup"? I fucking didn't. I just (barely) learned what "bone-dry" means. I'm too immature to graduate to the land of syrups and cold foams!

I recently started buying myself iced oat milk lattes because it's fun to say and also tastes pretty good without having to add a bunch of sugar to it, which is what I want to do but am too embarrassed to do because real coffee drinkers drink that shit black with no additives presumably because it makes them feel cool to pretend to like the taste. And I'm sorry but "bitter bug and dirt water" is never gonna be palatable to me, so I have to add something to blunt the terrible taste of my caffeine-delivery system. But I'm too embarrassed to ask for whatever number of sugars will make it taste like a milkshake. And it's so quick to say, it only takes a second, so I can easily get out of the way of the gentleman ordering a "venti double ristretto half-soy nonfat decaf double-shot Frappuccino double-blended with one NutraSweet" behind me.

Red Lobster is fancy and good.

When I brought home a good report card in elementary school, my mom would reward me with a trip to Red Lobster and that incentive, plus the unyielding desire to be loved and petted by women over forty, is why I got good report cards. I'd come home wagging my report card, and that weekend, we would get dressed in our church clothes (for me: a dress, a patent leather shoe, a lace-edged white sock) and drive to the mall. I would get popcorn shrimp and rice pilaf and feel like the luckiest person in the entire world.

As an adult I've discovered that Red Lobster makes the only kind of drinks I ever want to drink, so that is why I regularly put a nice shirt on and go. You know how everybody now drinks old man cocktails that taste like rancid cough syrup? Or they order whatever's on the bar menu that has mezcal in it and therefore tastes like burning newspaper? When did we start doing that? Why can't I be a grown-up *and* order a cocktail that tastes like an alcoholic juice box?

Literally what is the point of growing up and going into credit card debt if I still have to get the approval of weird booze snobs rather than buy what I actually want?

If I gotta be outside my house and drinking, then I want that drink to be called something like a "Sunset Passion Colada," not a "Poet's Lament" or whatever these fancy-ass places name their drinks. If I order a Frozen Favorites™ Bahama Mama, I know it's gonna taste like orange pineapple juice from the store with a splash of watered-down rum on top; but if I make my way down to the bespoke artisanal modern-day speakeasy (WHAT), and order a "Smirking Priest"? I have no idea what the fuck that drink is gonna taste like.

I went to a bachelorette party at a Red Lobster a few years ago and it was a busy Saturday night, so our large, shrieking party had to wait at the bar for a couple of tables to open up, so they could push them together for us to scatter with penis straws and paper crowns. While we waited, I noticed that the bartender looked like a dude I'd grown up with, like a kid-who-was-in-my-*kindergarten-class*-with-me kind of grown up with, and I walked over to say hi. There were several older women seated at the bar, dressed like they were trying to get fucked that night, and I was instantly smitten. This is what I want for my future.

My man was giving these ladies the full *Cocktail* experience: shaking his tightly pants'ed ass, flipping and twirling a bottle of mango Malibu rum, really emphasizing the ASS when he delivered one of them her Tiki Passion Punch™ as she squealed in delight. I need to remind you that this isn't a sultry beachside cocktail lounge in Jamaica. I was standing in a too-bright mall bar in Lincolnwood, Illinois. And it was still somehow sexy and glamorous! As the women whispered conspiratorially over their drinks, I went to the other end of the bar and said, "Oh my God, [*paste-eating child friend*], you are gonna get your dick sucked!!" And he was like, "Sam, I fuck at least three women a week? And you should see my tips!" I resisted making a joke about giving *me* some tip and mourned a future in which I would not be tits up to a Red Lobster bar, slurping seductively on a Berry Mango Daiquiri, trying to bone a dude who smells like Clamato and is young enough to be my son.

The hot bar

"What kind of person am I going to be today?" I think to myself as I sidle up to the salad bar at the local Overpriced Fresh Vegetable Emporium, my single seltzer (do I wish it was a Diet Coke? I absolutely do, but they don't sell that poison here) and modestly sized square of wholesome dark chocolate (revolting!) rolling around my basket. Salad bars offer the opportunity to reinvent yourself in the time it takes to wolf down a bowl of damp lettuce while hunched over the important papers strewn across your desk, or during the sad and lonely night meal shoveled into your mouth over the kitchen sink while you watch makeup tutorials you will never attempt to follow on your phone.

The possibilities are endless! Am I healthy today? Do I give a shit about being alive? Do I spend half a paycheck on minerals and fiber when my doctor can't even see me or should I just buy three pounds of croutons with organic ranch dressing poured over it, which is what I *actually* want to eat? Am I a marinated-artichoke person? Should I pretend to be interested in beets? Do I care about vitamin K? And, a follow-up: Do I care enough about vitamin K to spend fourteen dollars on an environmentally friendly (read: rapidly disintegrating) clamshell filled with the kind of dark leafy greens magazines are always insisting I try? Is that guy peering skeptically through the sneeze guard at the thirty-seven different varieties of olives judging how many scoops of chickpeas I'm getting? Do I want grains? Do I want grains on top of lettuce? Should I mix different types of lettuce or is that just showing off? I got too much farro last time, let me not repeat that mistake. What does golden squash taste like, and do I want to risk finding out it tastes bad in this way? How much meat and cheese disqualifies this from being labeled a "salad"? Do I like nuts on salad or do I just like the *idea* of nuts on salad? Do I have enough money in my checking account to risk this much herb-roasted salmon? How much does a hard-boiled egg weigh? Baby kale begs the question of whether mother kale exists. Why do bacon bits taste like burnt charcoal, and why can't I stop myself from sprinkling them on everything? The nuts keep calling me! This cabbage is gonna give me diarrhea, right? What is the difference between a "green" and a "lettuce," and why am I the kind of asshole hipster who is leaning toward the "greens"? Hang on, what was that NPR thing about phyto-nutrients from the other day? That healthy-looking yoga lady is getting so many radishes, and, damn, I wish that was my ministry. Will onions ruin this concoction I've slopped together or make it 100 percent better? I gotta swing by the bakery and grab one of those chocolate chip cookies that I deserve. If I use as much of this dressing as I want, the cashier will think I don't love myself. Ugh, why would she care? Did I miss the beans? Ooh, they have peas! Broccoli is a clear gastrointestinal mistake and yet, I cannot resist it. Hang on, before I go to the register should I actually get the nuts?!

I saw Bill Clinton in a Maggiano's.

In a former life, I "worked" in "politics." When I was twenty, I needed a job that wasn't in food service, because I'd had my fill of getting screamed at over custard cakes and fondant cookies. I was walking around Andersonville one day and saw that this little boutique called Presence had a sign in the window announcing that they were looking for help. So I went in and introduced myself before inquiring about filling out an application. I am . . . . not a clotheshorse. But this wasn't really that kind of spot, you know? It was, how should I put this, tiny shirts for "alternative" high school juniors and lots of cheap jewelry and candles and tote bags and journals, with Alanis and the Cranberries playing over the sound system to prove that they were hip and relevant. *That* kind of store.

A few days later I go in for my interview and I talk to Phyllis, the owner, and we're really hitting it off. Instant best friends, but maybe I'm more like her instant foster daughter, since she was easily in her fifties, and I wasn't even old enough to have a legal beer yet. So, I leave there floating on air, thinking about the 30 percent discount I was gonna get on all the clothes I couldn't fit into, and by the time the bus dropped me off down the street from my apartment, I had a message on my machine telling me that though she'd loved spending time talking to me, Phyllis thought I was way over-qualified for her little job.

I was shocked, for real shocked, because why wouldn't you want someone to work for you who you felt was over-qualified for the position but seemed to genuinely want, no *need*, that job anyway? Wouldn't that elevate the workplace? I understand now that she needed someone who just wanted some extra spending money and wouldn't mind folding rhinestoned hoodies on the afternoons she didn't have class, not a person who was gonna be dependent on that money to pay rent and support a real life. But I was bummed.

A couple of weeks later, I got another message from Phyllis on my answering machine (God I miss the 2000s), this time asking if I'd be interested in working for her husband, Peter, who was working on John Schmidt's primary campaign for Illinois attorney general. What had I said in that interview that made this woman think I was a good candidate for a job that didn't involve a mop or a cash register? I called her back and stammered some excuse about my poor performance on the Constitution test, but she shushed me and told me I'd be fine, that the job would be in the campaign's "research department" and required no prior knowledge of politics and/or law. Joseph, my roommate, stood across the living room mouthing "SAY NO" over and over, but I don't know how to do that. I hesitantly agreed to an interview that I regretted the minute I hung up when I realized I didn't even have anything appropriate to wear to the interview, let alone to the everyday downtown *job*.

I went to the interview, dutifully, and to my surprise was hired on the spot. After I made an emergency trip to Lane Bryant to buy a couple of black pencil skirts and button-down office shirts I never looked right in, I learned that the main component of my job was to get to the office at 7:00 a.m., three hours before the rest of the staff arrived, then I had to scour every Illinois newspaper available online and send a link-roundup email to all the fancy people in charge of the campaign to keep them updated on all the big news stories happening around the state.

I would take the red line down to Grand, walk up all those goddamn stairs in my Payless office pumps, then walk to the office, which was above the old Jazz Record Mart on Wabash, across the street from the *Sun-Times* building. (These details are only for the benefit of people in Chicago, who are undoubtedly pointing to this page and screaming "I know where that is!" right now.) In our suite I had a little office that I shared with this very nice man named Nick, who I'm pretty sure is a congressman now. I would leave all the lights off and get to work, logging on to my little computer and scrolling through, I don't know, the *Peoria Journal Star* (?) looking for stories that would be relevant to the candidate or the campaign. It's so funny thinking about that because I'm like, "Could I even do that now?" How did I know which downstate hotbed issues the former #3 lawyer under Janet Reno should be made aware?

I had to get the email out by 9:00 a.m., I'm pretty sure, and then I would hang with Patrick Botterman, the campaign manager, until everybody else got to work, and he had to make himself look busy. Hoo boy, did I have a crush on Pat. He was the best and so effortlessly funny. He taught me a lot about Illinois politics, mostly that it's a thankless job I should get out of as soon as I could. Okay, so I had to do the news links every morning and also read tons of stuff about cities in southern Illinois that I had never heard of, plus I made fliers for fundraisers and spent a lot of time running across the street to have diarrhea at Nordstrom, because the bathroom on our floor was too small and conspicuous. I also had to do all the regular boring campaign shit like collecting signatures and spending hours at the secretary of state's office trying to verify them. I was knocking on doors on the northwest side, which guaranteed I was gonna get meanly grunted at by no fewer than ten off-duty cops, and sitting through many black church services trying to apologize to the congregation with my eyes for being there with this white man who was interrupting their salvation to talk about consumer protection.

Let's circle back to the fundraisers. All you do when you are running for office is raise money, or try to raise money—constantly. You give speeches, you film attack ads, you try to get on the news, and you raise money. There was a whole team of fundraisers that sat in a different part of the office from the rest of us. Sometimes I could hear their voices echoing from the back, "Hey, Bill, it's Howard over at the Schmidt campaign calling to see if you'd be able to donate . . ." I wasn't allowed back there where the important work was getting done, but I like to imagine twenty people wearing green visors hunched over their adding machines, furiously tapping the keys and occasionally looking up to scream, "WE NEED MORE MONEY FOR LAWN SIGNS!"

The candidate had worked in Bill Clinton's Justice Department, which means he knew Bill Clinton, and when Pat told us the president was coming to town to help John raise money by hosting a dinner at Maggiano's, I was like, "Can I go???" The president of the United States in the same chain restaurant I'd saved up my babysitting money to go to the year before? Amazing. I couldn't wait to watch that dude eat mozzarella sticks. The fundraiser plates were like ten thousand dollars apiece or some other obscene amount, and I'm not sure I even had ten dollars at the time, but I wasn't even thinking about Bill Clinton, I was trying to get one of those delicious chopped salads and, also, do you remember that deal they had where if you bought a pasta, they would automatically make a second one and box it up for you to take home? If I played my cards right I could have finessed *three separate meals* out of that dinner!

Of course I couldn't go. No one was gonna spend ten grand for me to get a fucking lasagna. But they did tell me I could work the coat check if I promised not to speak or take any bread off anyone's table, and of course I said yes. How could I resist getting dressed up on my night off and spending my own $2 to take the train downtown and walk through cold, sleeting bullshit to catch a glimpse of what I thought might be Bill Clinton's tuxedoed elbow through a clot of armed Secret Service officers as they breezed past our little skirted table littered with carnival tickets and mismatched hangers? Anticlimactic for sure, but at the end those of us who'd struggled under the weight of so many pounds of luxurious black-and-navy wool got to eat the congealed chicken marsala all the senators' wives left behind, which I'm counting as a win. The only win, since we got fucking *slaughtered* in that election.

A eulogy for the Kentucky Fried Chicken little bucket parfait

Rest in peace my little thick layer of cream atop a thick layer of hospital cafeteria pudding atop a thick layer of damp sand. Finger-lickin' goodness, indeed. Come on, Colonel. Bring her back.

please invite me to your party

I'm a great guest. I will appreciate all of your deep cleaning! The baseboards you scrubbed, the silverware you polished to a high gleam, the corners you awkwardly maneuvered the Swiffer into to sweep the last of the crumbs and cat hair out of sight. I, too, have stood panting in the middle of a room no one coming to my house is even supposed to enter, worried what someone who stumbles in mistakenly looking for the bathroom is going to think because there's dust on the back of the TV.

Speaking of the bathroom, I will notice that you wiped all the toothpaste flecks off the mirror, ran a wet washcloth across the scale you hide under the radiator, and I'll appreciate that your toothbrushes are standing up straight in the new toothbrush cup you ran out to Target to get three hours before your first guest arrived. I will see your Anthropologie shower curtain and think, "Damn, she's fancy enough to get her shower curtains at Anthropologie?" Your Aesop hand soap won't be lost on me, either, and I know you really want me to peek at your unpronounceable shampoo brand, so rest assured that I will do that.

When I squeeze past the couple having an under-their-breath fight in the kitchen, I'm gonna notice that you sprayed some diluted bleach on the faucet. I promise I will *see* the recently purchased fruits on the counter to let me know that not only are you getting your fiber, but I will know that that fiber is organic, and rode in the back of a Lyft in an earth-conscious compostable bag. You didn't wipe down the stove-top or the refrigerator handle in vain, because I'm noticing them, and I am impressed. I'm clocking your matching silverware sets and your tulips in a real vase and that loaf of crusty bakery bread you bought to trick people into thinking you prefer to slice your own artisanal sourdough. If you do, that's cool, but I bet you actually don't!

I'm so fun. I'll talk to everybody. I'll charm your mom, telling her that she looks hot in fuchsia and joke with her that she should adopt me because you're such an asshole, and when your dad corners me aggressively into talking about sports, I will gently remind him that I'm not exactly that kind of lesbian. But also, I've seen enough of Skip Bayless to fake my way through a convincingly knowledgeable conversation about Ezekiel Elliott's rushing yards last season and that will win him over. He will suggest that we go to a football game together, an invitation I will dodge until one of us dies.

I'm gonna try all your weird party foods without spitting any of them out or hiding them in your plants. Even the stuff that looks homemade, which goes against one of my primary guiding principles. I'm gonna sample that gritty breadstick-looking thing, even though I know before I touch it that it's going to shatter into particles of sharp dust down the front of my nice party shirt the second my teeth make contact. I'm gonna take a handful of chips even though there's no good way to eat them at a party; if I take as many as I want, then it's just my greedy ass rudely walking around making small talk with a Miss Vickie's salt-and-vinegar bag strapped to my muzzle like I'm a horse, but if I take a socially accept-able amount, I'm standing in the middle of a crowded room balancing two and a half thin-sliced potato crisps on an itty-bitty cocktail napkin.

The aesthetic uniformity of carrot sticks is appealing to me, and I find them to be an excellent vehicle for delivering ranch dressing to my mouth and even though doing so will cause me to horrify anyone who attempts to talk to me. If you take even one bite of a raw carrot you will have carrot flecks in your mouth for at least a week afterward. I will eat them for you, so it doesn't look like you don't know what people want to eat. The hot dip? I'm trying that. The guaca-mole that's gone gray? I'll have some of that, too. I will take just enough of each proffered food item that you don't feel like you've wasted $400 on people who just want to clean out all your booze.

And I will bring good shit. I have a serious lack of confi-dence and am always trying to prove that I have good taste and like nice things, especially at a celebration. I'm gonna go to the boutique grocery and stuff my humiliation in my back pocket long enough to ask the person behind the counter to recommend something in the $30 range, then I'm gonna slide to the cheese counter and get one of those logs of goat cheese that has blueberry goo in it because that looks fancy to me. I'll make my way to the cracker section and get a couple pricey boxes of sturdy-looking health crackers covered in nuts and seeds that I would never ever buy for myself, and am mostly convinced you don't want either, but they are gonna look so nice and expensive on your cheese tray and that makes it worth it to me.

If you'd prefer a dessert I could certainly pick up a "torte" of some kind on my way over, a thing I would never purchase for myself because if I'm getting a cake, I am getting a slab of moist chocolate children's birthday cake slathered with an inch of thick, tooth-disintegrating grocery store buttercream. But that's a weird thing to show up with unless the guest of honor is a seven-year-old.

My clothes will be ugly, allowing you to shine. I understand that as the host, you need to be the best-looking person in your apartment. So if you invite me to your party I will arrive early enough that you don't panic about no one showing up, and I will be wearing some sort of shapeless black reaper-style garment that will easily fade into the background of every picture. "Who is that fat ghost?" your friends will ask as they swipe through the pictures you posted to prove to everyone that you know people and like to have a good time. Then they'll immediately forget they saw me and swipe to you in your sequined celebration frock and sigh in contentment while witnessing your glory.

And if you need someone to play tunes? I can do that. I know how to create a chill and sexy vibe, if that's the kind of vibe you're into, but I am also familiar with other vibes, *and* I pay for Spotify Premium. I don't remember what payment method or email address it's attached to, so I will never be free of it. All that to say you won't have to worry about annoying commercials interrupting the flow. I can play fast songs for dancing or slow songs for smooching or oldies for old people, and I'm the kind of freak who'll put twenty-seven hours' worth of songs on a playlist, so if your party happens to go on for an entire day, you won't have to listen to the same song twice.

If it's less of a "hey, let's marvel at what good music taste I have" party, and more of a "passive-aggressive storytelling competition" party, I'd be great at that, too. I have so many good stories. I won't say weird, off-putting, or challenging shit to casual acquaintances of yours, threatening to make your future relationships with them awkward as hell. I have a deep reservoir of jokes and funny anecdotes that'll thaw even the chilliest of the coworkers you invited just to be nice. And I know how to land a fucking punch line!

You also won't have to worry about me posting all your business online. That's right, you're never gonna log on to be confronted by the ten worst pictures of you and/or your apartment you've ever seen in your whole fucking life, posted by me, not even with the decency to put a flattering filter on your mismatched furniture and trash. If my phone is out, it's because I'm trying to find a meme to show someone, so I won't be that person trying to explain a visual medium to a person who is already bored, *not* because I am taking shadowy pictures of all your stuff that I plan to post at three in the morning when I know you're not going to see it for at least twelve hours, by which point everyone you know will have seen that you (1) had a party and didn't invite them, and

(2) should probably run a dustrag over your coffee table. That's rude.

I can also keep your cat company if you need me to. I mean, if Pickles is getting stressed out in the darkened bedroom you stashed her in with only an empty tuna can for company, I would not at all mind creeping in there and petting her for many hours, until the party is over and you forget I'm even in there, which sounds awkward in theory but will come in very handy when you find out that I don't mind helping clean up. I love party aftermath; I love seeing who congregated where and how many drinks they had and speculating about who kissed what and who went home with whom, even if it means collecting stacks of little plates covered in globs of unidentifiable cream-based goo and half-eaten celeries with their little unruly celery hairs sticking up.

So, you'll invite me, right? You're gonna text me the address and your favorite brand of tequila, right? I need to be invited more than anything I've ever needed in my life. Because trust me, I really am great at a party. Seriously, though, invite me. I'm the greatest party guest there is, especially since I won't come.

ACKNOWLEDGMENTS

HELL YEAH, BROTHER, thank you times a million to everyone I deeply love who loves me deeply in return.

I can't do shit without my pals and my lads and family, and this book is a testament to how cool and funny and supportive they all are. I've been extremely lucky to work with some incredible people over the past few years, and I'd be an asshole not to give juicy smooches to Abby McEnany and Lilly Wachowski, Lisa Hanawalt and Raphael Bob-Waksberg, Michael Patrick King, Julie Rottenberg, Elisa Zuritsky, and Susan Fales-Hill.

I would literally be dead and also this book would not exist in its current form without: Jessie Martinson, Lindy West, Rachna Fruchbom, Lucas Froelich, Melissa Fisher, Jared Honn, Ian Belknap, Kelsey McKinney, Fernando Meza, Nick Kreiss, Helen Williams, Carl Cowan, Amanda Rosenberg, Mimi Stringfield, Alexis Wilson, Sarah Rose Etter, Emily Kastner, Jenn Romolini, Cara Brigandi, Ted Beranis, Amy Hagedorn, Mike Verdi, Flea Fasano, and Megan Stielstra.

Thank God for Maria Goldverg, the greatest and smartest and most patient editor in history, and also for everyone at Vintage/Anchor who work so hard and do such a good job. Thank you to Jason Richman (and Maialie!!) for helping me navigate the shark-infested waters of Hollywood, and I am nothing without Kent Wolf, the best literary agent on the planet.

Mel Winer and Jim Hagedorn continue to be the best substitute dads in the business.

And to Kirsten, my magnificent, superlative ol' lady: Thank you for riding the wave. I owe you one fully dressed hot dog.

Read more from **Samantha Irby**
Because sometimes you just have to laugh— even when life is a pile of garbage.

Available in paperback and eBook

Available only in eBook

Available wherever eBooks are sold 🦁 VintageBooks.com